Managing Capital Flows

Managing Capital Flows

Issues in Selected Emerging Market Economies

edited by
BRUNO CARRASCO,
SUBIR GOKARN,
AND
HIRANYA MUKHOPADHYAY

Copublication of the Asian Development Bank
and Oxford University Press India

OXFORD
UNIVERSITY PRESS

Oxford University Press is a department of the University of Oxford.
It furthers the University's objective of excellence in research, scholarship,
and education by publishing worldwide. Oxford is a registered trademark of
Oxford University Press in the UK and in certain other countries

Published in India by
Oxford University Press
YMCA Library Building, 1 Jai Singh Road, New Delhi 110 001, India

The moral rights of the authors have been asserted

First Edition published in 2014

ISBN-13: 978-0-19-945334-4
ISBN-10: 0-19-945334-9

Typeset in Dante MT Std 10.5/13
by The Graphics Solution, New Delhi 110 092
Printed in India at Sapra Brothers, New Delhi 110 092

Contents

Tables and Figures

Tables

Figures

Foreword

Across most Emerging Market Economies (EMEs) the last decade has witnessed a significant and unprecedented increase in cross-country capital flows. Sharp and rapid increases in private capital flows to EMEs in the run-up to the global financial crisis (2003–7) was followed by sudden stops, sharp sell-offs in selected economies, and flight to quality. In 2010 and early 2011 a combination of push and pull factors led to another burst of strong capital inflows into EMEs. However, this recovery was short-lived and was brought to a halt by increasing global risk perceptions following on the euro area sovereign debt crisis in the second half of 2011.

These sudden and sharp changes in capital flows and the ensuing volatility led to serious challenges to macroeconomic management. High inflation, overheating, real exchange rate misalignments, and current account imbalances are some of the challenges associated with large and volatile capital inflows in EMEs. While capital flows can lead to important gains to the economy and for the financial system as a whole, taking into account such factors as its composition, scalability, and a country's absorptive capacity, it can also amplify asset prices, generate credit boom–bust cycles, and destabilize the financial system and, in turn, the economy.

Against this backdrop, this volume analyses capital flow management from two distinct vantage points, namely theoreticians and practitioners. This set-up provides for a very useful synthesis of key findings from both the recent academic literature on capital flow management, as well as from the practical operational side. The objective of this exercise is to build a consensus on important learnings on capital flow management in order for policymakers to be better prepared to safeguard the economy and the financial system in the future. This is of particular importance not just to EMEs but also to institutions such as the Asian Development Bank (ADB) in order to ring fence the gains in socioeconomic development of Asia's emerging economies achieved over the years.

An important theme analysed in this volume focuses on the optimal level of management of capital flows and the relative effectiveness of various policies and instruments to manage capital flows across the public policy space. This analysis had been informed by the broader debate on capital account liberalization and the more specific debate on capital controls. The volume highlights important findings of this debate in the context of the degree of capital account liberalization in pursuit of public policy objectives.

ADB and the Reserve Bank of India (RBI) held a conference in Mumbai on 19–20 November 2012 to deliberate on these issues to develop a converging conceptual framework building on the perspectives of the theoreticians and the compulsions of the practitioners. This volume *Managing Capital Flows: Issues in Selected Emerging Market Economies* contains the papers presented in the conference.

I thank the team led by Subir Gokarn (former Deputy Governor of RBI) and Bruno Carrasco, Hiranya Mukhopadhyay, and Rosa Mia Arao from ADB and, of course, the contributors for their dedicated time and effort leading to this publication.

W. Y.

Wencai Zhang
Vice President
Operations 1
Asian Development Bank

BRUNO CARRASCO
SUBIR GOKARN
HIRANYA MUKHOPADHYAY

Overview

The difficulty lies, not in the new ideas, but in escaping the old ones, which ramify, for those brought up as most of us have been, into every corner of our minds.

John Maynard Keynes, *The General Theory of Employment, Interest and Money*, February 1936.

I. Introduction

The motivation behind this work is to review how countries performed in capital flow management in the face of an unprecedented episode of volatility in global capital flows over the period 2003–12. As part of this work, the objective is to compare and contrast the experiences and findings of theoreticians and practitioners—mostly central banks—focusing on emerging market economies (EMEs) in a bid to forge a consensus on how to best manage international capital flows.

Indeed, looking back as recently as 2007–8, capital inflows to EMEs peaked with net capital flows reaching almost 9 per cent of GDP in India alone. India was, thus, the highest global recipient of net capital flows in that year only after the US and Spain (Mohan et al. 2011b). With the advent of the global crisis the following year, net capital flows fell drastically across the globe—slumping to 0.6 per cent of gross domestic product (GDP) in India—proving a major challenge for policymakers across the globe.

More generally, the 2003–12 period provides a snapshot of an even larger undercurrent of gross capital flows from large inflows to sudden stops and sell-offs to recovery and back to retrenchment. Four distinct periods are noteworthy. In 2003–7, in the run-up to the US subprime mortgage crisis, the under-pricing of risk and easy money led to large inflows of capital to EMEs. This period was known as the Great Moderation for the largely moderate rates of inflation that prevailed and characterized by ample liquidity and low interest rates across global markets. In late 2008, with the advent of the sub-prime mortgage crisis, there was a sudden stop and massive exit of capital out of EMEs and into safe havens given high counter-party risk, deleveraging, and repatriation of capital to plug holes back in the advanced home markets. In 2010–1, the introduction of quantitative easing (QE) by the Federal Reserve (FED) led to a resurgence of net capital inflows to EMEs, particularly to those economies that had best weathered the storm of the global financial crisis. However, this recovery was punctured in the second half of 2011, when worsening debt problems in the periphery of the Euro-Zone led to a further retrenchment and capital flows once again reversed direction towards safe havens.

Figure I.1 presents the evolution of net capital flows across emerging economies over the past three decades. In the five years from 2002 to 2007, net capital flows more than tripled from $200 billion to over $600 billion, driven by direct investment. While 2007 marked a peak which has not been surpassed until 2013, net capital flows have remained strong, averaging $325 billion over 2011–13.

Figure I.2 presents a breakdown of net capital flows broken down by countries. BRICS countries[1] (excluding South Africa) experienced a rapid growth of net capital inflows during 2005–7, leading to a peak in 2007,[2] followed by a steep decline through 2008, and once again a rapid acceleration in 2009–11. The dip in net capital flows, however, is more pronounced in the Russian Federation compared to other BRICS countries with no sign of recovery in 2011. Indonesia, to a lesser extent, also faced rapid growth, although later in time (2009–10) and with no evidence of much of a recovery. Chile and South Africa, by contrast,

---

[1] BRICS countries refer to Brazil, the Russian Federation, India, the People's Republic of China (PRC), and South Africa.

[2] The PRC reaches its peak earlier, in 2004.

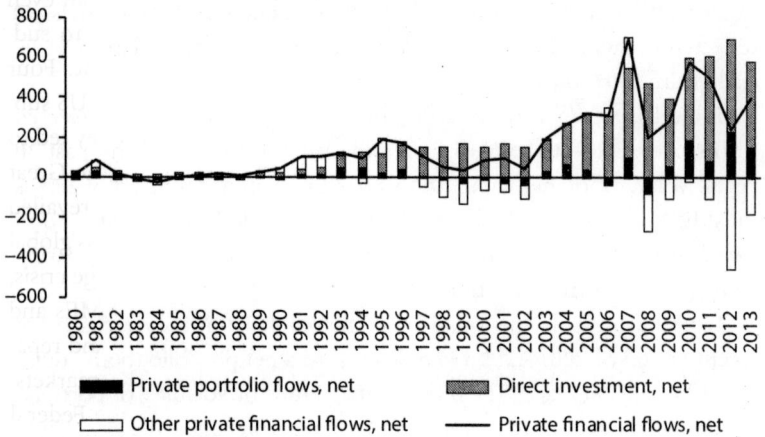

FIGURE I.1   Net Capital Flows to Emerging Market and Developing
Economies, $ billion
Source: International Monetary Fund. 2013. World Economic Outlook Database,
October.

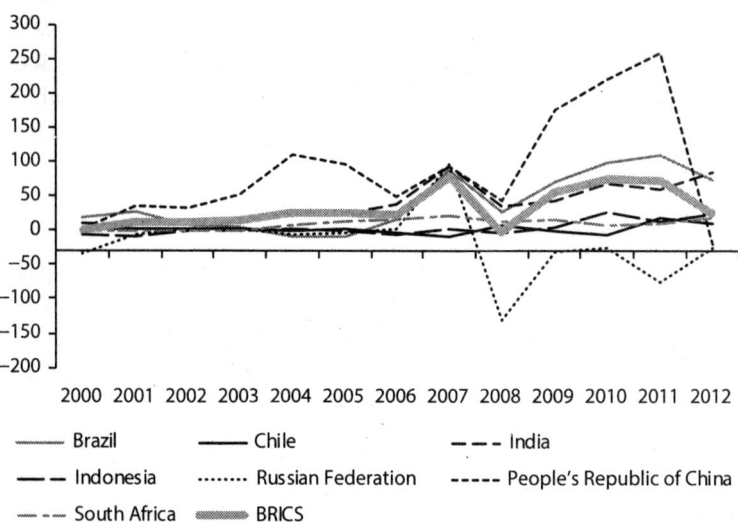

FIGURE I.2   Net Capital Flows ($ billion)
Note: 2012 values taken from IMF BPM6 adjusted to create a historical series.
Source: CEIC Data Ltd.

experienced a more modest and less volatile trend of capital inflows. As reflected in Figure I.3, portfolio flows experienced large volatility especially from 2005 to 2012.

Table I.1 presents the volatility of net capital flows across selected EMEs over 1980–2011. With increasing capital flows over the past 30 years, volatility of net capital flows has fluctuated significantly across most EMEs. Indeed, volatility declined in the period 1991–2000 as compared to 1980–90 and was followed by much greater volatility during 2001–12, with some exceptions.

Table I.2 presents the volatility of net capital flows over the more recent period of 2001–12, broken down across net portfolio (both equity and debt) and net loans. The order of magnitude of volatility of portfolio investments across Asia as compared to net loans highlights the underlying characteristic of this type of capital. However, in some other emerging markets, net loans turn out to be more volatile than portfolio investments.[3]

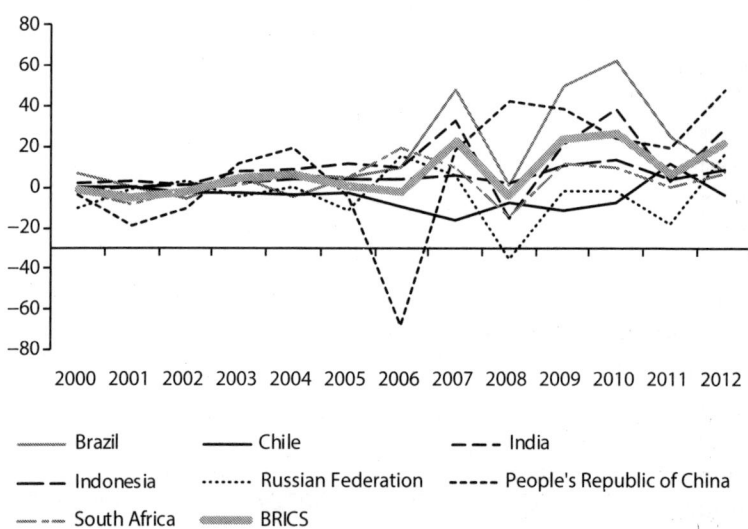

FIGURE I.3 Net Portfolio Investment Flows ($ billion)
Source: CEIC Data Ltd.
Note: 2012 values taken from IMF BPM6 adjusted to create a historical series.

[3] See also ADB (2011), which reported that from 1990, volatility of other investment flows (which includes loans) has exceeded that of portfolio flows in emerging Asia.

TABLE I.1   Volatility of Net Capital Flows Across Emerging Market
Economies, 1980–2012

Country	1980–90	1991–2000	2001–12
India	0.20	0.11	0.46
Indonesia	0.20	4.40	6.40
Malaysia	1.49	4.56	1.64
People's Republic of China	0.95	1.07	0.77
Philippines	0.83	0.33	5.34
Republic of Korea	118.38	1.26	33.43
Thailand	0.77	5.21	3.84
Asia	1.85	5.62	16.97
Brazil	0.93	0.37	1.06
Chile	0.42	0.58	23.88
Mexico	2.29	0.21	0.26

Source: CEIC Data Ltd.
Note: Net capital flows refer to the sum of net direct investment, net portfolio
investment, net financial derivatives, and net other investments.

   Volatility is computed as the square of the coefficient of variation (standard
deviation / mean).

   Asia includes Hong Kong, China (1998), India, Indonesia (1981), Malaysia,
the People's Republic of China (1982), the Philippines, the Republic of Korea,
Singapore, Taipei,China (1981), and Thailand. Year in parenthesis after country
refers to the first available year of observation in the dataset.

   Capital flow management has reflected various trends across the public policy space. Two prominent, if not controversial, debates that have
certainly shaped the approach to capital flow management include the
broader debate on capital account liberalization and the more specific
debate on capital controls. The motivation on either side of the debate
has been on the optimal level of liberalization or deregulation required
to attract large flows of capital to EMEs in order to finance investment
while safeguarding macro-management and averting sudden stops,
flight to quality, and resulting destabilizing forces on the economy.

   The debate has been particularly fluid between theoreticians and
practitioners and perhaps came most clearly into focus in the context of
the Asian Crisis. In 1998 Malaysia decided to introduce capital controls
to shield its economy from destabilizing outflows of capital and thereby
temporarily disconnect interest rate from exchange rate policies.

TABLE I.2   Volatility of Net Capital Flows across Emerging Market
Economies, 2001–12

Country	Net Capital Flows	Of which Net Portfolio Investment	Of which Loans
India	0.46	1.46	1.22
Indonesia	6.40	0.63	8.10
Malaysia	1.64	16.18	1.33
People's Republic of China	0.77	10.21	41.03
Philippines	5.34	2.59	24.26
Republic of Korea	33.43	9.15	9326.56
Thailand	3.84	15.13	56.61
Asia	16.97	1971.38	3490.62
Brazil	1.06	1.91	10.92
Chile	23.88	2.28	1.22
Mexico	0.26	3.22	36.98

Note: Volatility is computed as the square of the coefficient of variation (standard
deviation/mean).
Asia includes Hong Kong, China (1998), India, Indonesia (1981), Malaysia,
the People's Republic of China (1982), the Philippines, the Republic of Korea,
Singapore, Taipei,China (1981), and Thailand.
Source: CEIC Data Ltd.

In 2012, 14 years later, and following a multitude of crises across the
world, the International Monetary Fund (IMF) finally recognized that
the use of direct controls can serve to calm volatile cross-border capital
flows particularly in EMEs, with the caveat that these controls should be
targeted, transparent, and generally temporary.

II. Three Important Messages

In attempting to forge a consensus between theoreticians and practitioners, this volume seeks to shed light on three important messages that
are critical to the debate on the merits of international capital flow management. The contributors to this volume have provided their thoughts
and views on these messages, highlighting important considerations.
We hope that the findings presented in the chapters of this volume will
help develop a converging conceptual framework to improve capital
flow management.

Message 1—The Importance of Capital Flows

Economic theory tells us that if net capital flows can be effectively absorbed and given the right composition of capital—favouring Foreign Direct Investment (FDI), and mitigating against the more volatile portfolio flows—economies stand to gain. Standard arguments tend to invoke reference to (a) allocative efficiency between the world's savers and investors given the higher return to investments in capital-deficient economies and (b) consumption smoothing over the medium term.

However, and perhaps surprisingly, empirical evidence does not lend support in favour of the virtues of financial openness (Obstfeld 2009). Indeed, on average, over the past 25 years there have been three to four systemic banking crises per year. Moreover, in a sample of 40 financial crises, one quarter of them resulted in a cumulative output loss in the economy in excess of 25 per cent of pre-crisis GDP and in one third of the crises, economic contraction lasted more than 3 years (Cecchetti et al. 2009).

What should we take away from this debate? Part of the answer lies in how policymakers can effectively harness capital flows. FDI is generally associated with additional spillovers such as productivity growth from technological advances over and above capital formation. If policymakers can ensure that the economy has sufficient absorptive capacity and avoids overshooting of critical prices, then risks to financial stability can be significantly contained, thereby avoiding the crises that undermine the benefits of capital flows on investment and growth in the first place.

Message 2—Price Stability Does Not Guarantee Financial Stability

Volatile capital flows can impact financial stability. Large capital inflows are often associated with subsequent inflation, overheating, real exchange rate misalignments, and current account imbalances. Sudden stops can further complicate matters. Moreover, as EMEs have proceeded to further liberalize their capital accounts—particularly, in a financially integrated world—central bankers have faced an increasing challenge in trying to pursue both price and financial stability.

It is clear that the pursuit of price stability does not guarantee financial stability. Indeed, the old doctrine whereby monetary policy should not respond to asset bubbles—unless it had a potential impact on inflation—has now been cast aside. While this doctrine, as espoused by the 'Greenspan put', worked well during the 1987 market crash and the subsequent bust of the 2001 dot com bubble in the US, it was not able to withstand the test of time as witnessed by the 2008 post-Lehman Brothers debacle.

The new norm is that macroprudential regulation—together with efforts to strengthen financial systems—should be the first line of defense against the rapid build-up of asset prices, and thereby complement monetary policy. The Basel Committee on Banking Supervision has acknowledged the importance of macroprudential regulation and is working towards creating a Basel III framework for dealing with systemic risks and, consequently, with financial stability issues. The key is to ensure that banks have a sufficient pool of capital and liquidity levels particularly when the economy is in a downturn to avoid externalities related to systemic risks and the potential adverse impact on the real economy.

While the global economy rebuilds and capital and liquidity buffers in the banking system strengthen, the stakes remain high, especially in EMEs. Indeed, interest and exchange rate volatilities have a potentially higher impact on EMEs—in terms of economic activity, employment, and even distributional considerations—than in advanced economies. Why is this so? There are two main arguments to support this claim, one pertaining to the real side and the other to the financial side. On the real side, general profit margins across the bulk of the export sectors in EMEs tend to be thin (consider assembly-type labour-intensive work based on competitive wages producing intermediate technology products) and hence more susceptible to interest and exchange rate swings, and reinforced by the fact that hedging capacity and instruments in general are not as well developed. On the financial side, EMEs tend to have less developed financial systems. Accordingly, foreign capital is more likely to be channelled towards easily collateralized nontradable investments (that is, real estate) leading to a propensity to fuel asset price booms followed by busts impacting growth in the real economy (see Prasad and Rajan 2008).

Message 3—Active Policy is Critical to Stem Financial Headwinds

Proactive policy is critical to avoid persistent exchange rate and interest rate misalignments as it can lead to economic and financial fragilities. However, data remains weak on two critical fronts. First is the absence of available and reliable data on gross—as compared to net—capital flows, which is essential for timely intervention. Second, there is often limited data to verify whether 'pull' factors reflecting strong fundamentals as compared to 'push' factors reflecting conditions closely associated to source counties such as incentives for carry trades are at work.

Following the 2008 global financial crisis and the ensuing period of global financial turbulence, many EMEs, including India, followed a multi-pronged approach to crisis management. For example, policy measures in India included calibrating the policy regime with regard to the debt component of capital inflows/outflows, distinction between financial intermediaries and other resident entities, liberalization of policies in regard to capital outflows, flexibility in exchange rate movements, and interventions to smoothen volatility. Foreign exchange market interventions were also sterilized through changes in the cash reserve requirement and open market operations.

More generally, important lessons for EMEs include how to 'navigate' the Impossible Trinity by moving away from hard corners to middle grounds. Indeed, most Asian, including India, and Latin American countries have gained wisdom from their respective crises and have practised different degrees of management of the capital account. However, in Asia, India and the PRC remain among the least open and are likely to require fine-tuning of their policy framework as they pursue financial liberalization. In addition, there has been a certain acceptance of flexibility in exchange rate management with, for example, the Indian rupee depreciating by more than 12 per cent during 2011–12. A series of policy measures were also introduced by Reserve Bank of India (RBI) and the Ministry of Finance (MOF) to moderate volatility by encouraging capital flows while imposing restrictions on speculative 'one-way bets'. These measures, as a whole, allow EMEs—unequivocally so in the case of India—to maintain a degree of desirable monetary independence.

This takes us to arguably the most debatable topic in capital flow management, namely, capital controls. The current literature suggests that countries should first try various macro policy options before implementing capital control, and there is no 'one-size-fits-all' strategy for managing volatile capital flows. However, much more clarity is needed on two issues. First, our understanding about the functional mapping between the initial conditions and responses to shocks are generally weak. Without such mapping, there is a risk that policy responses can exacerbate the problem rather than mitigate it. Second, the literature is still evolving on the effectiveness of capital controls on the movements of key macro variables and the implications in terms of cross-country spillovers.

III. The Theoreticians and the Practitioners

With greater financial integration of the world economy, as well as greater leveraging and more complexity, capital account management in the larger context of macroeconomic stabilization has become a challenge for policymakers. Financial stability considerations can no longer be considered as a side event displayed on the rear-view mirror of the central bank dashboard. This was the case in the old central bank handbook where asset price build-up was a concern to the extent that it had potentially indirect effects on inflation. In fact, financial stability considerations can have very direct effects on the real economy, as we have witnessed with the bursting of the housing and bond bubbles in the US in 2007. The critical question is: how to unify the conceptual framework that links price, output, and financial stability considerations? Understanding the linkages will contribute towards putting together policy instruments that provide greater predictability in managing or steering the economy away from destabilizing dynamics.

Management of this volatility in capital flows generally involves actions across the monetary policy, fiscal, and capital account management spectrum. Furthermore, financial market regulation cannot be considered a spare tyre in the trunk but an increasingly important part of this framework. Indeed, macroprudential regulations will have to be effectively in place to avoid systemic risks where the economy in the presence of a small shock can be derailed from a potential narrow path and lead to important real effects. The debate, therefore, has focused on how to attract larger flows of capital to finance investment while safeguarding macro-management and minimizing destabilizing forces to the economy including output losses resulting from reversals in capital flows.

This fluid debate can be better understood across two important constituents, namely, theoreticians and practitioners. The first section of the volume presents the theoreticians' views while the second section presents the practitioners' views. This allows the reader to get a better sense of how the central bank's playbook is influenced by the theory and, to a certain extent, how central bankers have to, at times, write a new page in the gameplan. The practical reality and real time implications lead central bankers to try and make informed decisions in situations that may be categorized as being short of complete information with policy tools that may not be as refined as would be ideally desired. This, hence, brings up the importance of using judgment. This judgment under certain conditions may perhaps succeed in influencing market behaviour with the objective of targeting better policy outcomes. In some ways the analogy reverts back to the old Chinese saying of crossing the river by feeling your way one stone at a time.

A. The Theoreticians

In the first section, the theoreticians present their views on two important questions. First, can capital control measures be effective in moderating exchange rate volatility to prevent output losses, altering the maturity composition of inflows, and providing additional monetary policy independence? Second, how to introduce capital control measures in conjunction with other measures and when?

In this context, Kristin J. Forbes' paper ('Capital Flow Volatility and Contagion: A Focus on Asia') addresses some critical issues concerning the management of volatile capital flows. The recommendations of the paper are based on four important trends in Asia: the increase in the magnitude of gross capital inflows and outflows, the larger magnitude of gross capital inflows relative to outflows in some countries, the increase in the volatility of these capital flows, and the steady increase in the co-movement between equity markets over time. She suggests that the best approach involves attention to the form of these capital flows and strengthening the domestic financial system rather than directly controlling total capital flows. For example, supporting capital flows in the form of equity, instead of debt, provides natural risk sharing and reduces domestic vulnerabilities. Supporting outward capital flows by domestic investors can also provide an important form of stability, as domestic investors often 'retrench' and bring money invested abroad home during periods of heightened risk. Finally, one of the most powerful methods to stabilize economies against capital flow volatility is to reduce leverage in domestic banking systems.

Joseph E. Gagnon's paper ('All Currencies Are Reserve Currencies') deals with the fundamental question of how to attract foreign capital for productive investment while minimizing the risk of output losses from sudden stops. This paper begins with the proposition that currency mismatch has a statistically significant impact on growth performance after the financial crisis, and then recommends that the Local Currency Bond (LCB) markets have the potential to reduce financial vulnerability from the currency mismatch. To encourage the development of LCB markets, Gagnon recommends that IMF should create synthetic SDR bonds backed by medium-term sovereign bonds denominated in the currencies of the SDR basket. SDR bonds would make the international monetary system more symmetric: provide investors, including central banks, with a standardized asset that provides both a high degree of diversification and a deep and liquid market; reduce the distortions caused by excessive reliance on the US dollar as the main reserve asset; and assist in the development of LCB markets in developing economies. IMF's role is essential because no other institution has the expertise and the impartiality to choose the composition of the new SDR basket.

Michael W. Klein's paper ('Capital Controls and Real Exchange Rates') claims that there is little evidence that either longstanding or episodic controls on capital inflows tempered real exchange rate appreciations. PRC and, to a lesser extent, India—two countries with longstanding controls on capital inflows—had lower rates of appreciation than that consistent with real GDP growth, but there is no evidence of systematically lower appreciation for other countries that imposed controls on capital inflows. The analysis in his paper uses a new data set that differentiates between controls on inflows and outflows and also includes separate measures of inflow controls on six categories of assets. Thus, the results appear to suggest that capital controls may not be an effective tool to stem appreciations, especially the episodic controls.[4]

Jonathan D. Ostry's paper ('Capital Controls: When Are Multilateral Considerations of the Essence?') also addresses issues pertaining to the management of the volatile capital flows, but adds another dimension related to capital controls—multilateral dimension. His paper recommends that there is no surefire one-size-fits-all way to deal with the impact of potentially destabilizing short-term capital flows. In some circumstances, the usual macro-policy remedies will not be appropriate, in others, it may not be possible to address financial-fragility concerns through the domestic prudential framework alone. For both macroeconomic and financial-stability reasons, therefore, there may be circumstances in which capital controls are a legitimate component of the policy response to surges in capital inflows. However, Ostry suggests that capital controls should only be imposed in response to macroeconomic concerns when the flows are expected to be temporary. Persistent flows require stronger policy interventions. Moreover, capital controls could also be multilaterally problematic for various reasons including when capital controls are used to sustain undervalued currencies; and capital controls are used for manipulating the world interest rate. Thus, a multilateral framework governing the reimposition of controls, balancing the various considerations, could be helpful in managing possible cross-country spillovers.

B. *The Practitioners*

The practitioners' approach is captured in this volume by three central bankers from India, Brazil, and Indonesia, and a related paper on India. The three deputy governors were at the operational forefront and directly involved in finding practical solutions to stabilize their economies against a backdrop of very high volatility in capital flows in the recent past, especially in India, Brazil, and, to a lesser extent, Indonesia.

Subir Gokarn and Bhupal Singh's paper ('Costs and Benefits of Capital Account Management in India: A Practitioner's Perspective') brings out a

---

[4] However, it does not rule out the fact that controls can tilt the composition of inflows towards less volatile items (De Gregorio et al. 2000). See also, Table I.1 for a good survey on capital controls and the impact in Ostry et al. (2010).

thesis, common to all three practitioners, highlighting that flexibility and pragmatism is required in episodes of heightened volatility rather than adherence to strict theoretical rules. The paper provides a rich account of decision-making at work to stem the large inflows of capital—as well as subsequent outflows—and how the various instruments and measures at the central bank's disposal were activated during the 2007–12 period. In the case of India, the country was facing strong inflationary pressures during this period together with an increasing current account deficit, which made matters more challenging. The authors stress the importance of maintaining market-based exchange rates recognizing, however, the merits of exchange rate intervention to manage excessive volatility.

In the case of India, capital controls on *inflows* have reflected a combination of 'quantity' and 'price' based controls while controls on *outflows* have been mainly 'quantity' based. The authors' own experience suggests that the effectiveness of capital controls is both 'time' and 'situation' specific. However, there are both benefits and costs to capital account management including in (i) forming market expectations, (ii) development of the market, and (iii) impact on categories of stakeholders. Indeed, often news-based expectation can set in and prove destabilizing, leading the economy away from fundamentals. This can lead to excessive foreign exchange volatility and, in the case of EMEs running current account deficits, and higher depreciation.

Abhijit Sen Gupta and Rajeswari Sengupta's paper ('Negotiating the Trilemma and Reserve Management in an Era of Volatile Capital Flows in India') provides an analysis of India's recent experience in capital flow management. Various findings are presented in an effort to better understand how and why policymakers reacted the way they did. According to the authors, faced with the Impossibility Trinity, India decided to opt for a middle ground—an intermediate regime avoiding corner solutions—that sought to juggle various policy objectives as per the macroeconomic context. In recent years, there has been a shift towards greater weight on monetary policy independence to contain inflation pressures at the cost of a more flexible exchange rate. The exchange rate has served as the shock absorber in periods of volatile capital flows. This has been buttressed by selective capital flow management measures on both inflows and outflows.

Another finding is that the intervention in the foreign exchange markets has been asymmetric, with RBI intervening mostly to prevent appreciation of the currency but adopting a hands-off approach in a period of depreciation. Two clear periods of capital flow management can be discerned from the data. There is evidence that points to effective sterilization during 1998–2004 where increases in Net Foreign Assets (NFA) were offset by declines in Net Domestic Assets (NDA), insulating the money supply from intervention in the foreign exchange market. This coincides with a period of greatest accumulation of foreign exchange reserves. However, post-2004, sterilization was less effective with only 30 per cent of NFA increase offset by declines in NDA, which the authors attribute to increasing fiscal costs of sterilization. Finally, during 2007–11, India witnessed one of the highest erosions of reserve cover across a spectrum of EMEs.

Luiz Awazu Pereira da Silva and Ricardo Eyer Harris's paper ('Sailing through the Global Financial Storm: Brazil's Recent Experience with Monetary and Macroprudential Policies to Lean against the Financial Cycle and Deal with Systemic Risks') provides an account of Brazil's experience in 2008 and again in 2010–11 and how it sought to 'sail through the global financial storm', including the impact of the FED's QE program. The Central Bank of Brazil, like the RBI, adopted both inflation and financial stability goals. Macroprudential regulations were introduced not as a substitute for monetary policy action but to primarily deal with financial stability risks. Since 2010, application of macroprudential measures sought to 'lean against the wind' in dealing with the cyclicality of the financial system.

Brazil managed its massive capital inflows in standard textbook fashion with aggregate demand contraction through fiscal and monetary policies allowing for sufficient currency appreciation, while smoothing movements through sterilized reserve accumulation, which reduced volatility of the exchange rate without aiming at distorting its structural trend. The paper brings out a common theme among practitioners in that 'decisions cannot be as firmly grounded on theory as one might desire'. Policymakers are, therefore, forced to make 'genuine policy judgments' drawing on analysis, market intelligence, and modelling while adopting a 'step-by-step' approach 'weighing the trade-offs inherent to those measure and to avoid excessive distortions and undesirable side effects'. The chapter presents a conceptual framework on the goals and instruments that a central bank faces between monetary and macroprudential policies and how these interact with one another.

According to the authors, the ongoing analytical framework is deemed to be a work in progress where effective indicators will have to be developed to assist in better monitoring cross-sectional risks related to the interconnectedness of the financial system and the real economy.

Hartadi A. Sarwono's paper ('Managing Capital Flows: Indonesia's Experience') presents Indonesia's experience in dealing with capital flows. It highlights the inadequacy of a purely macroeconomic policy response and/or conventional open market operations to address volatile capital flows. Capital flow management and macroprudential measures are equally important to limit the risks of short-term, volatile flows but are mere reinforcements of previous policies and cannot substitute for basic monetary policies. In line with the deleveraging process that took place after the global financial crisis and the resurgence of capital inflows in Indonesia in 2009, the central bank pursued the following broad and comprehensive policy mix: (i) maintaining a flexible exchange rate, (ii) enhancing monetary operation strategy, and (iii) conducting capital flows management, as well as imposing targeted macroprudential measures. Data suggests that the above policy mix was able to achieve its goal, that is, maintain the trend of capital inflows, shift the composition of investment in financial instruments, expand FDI, and contain exchange rate volatility in the country.

Epilogue: Currency Turbulence during May–October 2013

Events inevitably overtake publication cycles. While the scope of the conference, which provided the chapters for this volume, was developments until 2012, the following year saw another episode of global financial turbulence, which impacted all the countries whose experiences are described in 'The Practitioners' section. This was both an inconvenience and an opportunity; the former, because the book would risk being partially obsolete by the time of its publication, and the latter because all the authors had some time to add short sections to their chapters. Despite their preliminary nature, these sections add to the value of the chapters and the book itself by comparing and contrasting policy responses during the 2013 episode with earlier ones.

The shock that generated the turbulence in 2013 was, paradoxically, an indication that the US economy was recovering strongly enough for the authorities to consider rolling back their unconventional policy measures. When Chairman of the US Federal Reserve Board, Ben Bernanke, suggested in May that a reversal of the asset purchase programme labelled QE3 was now likely, it might have been expected that the news would be greeted with some relief by global financial markets looking for signs of a robust and sustainable recovery. Instead, turmoil ensued. Evidently, markets that had become used to abundant liquidity were not yet prepared to live without it, even when the fundamentals were starting to look good. The transition from liquidity-driven to fundamentals-driven investment decisions was always going to be a difficult one; the reaction to Bernanke's statement indicated that it could cause panic.

From the perspective of EMEs, including the three that this volume covers, recent currency dynamics, either unstable or stable, were significantly determined by global liquidity conditions. Not surprisingly, the developments in the US spread through this group of countries, resulting in turbulence in both domestic asset and currency markets. Further, there was a key difference between recent episodes, which have been analysed, in depth, in the chapters,[5] and this one. In the earlier episodes, central banks in the advanced economies initiated large liquidity enhancement measures, which smoothed global financial markets. However, in 2013, the turbulence was caused by the prospect of one such measure being withdrawn, so a similar stabilizing response could obviously not be expected. In this sense, the horizon of instability and, consequently, the potential damage it could cause domestic economies was far greater than in the earlier episodes.

The policy responses in these as well as other countries were undoubtedly shaped by this perception. As the newly added sections demonstrate, there were similarities across countries but also important differences based on domestic macroeconomic conditions. The episode is too recent to draw any substantial conclusions about the effectiveness of the policy responses. In any case, the period of turbulence was itself truncated by the same factor as in the earlier episodes: the US Federal Reserve deciding that the time was not right for the withdrawal of liquidity support. This has brought some stability and provided some breathing space for economies whose tendencies to currency instability are exacerbated by domestic conditions.

[5] Please see chapters 5 and 6 for India, and 7 and 8 for Brazil and Indonesia, respectively.

To conclude, we do hope that readers of this book will be able to better understand the practical realities in capital flow management as experienced by some of the central banks that were most strongly exposed to shifting capital flows and the ways in which theoretical underpinnings have provided a direction for policy initiatives within certain bounds.

References

Asian Development Bank (ADB). 2011. *Asia Capital Markets Monitor*. Manila: ADB.

BIS-Committee on the Global Financial System. 2010. 'Macroprudential Instruments and Frameworks: A Stocktaking of Issues and Experiences', *CGFS Working Papers N° 38*, Bank for International Settlements, May 2010.

Bank for International Settlements. 2012. 'Challenges Related to Capital Flows: Latin American Perspectives', *BIS Papers*, Bank for International Settlements, No. 68, October.

Cecchetti, Stephen, Marion Kohler, and Christian Upper. 2009. 'Financial Crisis and Economic Activity', *paper presented at Federal Reserve Bank of Kansas City's Symposium at Jackson Hole*.

De Gregorio, José, Sebastian Edwards, and Rodrigo Valdés. 2000. 'Controls on Capital Inflows: Do They Work?', *Journal of Development Economics* 69: 59–83.

Forbes, Kristin J. and Francis Warnock. 2012. 'Capital Flow Waves: Surges, Stops, Flight and Retrenchment', *Journal of International Economics* 88 (2).

Forbes, K., M. Fratzscher, T. Kostka, and R. Straub. 2012. 'Bubble Thy Neighbor: Portfolio Effects and Externalities from Capital Controls', *NBER Working Paper* 18052, National Bureau of Economic Research, Cambridge, MA.

Gokarn, Subir. 2010. 'Monetary Policy Considerations after the Crisis: Practitioners' Perspectives', *Plenary Lecture at the Conference on Economic Policies for Inclusive Development*, Organized by Ministry of Finance, Government of India and National Institute of Public Finance and Policy at New Delhi, December 1.

IMF Strategy, Policy and Review Department. 2011. 'Recent Experiences in Managing Capital Inflows–Cross-Cutting Themes and Possible Policy Framework', International Monetary Fund.

Mohan, Rakesh and Muneesh Kapur. 2011a. 'Managing the Impossible Trinity–Volatile Capital Flows with Indian Monetary Policy', in R. Mohan (ed) *Growth with Financial Stability Central Banking in an Emerging Market*. New Delhi: Oxford University Press.

———. 2011b. 'Liberalization and Regulation of Capital Flows: Lessons for Emerging Market Economies', in R. Mohan (ed) *Growth with Financial*

Stability Central Banking in an Emerging Market. New Delhi: Oxford University Press.

Obstfeld, Maurice. 2009. 'International Finance and Growth in Developing Countries: What Have We Learned?', *IMF Staff Papers* (56) 1.

Ostry, J.D., A.R. Ghosh, K. Habermeier, M. Chamon, M.S. Qureshi, and D.B.S. Reinhardt. 2010. 'Capital Inflows: The Role of Controls', *IMF Staff Position Note 10/04*. International Monetary Fund, Washington, DC.

Ostry, J. D., A. R. Ghosh, K. Habermeier, M. Chamon, M. S. Qureshi, L. Laeven, and A. Kokenyne. 2011. 'Managing Capital Inflows: What Tools to Use?', *IMF Staff Discussion Note 11/06*. International Monetary Fund, Washington, DC.

Ostry, J.D., A.R. Ghosh, and A. Korinek. 2012. 'Multilateral Aspects of Managing the Capital Account', *IMF Staff Discussion Note 12/10*. International Monetary Fund, Washington, DC.

Ostry, J.D., A.R. Ghosh, and M. Chamon. 2012. 'Two Targets, Two Instruments: Monetary and Exchange Rate Policies in Emerging Market Economies', *IMF Staff Discussion Note 12/01*. International Monetary Fund, Washington, DC.

Prasad, Eswar and Raghuram Rajan. 2008. 'A Pragmatic Approach to Capital Account Liberalization', *NBER Working Papers 14051*, National Bureau of Economic Research, Inc.

Rogoff, Kenneth S. 2002. 'Rethinking Capital Controls: When should we keep an open mind?', *Finance and Development*, December, 55–56.

COMPOSITIONAL SHIFT AND VOLATILITY OF CAPITAL FLOWS

KRISTIN J. FORBES[*]

Capital Flow Volatility and Contagion[†]

A Focus on Asia

I. Introduction

Gross capital flows into and out of many countries have increased dramatically since 2000. Increased capital flows and integration with global financial markets—when occurring gradually over time—can provide substantial benefits. This growth in gross capital flows and global financial integration, however, has occurred simultaneously with an increase in the volatility of these capital flows. Extreme movements in capital flows—whether in the form of sharp increases or decreases—can create substantial challenges for the financial sector and overall macroeconomy.

This paper attempts to better understand what drives these periods of extreme capital flow volatility, focusing on Asia but drawing on

* The author would like to thank Frank Warnock for his critical role in some of the research projects that provided background for this paper. Further thanks to participants in the RBI–ADB conference, and especially Thomas Moser, for helpful suggestions.

† Paper prepared for RBI–ADB conference on Managing Capital Flows held in Mumbai, India, 18–20 November 2012.

insights and comparisons from around the world. Section II begins this analysis by documenting four important trends in capital flows and financial markets in Asia: (1) the increase in the magnitude of gross capital inflows and outflows; (2) the larger magnitude of gross capital inflows relative to outflows in some countries; (3) the increase in the volatility of these capital flows; and (4) the steady increase in the co-movement between equity markets over time. It also shows that most of these trends are similar for Asia as the rest of the world, except that several Asian countries have substantially greater international capital flows driven by foreigners relative to flows driven by domestic investors.

Section III then attempts to better understand these trends. It documents periods of sharp movements or 'waves' in different types of capital flows in individual Asian economies. It moves on to discuss the more limited role of domestic investors in stabilizing certain economies (such as India) during these sharp swings in capital flows. Results from regression analysis suggest that most of the volatility in gross capital flows is driven by global variables (especially global risk) and contagion, and by sharp swings in debt flows (instead of equity flows). Since these global and contagion effects are shared across multiple countries, it is not surprising that many extreme movements in capital flows occur simultaneously in many countries, potentially explaining the increased co-movement across financial markets.

Section IV builds on these results by closely examining the role of global shocks, and especially contagion, in transmitting volatility around the world and within Asia. It discusses various channels of contagion and shows evidence that trends in Asia, such as increased trade exposure, international investment exposure, and banking leverage, could all be increasing the region's vulnerability to sharp movements in capital flows and market returns in other countries and regions. The analysis suggests that greater vulnerability of the countries is not necessarily simply because of a greater integration with global financial markets or due to greater international capital flows. Instead, the form of these capital flows has a more important role in determining vulnerability. Countries with a greater share of their international capital flows in equity (relative to debt) and a larger ratio of outward capital flows by domestic investors (relative to inward flows by foreigners) tend to be less vulnerable.

Section V concludes by discussing key implications for how Asian economies can best mitigate risks in the current era of large and volatile capital flows and strong market co-movement. One lesson is that reducing exposure to international capital flows would not necessarily reduce domestic volatility and vulnerability. Instead, greater attention to the form of these capital flows is required. Supporting capital flows in the form of equity, instead of debt, provides natural risk sharing and reduces domestic vulnerabilities. Supporting outward capital flows by domestic investors can provide an important form of stability, as domestic investors often 'retrench' and bring money invested abroad home during periods of heightened risk. This insight is particularly important for several countries in Asia, such as India, which have substantially lower gross capital outflows by domestic investors relative to inflows by foreigners. A final important lesson is that one of the most potent methods to stabilize an economy against volatile capital flows is to reduce leverage in domestic banking systems. The lower leverage in Asian banks for much of the 2000s helped reduce the region's vulnerability to negative shocks originating elsewhere. However, this leverage has been increasing steadily over the last decade, and this will increase Asia's vulnerability to sharp swings in gross capital flows in the future. As a result, it is becoming increasingly important for Asian countries to evaluate carefully how best to strengthen their economies in this era of large and volatile global capital flows.

II. Four Trends

This section documents four trends in capital flows and financial markets in Asia: (1) the magnitude of gross capital inflows and outflows has increased; (2) gross capital inflows are greater than outflows in many countries; (3) capital flow volatility has increased; and (4) equity markets commove more closely today than in the past.

The First Trend

Much attention has been paid to the increase in net capital flows in many countries around the world—often referred to as global imbalances—since the early 1990s. More recently, attention has shifted to the even greater increase in gross capital flows—the capital flowing into a country driven by foreigners and the capital flowing out of a country driven by domestics.[1] This trend is also true for Asia—although patterns differ across countries. Figure 1 shows net capital flows, gross capital inflows (from foreigners) and gross capital outflows (from domestics) for six Asian economies—with the sample chosen based on data availability and to represent the range of experiences in the region.[2] Gross capital flows are written using balance of payments (BOP) accounting, so that a negative value for gross capital outflows represents domestic citizens sending money abroad.

In most countries, the magnitude of gross capital flows has increased dramatically over time and movements in gross capital flows are substantially larger than for net flows. The panel for Australia in Figure 1.1 shows an example of this trend, with a moderate increase in Australia's current account surplus reflecting much larger increases in both underlying gross capital inflows and outflows. Japan, the Republic of Korea, and Taipei,China also show similar trends. In contrast, Thailand has seen a more moderate increase in gross capital flows, with gross inflows from abroad still below levels prior to the 1997 Asian crisis. India shows a striking pattern (discussed in detail later) of a large increase in gross capital inflows from foreigners that corresponds to a large increase in net capital flows and much smaller changes _ 1 gross capital outflows by domestics.

The Second Trend

In most advanced and emerging economies, gross capital inflows and outflows tend to move simultaneously in opposite directions and be roughly the same magnitude (allowing for any differential corresponding to any current account imbalance). Figure 1.1 shows this typical pattern for Australia and Japan. The other graphs in the figure show that today many Asian countries have gross capital inflows from foreigners that are substantially greater than gross capital outflows from domestics.

[1] For recent discussions of the importance of gross capital flows, see Broner et al. (2010), Forbes and Warnock (2012), Gourinchas (2012), Lane (2012a), and Milesi-Ferretti and Tille (2010).

[2] Capital flow data reflects private capital flows and does not include changes in reserves. Gross capital inflows are net purchases of domestic assets by foreign investors and gross outflows are net purchases of foreign assets by domestic investors. Quarterly flows are calculated as two-quarter moving averages to smooth lines.

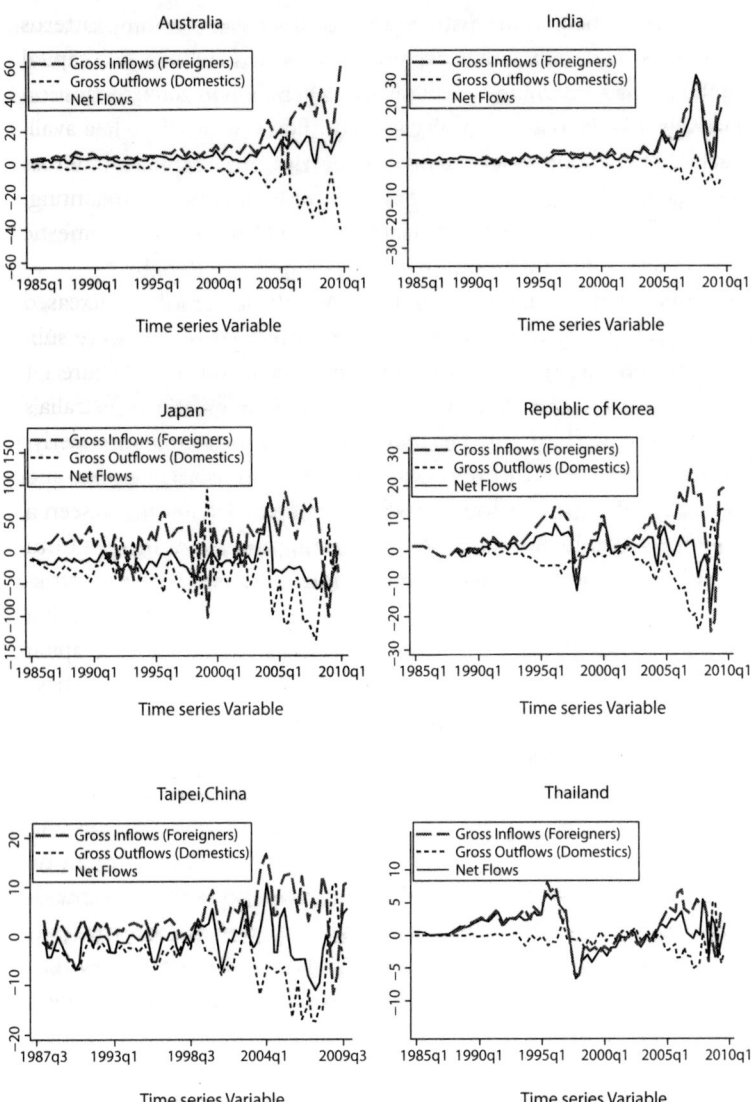

FIGURE 1.1   Net and Gross Capital Flows in Asia ($ billion)

Notes: These graphs show net capital flows and gross inflows and gross outflows from 1985 through 2010. Each flow is calculated as the 2-quarter moving average. Gross outflows are reported using standard BOP definitions, so that a negative number indicates a gross outflow. Gross outflows only include private capital flows and do not include changes in reserves. Capital flow data from IMF's BOP Statistics, augmented with country information.

The trends behind this pattern vary across Asian economies. At one extreme is India, which has experienced a sharp increase in quarterly capital inflows (reaching a peak of over $30 billion in 2008) but has had relatively little increase in gross capital outflows (which have never even reached $10 billion). In several other countries, gross capital inflows and outflows moved together in the past and were roughly the same magnitude, but since the Global Financial Crisis (GFC) inflows have increased substantially more than outflows. For example, the Republic of Korea had similar patterns in inflows and outflows through most of the 2000s; however, at the end of the decade it had quarterly gross inflows of close to $20 billion but gross outflows of less than $8 billion. Taipei,China and Thailand show a similar pattern of substantially greater inflows than outflows today. These patterns may reflect a number of factors: greater controls on the ability of domestic citizens in some Asian countries to invest abroad, a greater home bias in Asia due to a belief that domestic economies offer higher returns than investing abroad, or the active role of regional central banks in purchasing foreign reserves.

The Third Trend

Gross capital inflows and outflows have been extremely volatile in many Asian countries (as well as in most countries around the world). For example, as shown in Figure 1.1, quarterly net purchases of assets of the Republic of Korea by foreigners reversed from almost +$25 billion to −$25 billion (net sales) during the GFC. These sharp swings occurred not only in foreign capital flows, but also in flows by domestic investors. For example, net purchases of foreign assets by investors from Taipei,China reversed from almost −$18 billion (net purchases) to over +$10 billion (net sales of foreign assets with the proceeds being returned home to Taipei,China) during the GFC.

In order to assess, more formally, how this volatility has increased over time, Figure 1.2 graphs the volatility in gross capital inflows for several Asian countries.[3] The top panel shows a striking increase in volatility since the mid-2000s. The bottom panel of the graph shows, however, that in some countries (such as Indonesia and Thailand) recent levels of volatility are still not as high as experienced during the Asian crisis.

---

[3] Capital flow volatility is calculated as the standard deviation in quarterly gross capital inflows over the last two years (eight quarters) for each country.

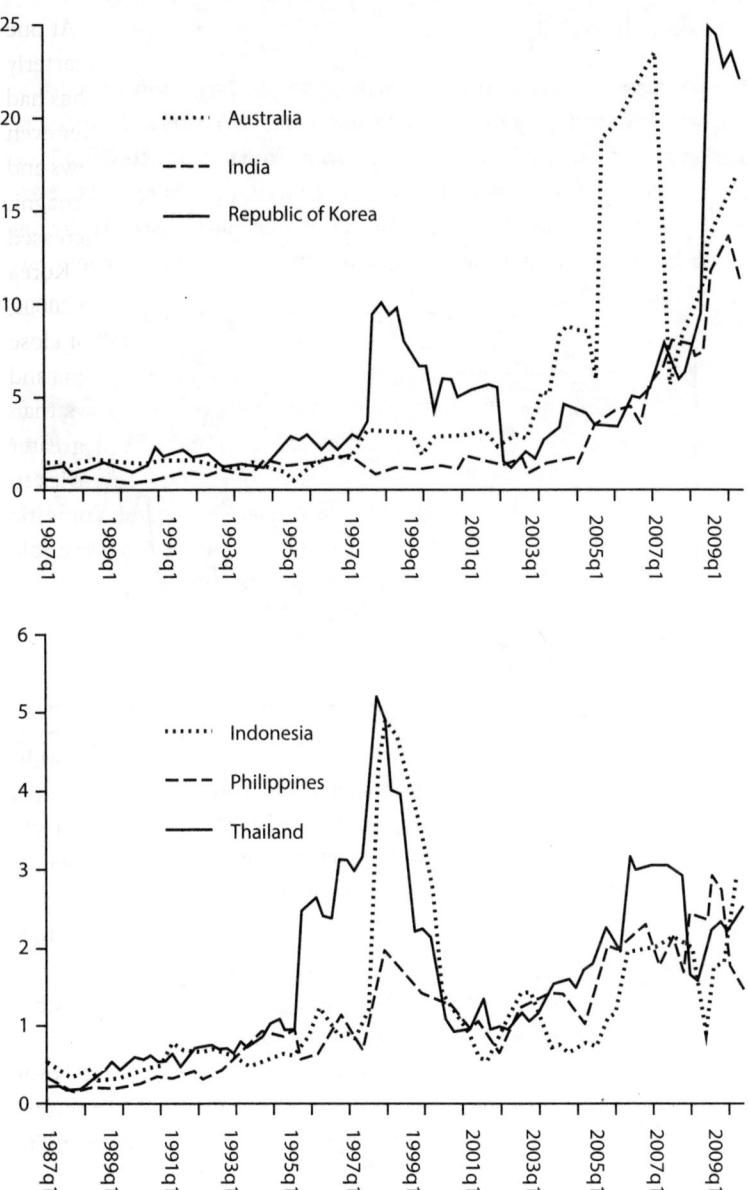

FIGURE 1.2   Volatility in Gross Capital Inflows in Asia
Notes: Capital flow volatility calculated as the standard deviation in quarterly gross capital inflows over the last two years (8 quarters).

The Fourth Trend

The co-movement across financial markets within Asia has increased substantially over time. Figure 1.3 shows this increased correlation in equity market returns for 14 Asian economies from January 1981 through June 2012.[4] It also shows the same correlation for a larger sample of 48 developed and emerging markets. Correlations are calculated based on moving 52-week correlations in local currency returns for each pair of countries.

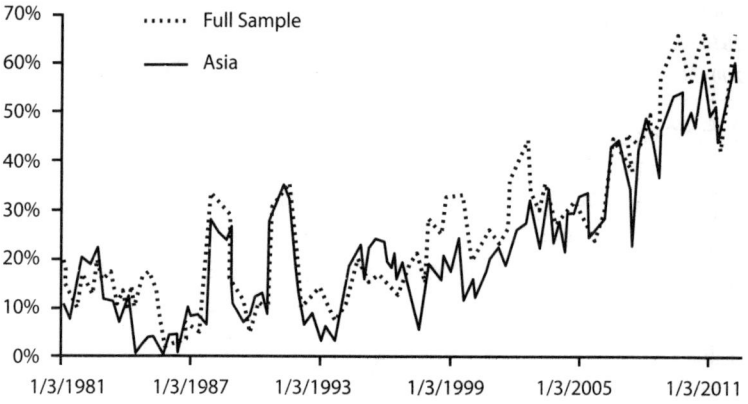

FIGURE 1.3   Average Bilateral Correlations in Equity Returns
Notes: Averages are 52-week moving averages of the bilateral correlations in equity (based on local currency stock indices) for countries in the specified group. See Table 1.1 for a list of countries included in the Asia group.

[4] Weekly stock returns are calculated based on the Friday closing price for each index as retrieved from Global Financial Data, Inc., accessed June 2012. The broadest equity index available is used for each country. I begin by calculating the moving 52-week correlations between local-currency returns for each pair of countries for each week. Each country must have return data for the previous 52 weeks to calculate this correlation. This generates a large matrix of bilateral correlations—of up to 1,128 country-pairs by 1,638 weeks—and I average the correlations for each week. I focus on local currency returns in order to exclude any increase in correlations resulting purely from similar exchange rate movements relative to the dollar. Cross-market correlations based on US dollar returns tend to be slightly higher than those based on local currency returns due to this exchange rate effect.

TABLE 1.1   Correlations in Equity Returns over Time

	Full Sample	Asian Economies
1981–4	0.140	0.113
1985–9	0.125	0.101
1990–4	0.180	0.157
1995–9	0.218	0.178
2000–4	0.301	0.238
2005–9	0.435	0.392
2010–June 2012	0.580	0.538
Change from 1981/84 to:		
2010/12	0.440	0.425
2005/09	0.295	0.279

Notes: Correlations are average 52-week bilateral correlations in weekly stock market returns based on indices in local currency. The territories included in Asia are: Australia, the People's Republic of China, Hong Kong, China, India, Indonesia, Japan, Malaysia, New Zealand, Pakistan, the Philippines, Singapore, the Republic of Korea, Taipei,China, and Thailand. See Forbes (2013) for more details on methodology and the list of the 48 countries in the full sample.

Table 1.1 further quantifies this increase in market co-movement by reporting average correlations over different time periods.

The graph and table show that correlations between Asian markets have increased dramatically over time and over each five-year window since 1985. More specifically, average correlations in Asian equity returns have increased by 43 per cent from the 1981–4 window to the 2010–June 2012 window, reaching a peak of 54 per cent in the latter period. The graph and table also show that this increase in correlations is similar to that experienced for the larger sample of markets around the world. More specifically, average correlations for the larger sample increased by 44 per cent over the same period, reaching a peak of 58 per cent in the last period. A number of reasons could have led to this increase in correlations, such as greater role of global shocks, increased volatility over time, or a greater role of contagion and other linkages across markets.[5]

---

[5] See Forbes and Rigobon (2002) for a discussion on how increased volatility in one country's stock market will automatically increase the unconditional correlation in returns between countries for purely statistical reasons.

To summarize, this section has documented four key trends in capital flows and financial markets in Asia: the increased magnitude of gross capital inflows and outflows; the larger volume of inflows from foreigners relative to outflows by domestics in many economies; the increased volatility of these gross capital flows; and the increased co-movement in equity markets. A key theme from this discussion, however, is that most of these trends are not unique to Asia and are common to many other countries and regions in the world. For example, most countries and regions have experienced large increases in gross capital inflows and outflows, an increase in the volatility of these gross flows, and an increase in the co-movement of their markets with other financial markets around the world. The one trend documented for many Asian countries, but which is less common in other parts of the world, is the substantially larger volume of gross inflows from foreigners relative to gross outflows by domestics.

III. Explaining Trends in Asian Capital Flows

In order to understand what has caused these four trends in Asian capital flows and financial markets, this section builds on the analysis in Forbes and Warnock (2012) (hereafter referred to as FW). FW develops a new methodology to identify and analyse what the authors call 'waves' in gross capital flows. More specifically, FW uses quarterly data on gross capital inflows and outflows to identify four types of episodes of extreme capital flow movements.[6] These four episodes are:

- 'Surges': a sharp increase in gross capital inflows (driven by foreigners);
- 'Stops': a sharp decrease in gross capital inflows (driven by foreigners);
- 'Flight': a sharp increase in gross capital outflows (driven by domestics); and
- 'Retrenchment': a sharp decrease in gross capital outflows (driven by domestics).

[6] An earlier literature uses a similar methodology to identify 'surges' and 'stops' in capital flows. FW is the first paper in this literature, however, to use actual data on *gross* capital flows in order to differentiate the movements in capital flows by foreigners and domestics (versus earlier work, which used aggregated data on net flows). This allows an identification of more episodes and improved understanding of what drives these episodes.

To provide a more concrete example of this methodology, consider the calculation of surge and stop episodes for India. Let C_t be the four-quarter moving sum of gross capital inflows (GINFLOW) and compute annual year-over-year changes in C_t:

$$C_t = \sum_{i=0}^{3} GINFLOW_{t-i}, \qquad \text{with } t = 1, 2, \ldots, N \text{ and} \qquad (1)$$

$$\Delta C_t = C_t - C_{t-4}, \qquad \text{with } t = 5, 6, \ldots, N. \qquad (2)$$

In Figure 1.4a, the solid line is this change in annual gross capital inflows as defined in equation (2). Next, compute rolling means and standard deviations of ΔC_t over the last five years. The dashed lines are the bands for mean capital inflows plus or minus one standard deviation, and the dotted lines are the comparable two-standard-deviation bands. A 'surge' episode is defined as starting the first month t that ΔC_t increases more than one standard deviation above its rolling mean. The episode ends once ΔC_t falls below one standard deviation above its mean. In addition, in order for the entire period to qualify as a surge episode, there must be at least one quarter t when ΔC_t increases at least two standard deviations above its mean.[7] A 'stop' episode, defined using a symmetric approach, is a period when gross inflows fall one standard deviation below its mean, provided it reaches two standard deviations below at some point. The episode ends when gross inflows are no longer at least one standard deviation below its mean.

Figure 1.4b shows the comparable framework for defining flight and retrenchment episodes, with these episodes calculated based on gross private outflows (by domestics) rather than the gross inflows (from foreigners).[8] More specifically, we use equations (1) and (2) to calculate the annual change in gross capital outflows, shown in Figure 1.4b as the solid line. A 'flight' episode is defined starting the first month that ΔC_t falls more than one standard deviation below its rolling mean and ends once ΔC_t rises back to one standard deviation below its mean, provided it reaches at least two standard deviations below the mean at some point. A retrenchment' episode is defined symmetrical, as when gross

---

[7] We also require that the ΔC_t must be above or below the relevant one-standard deviation line for more than one quarter to qualify as an episode.

[8] In BOP accounting terms, outflows by domestic residents are reported with a negative value.

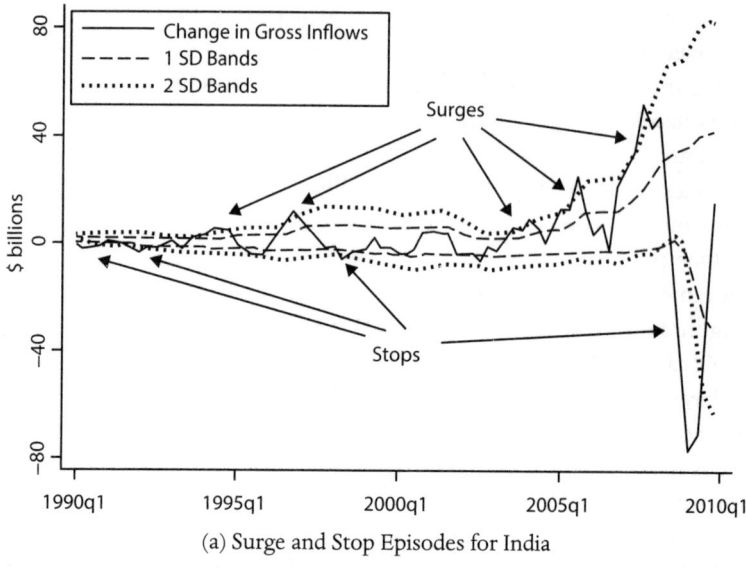

(a) Surge and Stop Episodes for India

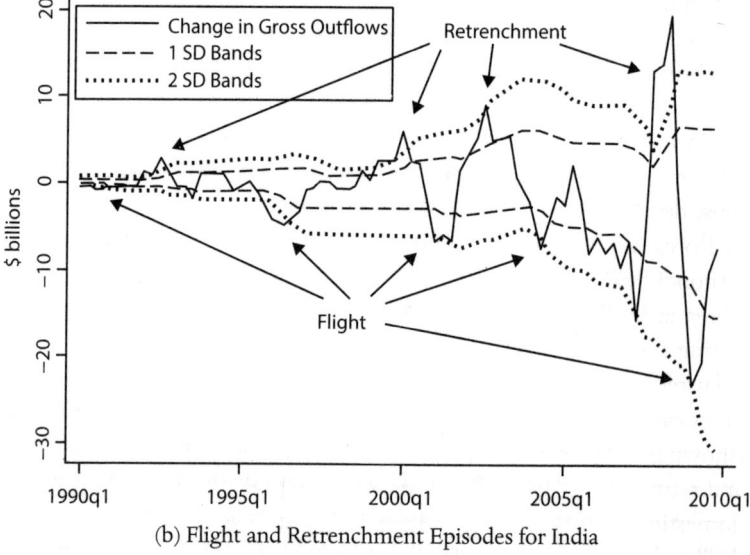

(b) Flight and Retrenchment Episodes for India

FIGURE 1.4   Capital Flow Episodes for India: 1990–2010

outflows increase more than one standard deviation above its mean, provided it reaches two standard deviations at some point.

Figures 1.4a and 1.4b show that during the period from 1990–2010, India had five surge episodes, four stop episodes, five flight episodes, and four retrenchment episodes. Table 1.2 lists the exact dates of these episodes, as well as the episodes for other Asian countries using the same methodology.

One pattern that stands out in these graphs of India's capital flow movements is the different magnitude of the flows by foreigners (Figure 1.4a) versus flows by domestics (Figure 1.4b). During the recent GFC, capital inflows from foreigners reversed sharply from large inflows to large outflows in a 'stop' episode. In early 2008 this was partially balanced by Indian's selling foreign investments and returning the proceeds to home in a 'retrenchment' episode. However, since investment abroad by Indians was lower than investment into India by foreigners, this retrenchment by domestic investors was not enough to balance the reduction in inflows from abroad, it led to India experiencing a sharp reduction in net capital flows. Moreover, as global financial conditions deteriorated during the GFC, domestic Indians stopped retrenching and bringing funds home and instead started to send capital abroad in a 'flight' episode.

This pattern is fundamentally different than occurred in most emerging markets during the GFC. Instead, a more typical pattern (in most developed and many emerging markets) is that for the Republic of Korea and Thailand in Figure 1.5 (with the exact dates of the corresponding episodes listed in Table 1.2). In both the Republic of Korea and Thailand, capital inflows from foreigners dropped sharply during the GFC, causing a 'stop' episode in Figures 1.5a and 1.5c (as occurred in India). However, in each of these countries, the 'stop' in gross capital inflows was largely balanced by a 'retrenchment' episode (shown in Figures 1.5b and 1.5d) as domestics sold foreign investments and returned the cash home. The magnitude of this retrenchment by domestic investors was so great that it helped cushion these economies during the GFC when global liquidity evaporated. More specifically, in the Republic of Korea, the ΔC_t measuring capital inflows from foreigners fell by over $100 billion, but this was largely counteracted by the ΔC_t measuring flows from domestics which increased by almost $90 billion. In Thailand, the fall in inflows from foreigners was just over $20 billion;

TABLE 1.2 Surge, Stop, Flight, and Retrenchment Episodes for Asia, 1990–2010

	Surges		Stops		Flight		Retrenchment	
	Start	End	Start	End	Start	End	Start	End
Australia	1993q4	1994q3	1990q1	1991q3	1995q4	1996q3	1990q1	1991q1
	1995q3	1996q3	1997q3	1998q1	2004q1	2004q3	1994q4	1995q2
	2002q3	2002q4	1998q3	1998q4	2006q2	2007q1	2003q1	2003q3
	2003q4	2004q3	2005q1	2005q4			2005q1	2005q4
	2006q2	2007q1						
India	1993q4	1994q4	1990q1	1990q4	1990q3	1991q2	1992q1	1992q4
	1996q2	1997q1	1991q3	1992q1	1995q4	1996q4	1999q2	2000q2
	2003q3	2004q2	1998q2	1998q3	2000q4	2001q3	2002q1	2002q4
	2004q4	2005q3	2008q3	2009q3	2004q1	2004q3	2007q4	2008q2
	2006q4	2008q1			2008q4	2009q2		
Indonesia	1990q3	1991q2	1993q2	1993q3	1993q3	1994q3	1997q2	1998q3
	1995q2	1996q3	1997q4	1998q3	2002q3	2003q2	2003q3	2003q4
	2005q4	2006q1	2006q4	2007q1	2004q1	2005q1	2006q3	2007q1
			2009q1	2009q3	2005q3	2006q2		
Japan	1993q4	1995q1	1990q4	1991q4	1993q4	1994q4	1990q3	1991q3
	2000q2	2001q1	1992q2	1993q1	2000q2	2001q1	1996q3	1996q4
			1998q1	1999q1			1998q2	1999q4
			2005q2	2005q3			2008q3	2009q3
			2006q3	2007q1				
			2008q3	2009q3				

Country								
Republic of Korea	1994q3	1995q4	1997q2 2008q1	1998q3 2009q2	1994q2 2002q4	1995q4 2003q3	1997q3 2005q1 2008q3	1999q1 2005q3 2009q3
Malaysia			2005q4 2008q3	2006q3 2009q2	2006q2	2007q4	2008q3	2009q2
New Zealand	2000q2 2006q3	2001q1 2007q3	1996q4 1998q3 2008q2	1997q2 1999q2 2009q3	1990q1 1993q3 2000q2 2006q3	1990q2 1994q2 2001q1 2007q3	2002q4 2005q3	2003q3 2006q1
Philippines	1994q2 1996q1 2005q2 2007q1	1994q3 1997q1 2005q4 2007q3	1992q1 1997q3 2008q1	1992q2 1998q4 2009q1	1991q4 1999q1 2007q1	1994q2 1999q2 2007q2	1997q3 2008q1	1998q2 2008q4
Singapore	2006q4	2008q1	2008q2	2009q2	2006q2	2007q4	2008q2	2009q2
Taipei,China	1999q2 2003q3	2000q2 2004q2	1995q3 1997q4 2001q1 2005q1 2008q4	1995q4 1998q3 2001q2 2005q2 2009q2	1996q1 2000q1 2003q3	1996q3 2000q4 2004q1	1997q1 2002q2 2008q2	1997q4 2002q3 2009q2
Thailand	1990q1 1995q2 2004q3	1990q3 1996q1 2006q1	1992q1 1996q3 2007q1 2008q3	1992q4 1998q2 2007q4 2009q3	1990q1 1993q2 2005q1	1990q2 1994q2 2006q1	1991q2 1994q4 1996q3 2008q1	1991q4 1995q1 1997q2 2009q3

Note: This table is an excerpt from Appendix Table 2 in Forbes and Warnock (2012). Data is not available for the full period for several countries and the table lists episodes only during periods for which data is available.

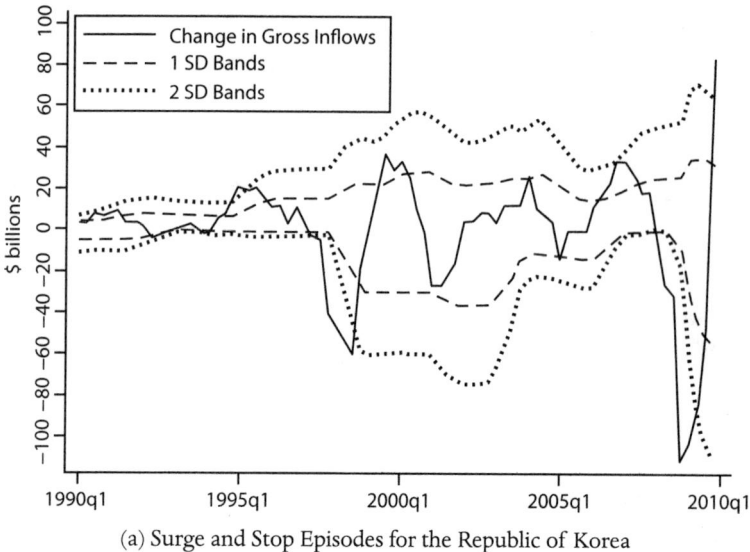

(a) Surge and Stop Episodes for the Republic of Korea

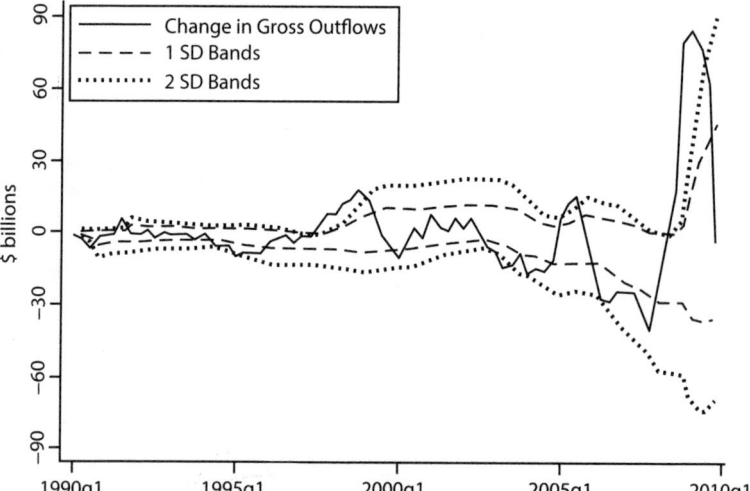

(b) Flight and Retrenchment Episodes for the Republic of Korea

(Cont'd)

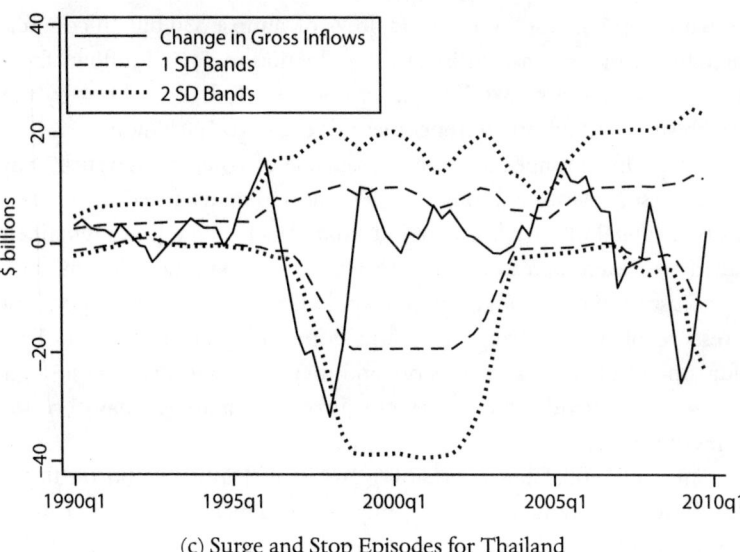

(c) Surge and Stop Episodes for Thailand

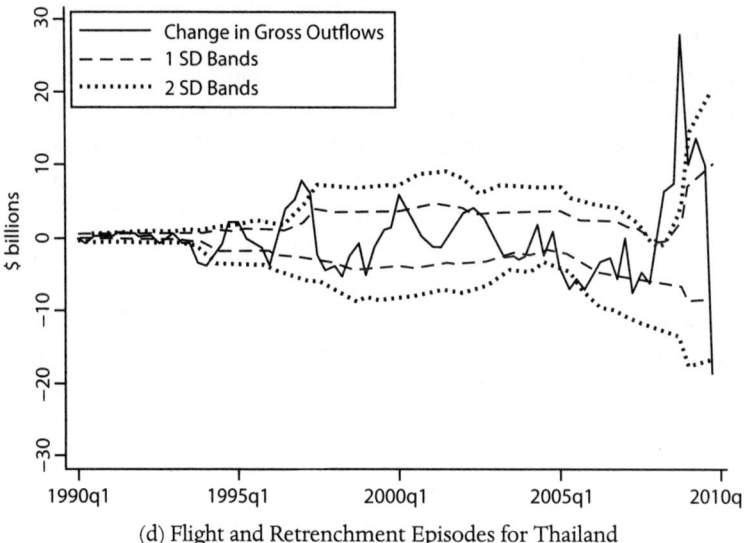

(d) Flight and Retrenchment Episodes for Thailand

FIGURE 1.5   Capital Flow Episodes for the Republic of Korea and Thailand:
1990–2010

however, an increase in domestic flows of almost $30 billion counter-acted this. By contrast, in India the reduction in capital inflows from foreigners of almost $80 billion, was not nearly balanced out by the much smaller domestic retrenchment of closer to $20 billion.

In fact, in a number of countries outside of Asia, this retrenchment by domestic investors during the GFC more than balanced the sudden stop in capital inflows from abroad, so that net capital flows remained steady (or even increased). As a result, these economies did not need to adjust to major changes in net capital flows and any corresponding pressure on the exchange rate and domestic financial system. This adjustment of domestic investors and their ability to draw on foreign investments provided an important source of stability for many economies during the GFC.

This differential behaviour of gross capital inflows and outflows can have important macroeconomic consequences—but what causes these differences across countries? Are these patterns driven largely by 'global' events that affect most countries in the world, such as changes in global risk aversion or liquidity? Or are these patterns driven by 'contagion'—by events in neighbouring countries or countries that are linked together through bilateral relationships? Or can a country's domestic policies strongly influence these patterns in capital flows? For example, consider the episodes of extreme capital flow movements in India shown in Figure 1.4 and listed in Table 1.2. Global changes in risk aversion and liquidity were undoubtedly important factors behind the surges in capital inflows from abroad to India in the mid-2000s, as well as the sudden stop in capital inflows during the recent GFC. Events in neighbouring countries—such as the Asian crisis—may have caused the sudden stop of capital into India in early 1998. Domestic challenges during India's 1991 crisis undoubtedly played a role in causing the sudden stop of foreign capital and the flight of domestic investors at the start of the graph. Similar stories can be constructed to explain the extreme capital flow movements for other countries, suggesting that some combination of global, contagion, and domestic variables may drive these sharp swings in capital flows.

In order to better understand the relative importance of different variables in driving these waves in capital flows, it is necessary to move from anecdotal country evidence to a more formal regression framework. Forbes and Warnock (2012) perform this analysis for a large set of countries and test for the role of global factors (global risk, global liquidity, interest rates in the largest economies, and global growth); contagion factors (through trade linkages, financial linkages, and geographic location); and domestic factors (a country's financial market development, capital controls, fiscal position, and growth shocks) in explaining the episodes of sharp movements in gross capital flows (constructed as described earlier). They find that the most important variables driving sharp capital flow movements are global factors (especially global risk) and contagion (especially through financial and trade linkages). In contrast, they find that most domestic variables do not have a significant effect on the probability of experiencing a sharp movement in capital flows. In particular, capital controls (measured a number of different ways) do not reduce a country's probability of having a sudden surge or sudden stop in capital flows from foreigners. Instead, there is weak evidence that countries with greater capital controls may be more likely to see capital 'flight' by domestic investors—potentially weakening the ability of domestic investors to help cushion the economy.

In a follow-up paper, Forbes and Warnock (2014) take this analysis one step further to see if these results apply to different types of capital flows. More specifically, they test if sharp movements in capital flows tend to be driven more by movements in equity (which they define to include equity flows and FDI) or debt (which includes bond and bank flows). They find that most of the extreme movements in gross capital flows are caused by sudden shifts in debt flows. For example, in Asia 80 per cent of the surges and 79 per cent of the sudden stops in capital inflows from foreigners are led by movements in debt flows. Similarly, 67 per cent of the episodes when domestic investors send money abroad and 68 per cent when domestic investors retrench are also led by movements in debt flows. When Forbes and Warnock (2014) use more formal regression analysis to explain what causes these sharp movements in debt flows and equity flows, they find that it is difficult to explain sudden shifts in equity flows. In contrast, sudden shifts in debt flows are driven by the same variables that determine sudden shifts in aggregate capital flows—largely changes in global variables (mainly global risk) and contagion variables (largely financial and trade linkages between countries).

To conclude, this section has focused on periods when gross capital inflows or outflows suddenly increase or decrease, discussing a framework by which to better understand these episodes as well as providing analysis on what causes these extreme movements. The discussion provides a number of insights to understand the four trends in capital flows discussed in Section II. Most of the volatility in gross capital flows appears to be driven by global variables—especially global risk—and contagion effects. Much of the volatility also results from changes in debt flows (instead of equity flows). Since variables shared across multiple countries—albeit through global or contagion variables—are the major drivers of these sharp movements in capital flows, it is not surprising that these sharp movements often occur simultaneously across countries and contribute to the high levels of co-movement in financial markets. Finally, one important difference across countries is the role of domestic investors. Although sharp movements in capital flows by domestic investors are driven largely by the same factors as sharp movements in foreign capital, domestic flows can provide an important benefit by partially counteracting sharp movements in foreign flows.

IV. Global Shocks and Contagion

The previous section showed that global variables and contagion are the most important factors driving extreme movements in capital flows. This section takes a closer look at the role of global shocks, especially contagion, using higher frequency information for a greater understanding of their role in transmitting volatility around the world, and especially within Asia.

Before beginning this analysis, it is useful to more concretely define key terminology. Global shocks are any significant change in global variables that simultaneously affect all countries in the world—such as changes in commodity prices or changes in global risk aversion. Defining contagion is more controversial.[9] This section will adopt what is becoming the most common usage of the term contagion—the transmission of an extreme negative shock in one country to another country (or group of countries). This definition is broader than the terminology used in much of the academic literature and includes examples when a shock to one country

---

[9] For details on various approaches to defining contagion, see Forbes (2013) and Claessens and Forbes (2001).

evolves into a global shock (such as by causing a contraction in global liquidity). This broad definition of contagion is closest to the meaning of the term when used by governments, citizens and policymakers—the fear that negative events in another country, outside of their control, could spread and have deleterious effects at home.

Contagion can occur through a number of different mechanisms, which can be categorized and grouped in several ways. For this section, I follow Forbes (2013) and divide the extensive theoretical and empirical literature into four main channels of contagion: trade, banks, portfolio investors, and wake-up calls. These categories are broad and there are important links between them—but this framework provides a useful way to summarize an extensive literature and directly test for the role of different channels of contagion.[10]

Trade

Trade can cause contagion through two effects: bilateral trade and competition in third markets. A crisis in one country can reduce income and the corresponding demand for imports, thereby affecting exports from other countries through bilateral trade. In addition, if a country devalues its currency, this can improve the country's relative export competitiveness in third markets. The greater use of global supply chains could magnify both of these effects.

Banks and Lending Institutions

One important financial channel for contagion is through banks and other financial intermediaries. A shock to one country can cause banks to reduce the supply of credit in other countries, reducing liquidity and raising the cost of credit. This could occur in a number of different ways. Moreover, the role of banks in causing contagion can be aggravated by characteristics of banking systems, such as the degree of leverage and their close relationship to the solvency of their sovereign. More specifically, negative shocks to banks are magnified in more leveraged financial systems, causing an even greater reduction in loans and unwinding of

---

[10] See Forbes (2013) for a much more detailed explanation of each of these channels and references to key theoretical and empirical papers.

positions.[11] This has been called 'liquidation spirals', 'rapid deleveraging', or a 'diabolic loop'.

Portfolio Investors

Another financial channel for contagion is portfolio investors.[12] An extensive literature explains various mechanisms by which investors can transmit shocks across countries. Moreover, recent research highlights that it is not only the *net* value of a country's international portfolio flows and investment positions that determines contagion; the *gross* flows and positions may be even more important.[13] Recent research has also highlighted the benefits of having a greater share of portfolio investment in the form of equities—which implies an automatic sharing of risk—rather than debt.

Wake-up Calls/Fundamentals Reassessment

A final (and closely related) mechanism by which contagion can occur is 'wake-up calls', that is, when additional information or a reappraisal of one country's fundamentals leads to a reassessment of risks in other countries.[14] These wake-up calls can involve many forms of reassessment including not only pertaining to the macroeconomic, financial, or political characteristics of the country but also the functioning of financial markets or the policies of international financial institutions.

As a preliminary look at whether these channels of contagion have played a role in the sharp movements in international capital flows and the increased co-movement in markets around the world, it is useful to

---

[11] For theoretical models and empirical evidence, see Greenwood et al. (2012), Van Wincoop (2011), and Shin (2012).

[12] Portfolio investors include hedge funds, mutual funds, pension funds, individuals, and some sovereign wealth funds. This includes investments in equities and debt (government and corporate) but *not* investments classified as foreign direct investment (when the investor owns 10 per cent or more of the entity).

[13] See Lane and Milesi-Ferretti (2007), Gourinchas and Rey (2007), Forbes and Warnock (2012), and Gourinchas (2012). This point also applies to contagion through banks, as highlighted in Shin (2012).

[14] Goldstein (1998) coined this term to capture the sudden awareness of risks in Asian financial systems during the 1997–8 crisis.

begin by examining trends in key variables. Figure 1.6 graphs several variables linked to these channels of contagion from 1980 through 2011 for Asian economies and a larger sample of 48 countries from all regions. More specifically, to capture the potential role of contagion through

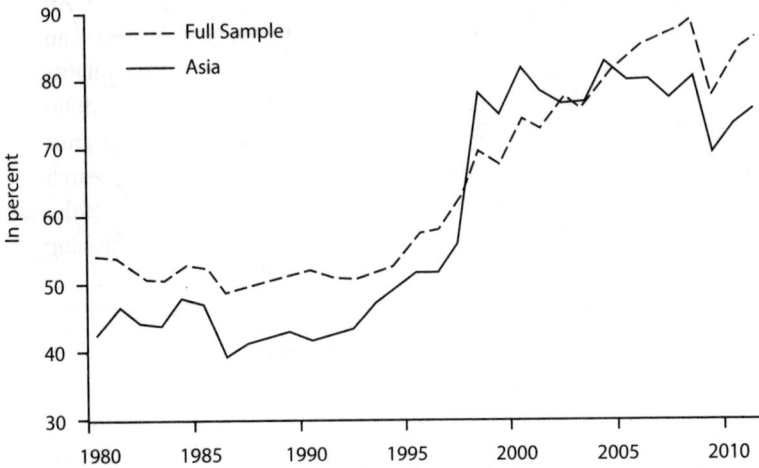

Note: Sum of imports plus exports as a percentage of GDP. Mean values exclude the two largest and smallest values for each.

(a) Total Trade as a Percentage of GDP

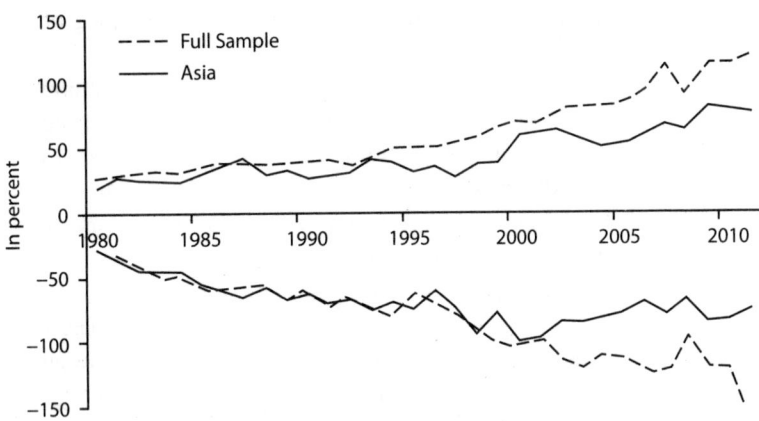

Note: Gross investment assets (positive) and liabilities (negative) as a percent of GDP. Includes portfolio investment, foreign direct investment, and other investment.

(b) Gross Investment Assets and Liabailities as a Percentage of GDP

(Cont'd)

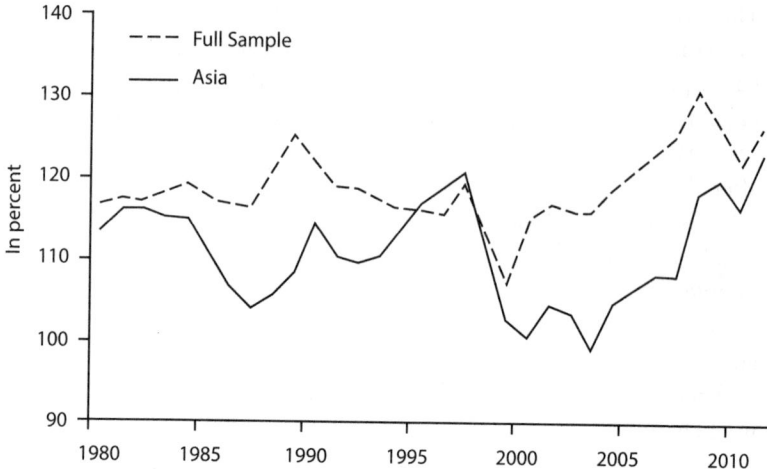

Note: Ratio of private credit by deposit money banks and other financial institutions to bank deposits, including demand, time and saving deposits in nonbanks. Mean values exclude the two largest and smallest values for each group.

(c) Leverage in Banking System

FIGURE 1.6   Channels for Contagion, 1980 – 2011

Notes: Asia includes as many of the following territories as possible when data is available: Australia, the People's Republic of China, Hong Kong, China, India, Indonesia, Japan, Malaysia, New Zealand, Pakistan, the Philippines, Singapore, the Republic of Korea, Taipei,China, and Thailand. Full sample is a group of 48 developed countries, emerging markets and developing economies from around the world.

trade, Figure 1.6a graphs mean trade exposures (measured as imports plus exports relative to GDP).[15] The graph shows the well-known trend that trade exposure has increased substantially for countries around the world since the early 1990s—and especially for Asian economies after the series of devaluations in the region in 1997. This increase in trade exposure—in Asia as well as the larger sample—could be a factor causing increased co-movement across markets.

The other two panels of Figure 1.6 focus on financial variables. Figure 1.6b graphs total exposure to international investments, measured as gross investment assets and liabilities relative to GDP.[16]

---

[15] Mean values are calculated after dropping the largest and smallest two values in each year in order to reduce the impact of extreme outliers.

[16] Investment includes portfolio investment, FDI, banking, and other investments, but not reserve accumulation.

The graphs show an increase in international investment positions since the mid-1990s for the full sample as well as for Asia, although Asia has experienced less increase in international investment assets and liabilities than for the full sample. Figure 1.6c shows leverage in banking systems.[17] There was a sharp decline in average bank leverage in Asia after the 1997 crisis, reducing Asian leverage well below that for the full sample for most the 2000s. Since 2004, however, bank leverage in Asia has been increasing rapidly, rising to almost the average for the full sample at the end of 2011. Increased market co-movements over time could also be explained by these trends of increased banking leverage and increased international investment exposure.

These graphs suggest several ways in which countries around the world have become more integrated—all of which could be causing the increased co-movement in their markets over time and the sharp, synchronized swings in capital flows. But which of the various channels of contagion appear to be more important in explaining recent volatility? And are there any policies which can stabilize countries experiencing this volatility? In order to better answer these questions, it is necessary to move to a more formal empirical analysis. Forbes (2013) provides a useful framework and estimates the conditional probability that a country has an extreme negative event in each week as a function of global shocks and the four channels of contagion.[18,19]

---

[17] Leverage is measured as the ratio of private credit by deposit money banks and other financial institutions to bank deposits, including demand, time, and saving deposits in nonbanks.

[18] Extreme negative events are defined as weeks when the country's stock return is in the bottom 5 per cent of the country's return distribution over the sample period (1980–June 2012). This analysis focuses on equity returns instead of capital flows in order to have higher frequency data to better identify the causes of sharp market movements. Equity returns are obviously not perfect, but they are a useful start as they should incorporate all available information on the expected future profitability of companies in a country—and therefore capture expected changes in real indicators. Other high frequency measures are generally not available for as long a time series or for as broad a set of countries as equity returns.

[19] The global shocks controlled for in the analysis are the change in commodity prices, the change in US interest rates, the TED spread, and the VXO. The channels of contagion are measured by total trade relative to GDP, total international banking flows relative to GDP, banking leverage, total portfolio investment exposure relative to GDP, gross portfolio inflows relative to GDP, and country credit ratings.

This analysis in Forbes (2013) yields two results that help explain the four trends discussed in Section II. First, the results suggest that in addition to global shocks, several channels of contagion are important in explaining extreme market movements. More specifically, countries are more vulnerable to contagion and events in other countries if they are more reliant on trade (relative to GDP) and have more leveraged banking systems. Second, countries do not necessarily have greater vulnerability to events in other countries simply because they have greater international capital flows—whether measured by international portfolio flows or international banking flows. Instead, the form of these capital flows determines vulnerability. More specifically, countries with greater portfolio investment liabilities are more vulnerable to contagion, but a reduction in this vulnerability is possible if the country holds greater international portfolio assets. Also, countries with a greater share of their international portfolio investment in the form of debt are more vulnerable to contagion, while countries with a greater share in the form of equity are less vulnerable.

These key results support those in Section III on the drivers of sharp movements in international capital flows, but provide additional nuance that is useful when evaluating appropriate policies in this era of large and volatile capital flows and high levels of market co-movement. The simplistic interpretation that 'more international capital flows = more volatility' is not accurate and there are important subtleties in how international capital flows affect country vulnerability. Although greater international portfolio investment liabilities *increase* vulnerability, greater international portfolio investment assets *reduce* vulnerability. This supports the analysis in Section III on capital flow movements that shows that countries with large international capital flows by domestic investors (which contribute to the accumulation of international portfolio asset positions) allows a 'retrenchment' of funds which can provide stability during sharp reduction in foreign capital inflows. The results showing that greater reliance on international investment in the form of equity (versus debt) can be stabilizing, also supports the results in Section III that most of the extreme movements in capital flows are driven by movements in debt instead of equity flows.

Finally, for countries hoping to mitigate the effects of sharp movements in international capital flows on their economies, these results suggest that a key focus should be the extent of leverage in the financial

system. Countries with more leveraged banking systems are significantly more vulnerable to contagion and sharp negative events in other
countries. The lower leverage in Asian banks (relative to the full sample)
in the 2000s may have played a role in reducing the region's vulnerability to negative shocks originating elsewhere—such as the bursting of
the dot-com bubble and even the GFC. The recent increase in banking
leverage in Asia, however, suggests that Asia may be more vulnerable
to negative shocks and sharp swings in gross capital flows in the future.

V. Conclusions and Policy Recommendations

This paper began by documenting that gross capital flows in Asia have
increased over time and by substantially more than net capital flows.
This increase in gross capital flows is occurring simultaneously with a
sharp increase in the volatility of these flows and with a sharp increase
in the co-movement in market returns across countries. Most of this
volatility in capital flows appears to be caused by global shocks and
'contagion'—links between countries—and this is not surprising given
that extreme movements in capital flows and financial markets tend
to occur in multiple countries around the same time. This volatility in
capital flows can cause substantial challenges for financial systems and
overall economic stability—a concern that is especially potent when the
volatility is largely driven by factors outside the control of individual
countries.

The results in this paper, however, do not imply that countries
should respond by limiting their integration through trade and international financial flows. Instead, the paper's analysis suggests several
policies that can reduce a country's vulnerability to sharp movements in
capital flows and allow them to benefit from international financial integration. More specifically, countries should seek to promote a greater
share of international capital flows in the form of equity (relative to
debt).[20] Countries should support outward capital flows by domestic
investors—or at the very least not adopt policies to restrict this outward
investment—as international asset holdings by domestic investors
can provide an important buffer during periods of volatility. Last, but

---

[20] Lane (2012b) discusses how the shift towards equity instead of debt in
Asia after the 1990s may have reduced this regions vulnerability to the GFC.

certainly not least, countries should carefully monitor and limit leverage in their banking systems. Countries with less leveraged financial systems are in a better position to handle sudden shifts in capital flows from abroad—both positive and negative.

These lessons are particularly relevant for Asia today. Several Asian economies (such as India) have very limited outward capital flows by domestic investors relative to inward capital flows from foreigners. As a result, there was minimal 'retrenchment' by domestic investors reinvesting in India during the recent GFC to help counteract the sudden contraction in global liquidity. In other emerging markets, domestic investors provided an important source of stability and capital during this period. Asian economies should also carefully monitor the leverage of their domestic banking systems. Low levels of leverage during the 2000s undoubtedly helped provide stability to the region during this period, but the recent increases in banking leverage in Asia suggest that this source of stability may be eroding.

International capital flows will undoubtedly continue to increase in the future and continue to be highly volatile. This will make it even more important that Asian economies make optimal use of the policy choices that are within their control, such as limiting leverage in their financial systems, supporting international capital flows by domestic investors as well as foreigners, and encouraging capital flows in the form of equity. This combination of policies would help support growth and stability in Asia and allow the region to benefit fully from trends in international capital flows and financial markets in the global economy.

References

Broner, Fernando, Tatiana Didier, Aitor Erçe, and Sergio Schmukler. 2010. 'Financial Crises and International Portfolio Dynamics'. Mimeo.

Claessens, Stijn and Kristin Forbes (eds). 2001. *International Financial Contagion*. Boston: MA: Kluwer Academic Publishers.

Forbes, Kristin J. 2013. 'The "Big C": Identifying and Mitigating Contagion', *The Changing Policy Landscape*, Proceedings of the 2012 Jackson Hole Symposium hosted by the Reserve Bank of Kansas City, pp. 23–87.

Forbes, Kristin J., and Roberto Rigobon. 2002. 'No Contagion, only interdependence: Measuring stock market co-movements', *Journal of Finance* 57 (5): 2223–61.

Forbes, Kristin J., and Francis Warnock. 2014. 'Debt- and equity-led capital flow episodes', in Miguel Fuentes and Carmen M. Reinhart (eds), *Capital Mobility and Monetary Policy*, Santiago: Central Bank of Chile, forthcoming.

Forbes, Kristin J., and Francis Warnock. 2012. 'Capital flow waves: Surges, stops, flight and retrenchment', *Journal of International Economics* 88 (2) (November): 235-51.

Goldstein, Morris. 1998. *The Asian Financial Crisis: Causes, Cures, and Systematic Implications*. Washington, DC: Institute for International Economics.

Gourinchas, Pierre-Olivier. 2012. 'Global imbalances and global liquidity'. Paper presented at the 2011 Asia Economic Policy Conference at the Federal Reserve Bank of San Francisco, San Francisco, California, 28-30 November.

Gourinchas, Pierre-Oliver, and Hélène Rey. 2007. 'International financial adjustment', *Journal of Political Economy* 115 (4): 665-703.

Greenwood, Robin, Augustin Landier, and David Thesmar. 2012. 'Vulnerable banks'. NBER Working Paper no. 18537, November, http://www.nber.org/papers/w18537 (accessed on 27 May 2014).

Lane, Philip. 2012a. 'Capital Flows in the Euro Area'. Mimeo.

———. 2012b. 'Cross-Border Financial Integration in Asia and the Macro-Financial Policy Framework.' Mimeo.

Lane, Philip, and Gian Maria Milesi-Ferretti. 2007. 'The external wealth of national mark II: Revised and extended estimates of foreign assets and liabilities, 1970–2004', *Journal of International Economics* 73 (2): 223–50.

Milesi-Ferretti, Gian-Maria, and Cédric Tille. 2011. 'The great retrenchment: International capital flows during the global financial crisis', *Economic Policy* 26 (66): 289–346.

Shin, Hyun Song. 2012. 'Global banking glut and loan risk premium', *IMF Economic Review* 60 (2): 155–92.

Van Wincoop, Eric. 2011. 'International Financial Contagion through Leveraged Financial Institutions'. NBER Working Paper No. 17686, National Bureau of Economic Research.

JOSEPH E. GAGNON

All Currencies Are Reserve Currencies

I. Introduction and Summary

For the first time, significant volumes of foreign capital are flowing into developing economies denominated in the fiat currencies controlled by governments in those economies. The so-called 'exorbitant privilege' of the US dollar is now enjoyed by upwards of 40 countries, advanced and developing, and dozens more are poised to benefit. Official data from the International Monetary Fund (IMF) show that nontraditional currencies are slowly but surely gaining a share of the world's official foreign exchange reserves (Truman 2012). But private investors are moving even faster. This remarkable development will have profoundly beneficial consequences for economic stability in the developing economies and around the world.

Section II of this chapter documents the rise of local currency bond markets and the factors that underlie this development. Fiscal and monetary policy frameworks, in particular, have improved considerably in many developing economies. Section III shows that financial vulnerability from foreign currency debt has declined in most developing economies, but there is still room for improvement. Section IV shows that increased foreign currency assets and reduced foreign currency debt are very important in explaining the relatively strong economic growth rates of many developing economies after the global financial crisis of 2008–9. Section V concludes with a proposal for the IMF to accelerate the development of local currency bond markets by creating a synthetic reserve asset backed by bonds of many countries.

II. The Revolution in Developing-Economy Bond Markets

Foreign participation in local currency bond markets of developing economies has exploded in the past 10 years. Table 2.1 lists developing and newly advanced economies in which either (a) US investors hold at least $1 billion of local currency bonds or (b) data from Morgan Stanley

TABLE 2.1 Foreign Holdings of Emerging Market Government Debt Denominated in Local Currency

	2001 US Holdings ($ billion)	2010 US Holdings ($ billion)	2011 Percentage Held Abroad
Brazil	0	25	11
Colombia	0	3	NA
Czech Republic	0	0	14
Hungary	0	2	40
India	0	0	3
Indonesia	0	5	31
Israel	0	2	3
Republic of Korea	0	12	10
Malaysia	0	7	25
Mexico	0	8	43
Peru	0	0	20–30
Philippines	0	4	NA
Poland	1	10	30
Russian Federation	0	0	5–10
Singapore	0	2	NA
South Africa	0	4	29
Thailand	0	1	12
Turkey	0	0	17

Source: US Department of the Treasury, Reports on US Portfolio Holdings of Foreign Securities at 31 December 2001 and 2010; Morgan Stanley *EM Local Markets Guidebook*, March 2012.

show that foreign investors hold a nontrivial share of bonds issued in local currency. The first column shows that US investors held essentially no local currency bonds in these economies 10 years ago. The second column shows that US investors now hold more than $1 billion of local-currency bonds in each of 12 of these economies. The third column shows that foreign investors are major players in the local currency markets of Hungary, Indonesia, Malaysia, Mexico, Peru, Poland, and South Africa. Foreign investors hold small but significant shares of the local currency bond markets of most of the other countries listed.

The People's Republic of China (PRC) is notably absent from this list, reflecting the PRC's prohibition of most foreign investment except direct investment. But there is clearly great foreign appetite for Chinese local currency bonds as evidenced in the growth since its inception in 2007 of the 'dim sum' market for renminbi bonds in Hong Kong, China. India, too, has greatly restricted foreign access to its local bond market, and India's 3 per cent foreign share shown in Table 2.1 would, doubtless, be higher in the absence of these restrictions.

Development of corporate bond markets in local currencies has lagged behind that of government bonds, and is most advanced in Asia. According to Asian Bonds Online, local currency corporate bonds in Asia (excluding Japan) total about $2 trillion, mainly in the PRC and the Republic of Korea. It is not known how much of these bonds are held by foreign investors.

The World Bank, in conjunction with the consulting firm CRISIL, has developed indicators of investability for local currency markets. These are based on capital controls and taxes, market infrastructure and liquidity, investor protection, and the size of the domestic investor base. A higher degree of investability is associated with greater holdings of local currency bonds by US investors (Burger, Warnock, and Warnock 2012). Economic conditions also are likely to affect foreign participation. In particular, local currency bonds should be more attractive to foreign investors if a country's total debt is not too high and if it has a track record of maintaining low inflation.

Figure 2.1 shows that, in 2001, many developing countries had gross central government debt in excess of 100 per cent of GDP and average inflation over the previous 10 years in excess of 20 per cent. Rough and ready benchmarks for sound policy are debt below 50 per cent of GDP and inflation below 10 per cent, denoted by the lower

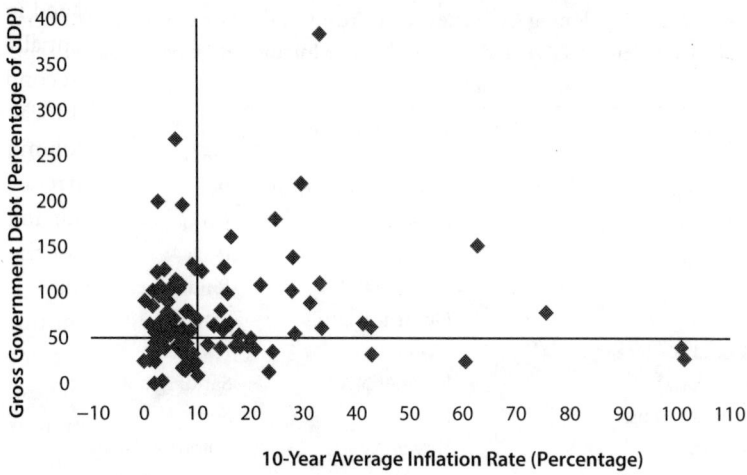

FIGURE 2.1   Debt and Inflation in Developing Countries, 2001
Source: IMF *World Economic Outlook* database.

left quadrant in Figure 2.1. Whereas most developing countries did not meet these benchmarks as of 2001, Figure 2.2 shows that roughly half of these countries did meet these benchmarks as of 2011. Table 2.2 lists the developing countries in the lower left quadrant of

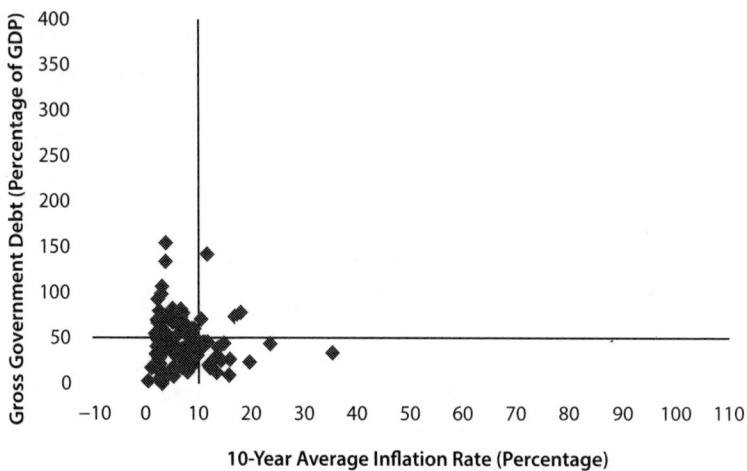

FIGURE 2.2   Debt and Inflation in Developing Countries, 2011
Source: IMF *World Economic Outlook* database and author's calculations.

TABLE 2.2   Developing Countries with Gross Central Government Debt Less than 50 per cent of GDP and 10-Year Average Inflation Rate below 10 per cent in 2011

Algeria	Czech Republic**	Niger
Armenia**	Ecuador	Oman*
Azerbaijan**	Equatorial Guinea*	Panama
Bahamas*	Gabon	Paraguay
Bahrain*	Georgia**	Peru
Benin	Guatemala*	Philippines
Bolivia	Guinea-Bissau	Qatar
Bosnia & Herzegovina**	Honduras	Rwanda
Botswana*	Indonesia	Saudi Arabia
Brunei Darussalam*	Kenya	Senegal
Bulgaria	Kuwait*	Solomon Islands**
Burkina Faso**	Lesotho	South Africa*
Cambodia	Liberia	Swaziland*
Cameroon	Lithuania**	Tanzania**
Central African Republic	Macedonia**	Thailand
Chad	Mali	Togo
Chile*	Mexico	Trinidad & Tobago
People's Republic of China*	Moldova**	Tunisia
Colombia	Montenegro**	Uganda
Congo, Republic of	Mozambique	United Arab Emirates*
Costa Rica	Namibia	Viet Nam
Croatia**	Nepal	

Source: IMF *World Economic Outlook* database. Inflation based on GDP deflator.
Note: *Country satisfied these criteria in 2001.
**Either debt or inflation data missing for 2001.

Figure 2.2.[1] Countries that were also in the lower left quadrant of Figure 2.1 are noted with an asterisk. Countries with missing data in 2001 are marked by two asterisks. Most of the countries listed in Table 2.2 did not meet the rough and ready benchmarks for sound policy in 2001, but the improvement since then has been remarkable. I believe that the adoption of sound macroeconomic policies in many developing countries is an important driver of foreign interest in their local currency bonds.

[1] This analysis excludes advanced economies, all of which had average inflation below 10 per cent but most of which had gross debt above 50 per cent of GDP.

III. The Reduction of Currency Mismatches

The main benefit of local currency bonds is to reduce the mismatch between the currency denomination of a country's liabilities and the currency denomination of its assets. There is widespread agreement that currency mismatches increase both the likelihood of a financial crisis and the economic cost of a financial crisis (Allen et al. 2002; Goldstein and Turner 2004). On the other hand, for countries that do not suffer from currency mismatches, Gagnon (2010) shows that large and sudden currency depreciations (which often occur during financial crises) never cause recessions and often lead to faster economic growth.

A currency mismatch occurs when a household's or a firm's liabilities are denominated in a different currency from that of the future stream of earnings available to service the liabilities or any assets that may back the liabilities. For example, an electric utility firm that bills customers in domestic currency may borrow in foreign currency to finance a new power station. The utility then faces the risk that its foreign currency liabilities may increase in value without any compensating increase in its domestic-currency revenues. In recent financial crises, many companies were driven into bankruptcy by the increased debt burden caused by a depreciation of the domestic currency. Note that an exporter or a producer of a good or service that is tradable may borrow in foreign currency without creating a currency mismatch, since at least part of the future revenues will be in foreign currency.

In the aggregate, economies should have positive net foreign currency positions rather than zero or negative net foreign currency positions. Having a positive net foreign currency position stabilizes an economy in the face of the most common macroeconomic shocks. Typically, bad news about economic growth depreciates a country's currency. Since revenues tend to move with domestic currency, debts denominated in foreign currency are especially prone to default in bad times, which compounds the economic harm. On the other hand, assets denominated in foreign currency increase in value when the domestic currency depreciates, thereby providing a cushion against hard times. Moving from negative to positive net foreign currency positions allows exchange rates to better perform their role of stabilizing the world economy (Gagnon and Hinterschweiger 2011).

Note that an economy can have a positive net foreign currency position regardless of whether it has a positive or negative net foreign asset position. For example, in 2009, Australia had a negative net foreign asset position equal to 71 per cent of its GDP, but it had a positive net foreign currency position equal to 31 per cent of its GDP (Australian Bureau of Statistics 2009).

Following Goldstein and Turner (2004), I define net foreign currency assets (NFCA) as

$$NFCA = NFAMABK + NBKAFC - NBKLFC - IBFC$$

NFCA equals net foreign assets of the monetary authority and deposit money banks (NFAMABK) plus cross-border claims of nonbank residents in foreign currency on Bank for International Settlements (BIS)–reporting banks (NBKAFC) minus cross-border liabilities of nonbank residents in foreign currency to BIS-reporting banks (NBKLFC) minus international debt securities (bonds) issued by domestic residents in foreign currency (IBFC).[2]

Errors and Omissions

There are several sources of error in the above measure of NFCA. First, the use of NFAMABK implicitly assumes that all cross-border assets and liabilities of the monetary authority and banking system are in foreign currency. Second, nonbank claims on and liabilities to banks outside of BIS reporting jurisdictions are not included. Third, domestically issued foreign currency bonds held by foreigners are not included. Fourth, international foreign currency bonds issued by domestic banks are double counted because they are included in IBFC as well as NFAMABK. Fifth, nonbank claims on foreign nonbanks are not included. Sixth, net positions in derivatives markets are not included. Seventh, exposures from current and expected trade flows invoiced in foreign currency are not included.

The second and third errors are likely to be small. BIS-reporting jurisdictions cover the vast majority of international banking activity. In most of these countries, almost all domestic bonds are in local cur-

---

[2] NFAMABK is from the IMF's *International Financial Statistics*. NBKAFC and NBKLFC are derived from source data for the BIS's *Locational Banking Statistics*. IBFC is derived from source data for the BIS's *Securities Statistics*. I thank Philip Turner and Emese Kuruc of the BIS for providing the data.

rency.[3] On balance, the remaining errors are probably negative, so that true NFCAs are more positive than those shown in the following lines. The fifth and sixth errors, in particular, may have grown rapidly. In recent years, the IMF has conducted coordinated surveys of portfolio investment that show rapid increases of nonbank claims on foreign nonbank firms. Not all countries participate, the data go back for only a few years in most cases, and little or no information is published on currency denomination of assets. Nevertheless, if portfolio claims are predominantly in the currency of the debtor, as seems likely, the NFCA estimates presented here understate the true NFCA. Also, as mentioned previously, derivatives contracts of Australian residents are skewed substantially towards long positions in foreign currency, so that the NFCA methodology used here understates the true Australian NFCA position. Anecdotal evidence suggests that Brazil may be another country for which derivatives contracts are importantly skewed towards long foreign currency positions.

Recent Developments

Figure 2.3 displays NFCA for 27 important developing and newly advanced economies. The grey bars refer to 2002 and the black bars to 2011. The vulnerability from a negative NFCA and the benefit of a positive NFCA derive in large part from a country's exposure to foreign trade. It is common to gauge a country's foreign exchange reserves in relation to its imports and to gauge its external debt in relation to its exports. For this reason, the NFCA positions are expressed as a percentage of total trade (exports plus imports of goods and services).

Negative NFCA positions are shrinking everywhere except in Eastern Europe. Most countries now have NFCA near zero or greater than zero. Especially large increases in NFCA occurred in Argentina, Brazil, the PRC, the Philippines, and the Russian Federation. Notable declines in NFCA occurred in India, Peru, and Venezuela, but NFCA remains positive in these countries. All of the Eastern European countries except Bulgaria and the Czech Republic have significant negative NFCA positions, as does Turkey. The PRC and Taipei,China have the largest positive NFCA. Other

---

[3] Table C5 in the BIS *Securities Statistics* reports survey results on the currency denomination of domestic government bonds in 23 developing and newly advanced countries. Only in Argentina and Peru are more than 5 per cent of domestic bonds denominated in foreign currency.

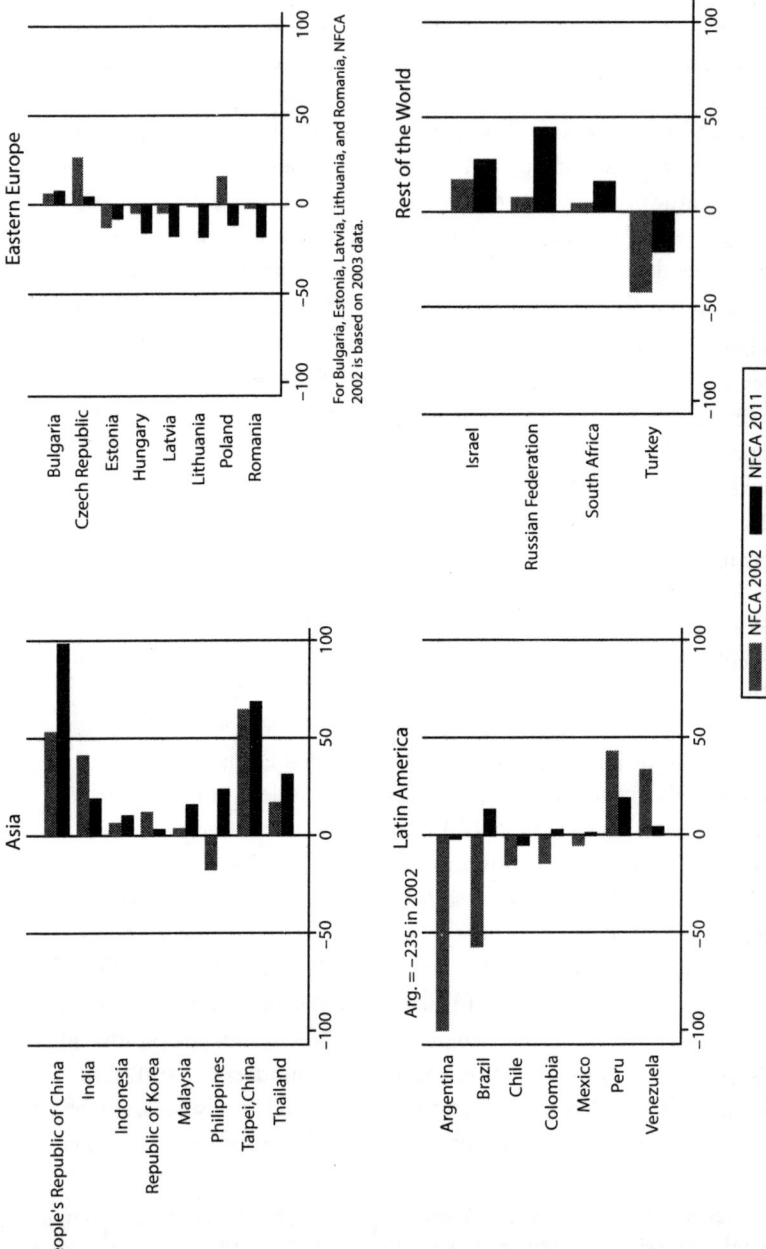

Figure 2.3 Net Foreign Currency Assets (NFCA) in 2002 and 2011 (Percentage of Exports Plus Imports)

Source: Correspondence with BIS, IMF *World Economic Outlook* database and author's calculations.

countries with notable positive NFCA include the Russian Federation, Israel, Thailand, the Philippines, Peru, India, and Malaysia.

Figure 2.4 displays the NFCAs of the public sectors of these countries, defined as foreign exchange reserves minus government debt denominated in foreign currency. In 2011, public sector NFCA positions were significantly negative in only five of these countries: Argentina, Hungary, Latvia, Lithuania, and Venezuela. There is a widespread, but not universal, trend towards more positive public sector NFCA positions. This is the result of rapid accumulation of foreign exchange reserves and reduced reliance on foreign currency debt.

Figure 2.5 shows private sector NFCA positions. Here the differences across countries are more pronounced. Most countries, including all of the Eastern European countries, have negative private NFCA positions. Only Argentina, the PRC, and Venezuela have large positive private NFCA. Large declines are observed in Brazil, Peru, the Russian Federation, Venezuela, and some of the Eastern European countries. It is possible that in some of these countries an apparent negative private NFCA position is measured incorrectly because it excludes nonbank portfolio assets and derivatives positions. Brazil and the Republic of Korea, in particular, have large derivatives markets.

To some extent, governments may use their foreign exchange reserves to bail out private firms in a crisis, so that a positive public NFCA position provides some insurance against the risks of a negative private NFCA position. But it is far better to have a positive private NFCA position, which would allow for smaller holdings of foreign exchange reserves, which usually have a high fiscal cost.

Overall, NFCA seems to be a good indicator of vulnerability to financial crisis. Mexico in 1994, Indonesia, the Republic of Korea, Malaysia, the Philippines, and Thailand in 1997, Argentina in 2001, and Brazil in 2002 all experienced major crises at times when their NFCA positions were negative. Studies have found that low levels of foreign exchange reserves are one of the best predictors of crisis and recession in developing countries (Frankel and Saravelos 2010).

IV. Currency Mismatches and Outcomes of the 2008–9 Global Financial Crisis

This section examines whether indicators of currency mismatches can help to explain differences in economic growth following the global

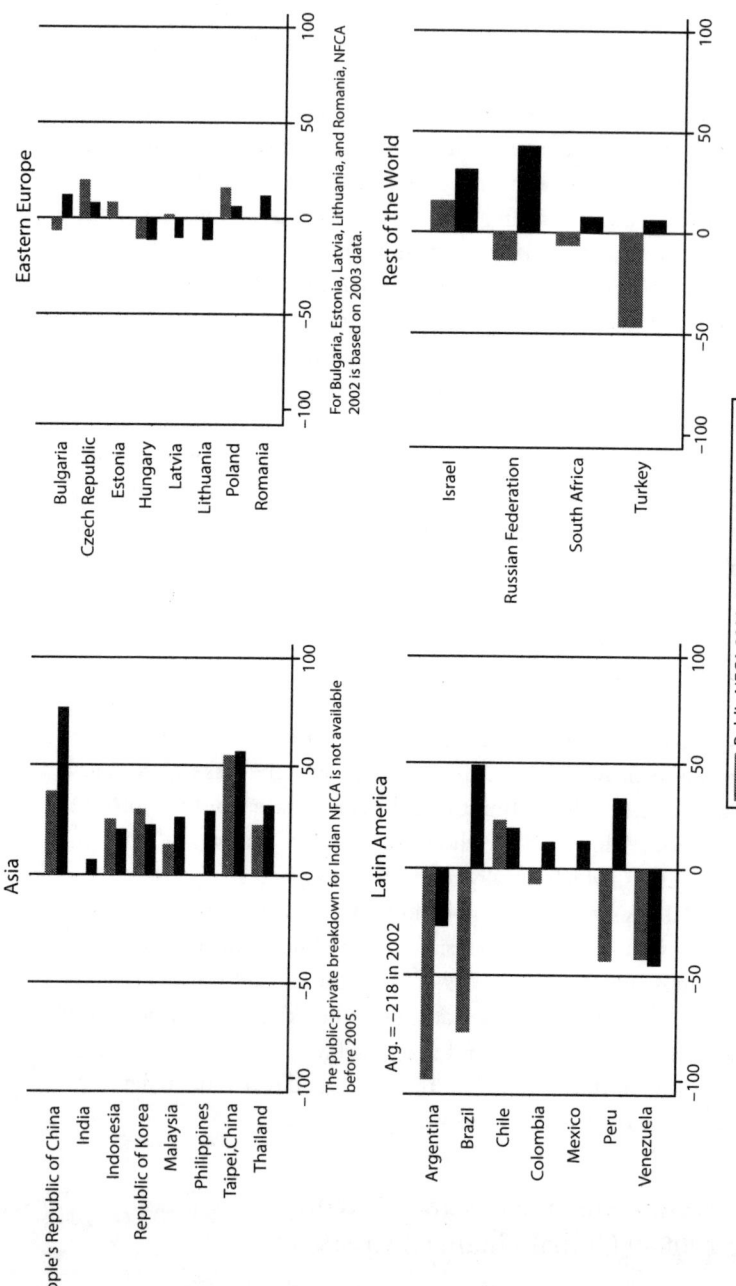

FIGURE 2.4 Public Sector NFCA in 2002 and 2011 (Percentage of Exports Plus Imports)

Source: Correspondence with BIS, IMF *World Economic Outlook* database and author's calculations.

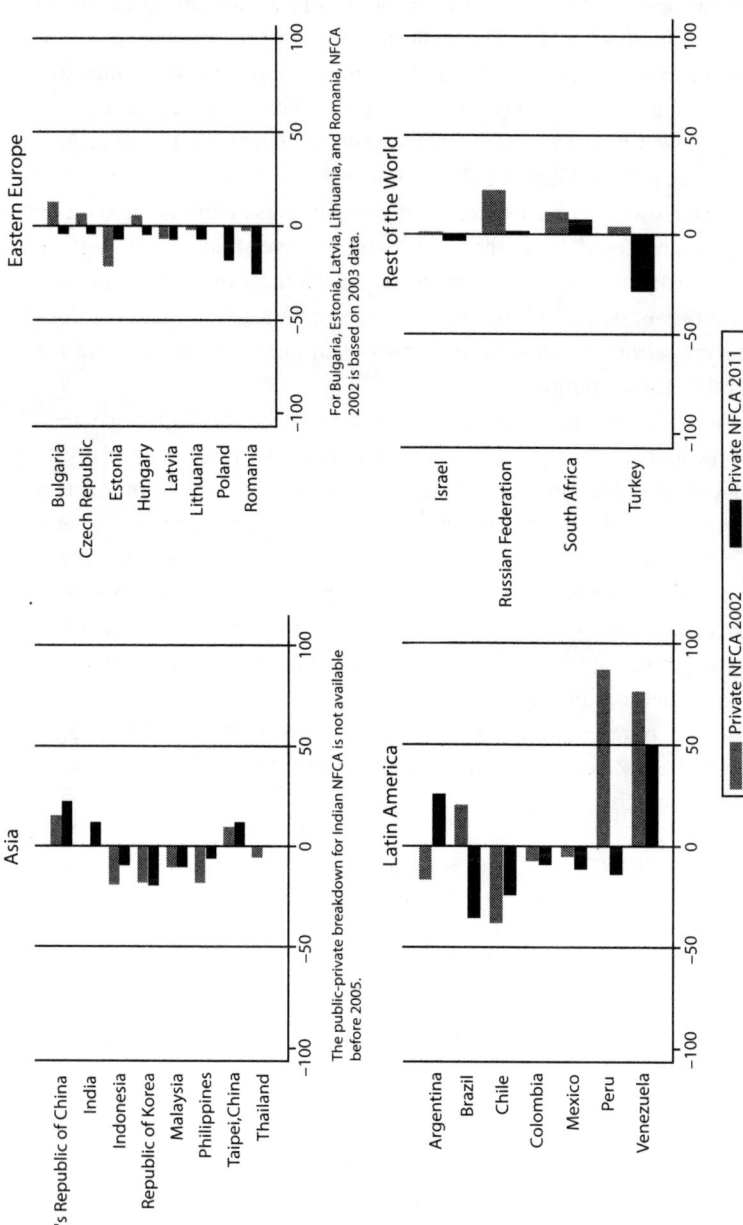

FIGURE 2.5 Private Sector NFCA in 2002 and 2011 (Percentage of Exports Plus Imports)

Source: Correspondence with BIS, IMF *World Economic Outlook* database and author's calculations.

financial crisis of 2008–9. The countries examined are the 27 countries shown in figures 2.3–2.5. The indicators of currency mismatch are (a) foreign exchange reserves, (b) public sector NFCA (reserves minus foreign currency debt), and (c) private sector NFCA. All three indicators are expressed in percentage of total trade (exports plus imports). As a pure mismatch measure, public NFCA is better than foreign exchange reserves. However, to the extent that governments do not need to repay foreign currency debt in the near term, reserves may better capture their short-run ability to intervene in the financial markets. This consideration suggests looking at reserves minus foreign currency debt maturing within 12 months, but short-term debt data are missing for several of these countries.

A good summary measure of a country's economic performance after the global financial crisis is its average growth rate of real per capita GDP between 2007 and 2010. Figure 2.6 displays the correlations of this growth rate with the three indicators of mismatch. There are strong positive correlations between growth and reserves and between growth and private sector NFCA. There is a weak positive correlation between growth and public sector NFCA. The fourth panel of Figure 2.6 shows a weak negative correlation between growth and average inflation in the five years before the crisis.

Table 2.3 presents the results of regressions of the following equation on these 27 countries. In addition to the three indicators of currency mismatch,

$$\Delta \text{PCGDP}(2007\text{--}10) = \text{FXReserves} / (X + M)(2007)$$
$$\text{PublicNFCA} / (X + M)(2007)$$
$$\text{PrivateNFCA} / (X + M)(2007)$$
$$\Delta \text{PCGDP}(2002\text{--}7)$$
$$\Delta \text{CPI}(2002\text{--}7)$$
$$\log \text{PCGDP(PPP)}(2007)$$
$$(X + M) / \text{GDP}(2007)$$
$$\Delta \text{M2}(2007\text{--}10)$$
$$\text{Constant}$$

(Δ denotes percentage change, average annual rate)

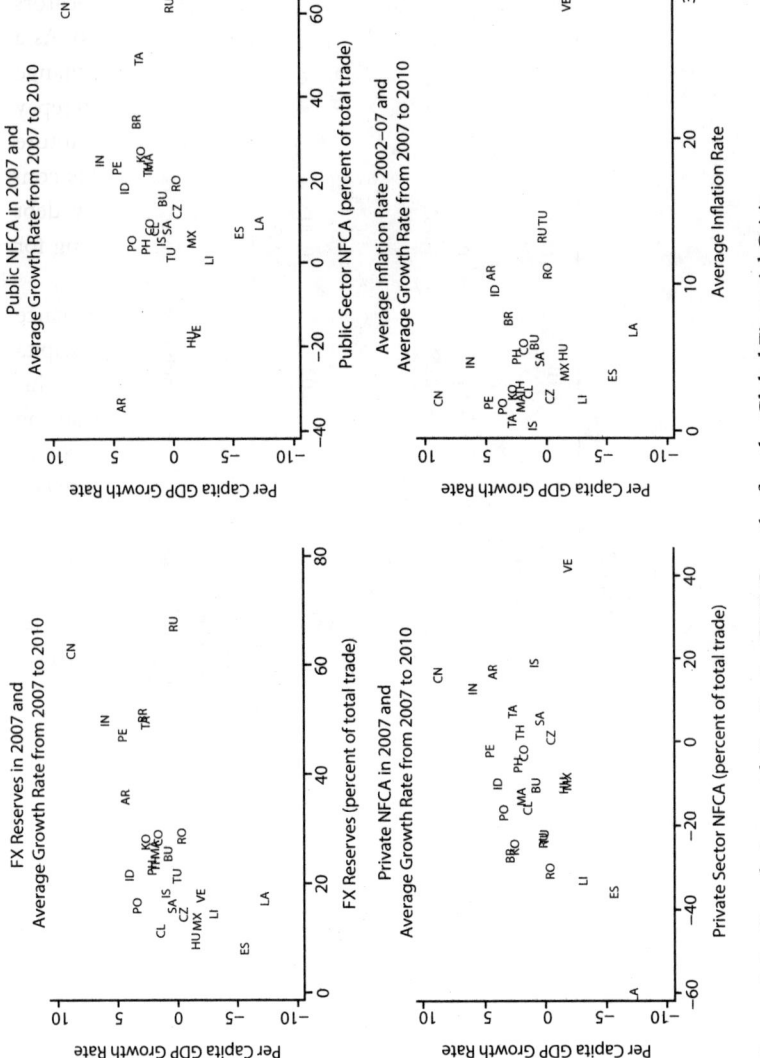

FIGURE 2.6   Correlations with Per Capita GDP Growth after the Global Financial Crisis

Source: Correspondence with BIS, IMF *World Economic Outlook* database and author's calculations.

TABLE 2.3   Emerging Market Growth after the Global Financial Crisis

FX Reserves	0.12***	0.11***		0.10***	0.10***	0.04	0.04*	
Public NFCA			0.07**					0.02
Private NFCA		0.07*	0.09**	0.06**	0.07**		0.04***	0.04***
ΔPCGDP				-0.22	-0.14	-0.27	-0.17	-0.11
ΔCPI				-0.19***	-0.22***	-0.46***	-0.43***	-.46***
PCGDP(PPP)				-0.02***				
(X + M) / GDP					-0.02			
ΔM2(2010)						0.35***	0.29***	0.33***
Constant	-0.02*	-0.02	0.01	0.18***	0.02	0.00	0.00	0.01
R^2	0.37	0.55	0.47	0.76	0.71	0.77	0.82	0.80

Source: Correspondence with BIS, IMF *World Economic Outlook* database, and author's calculations.

Note: Regression on 27 countries. See text for specification and countries.

***, **, and * denote significance at the 1, 5, and 10 per cent levels, respectively, based on robust standard errors.

the regressions include growth of real per capita GDP from 2002 to 2007 (ΔPCGDP), average inflation from 2002 to 2007 (ΔCPI), the logarithm of PPP-adjusted per capita GDP in 2007 [PCGDP(PPP)], the ratio of total trade to GDP in 2007 ((X + M) / GDP), and average growth of the M2 measure of the money supply from 2007 to 2010. Other auxiliary variables, not shown, included the ratio of the current account balance to GDP in 2007, the growth rate of bank credit from 2002 to 2007, and dummy variables for each region (Asia, Latin America, Europe, and Rest of the World). None of the results was sensitive to these alternative variables.

The first three columns of Table 2.3 show that all three measures of mismatch have a strong predictive effect on economic growth after the crisis. Column 1 confirms previous research that found that higher foreign exchange reserves are associated with stronger growth (Frankel and Saravelos 2010; Bussiere et al. 2013). Adding private NFCA along with reserves (column 2) raises the equation's R^2 from 0.37 to 0.55, which is quite high for an equation with only two explanatory variables and no lagged dependent variable. Substituting public sector NFCA for reserves lowers the R^2 moderately to 0.48. Apparently, reserves play a role independent of pure currency mismatch, but the mismatch effects may be the most important effects.

The fourth and fifth columns show that estimates of the effects of the currency mismatch variables on growth are not sensitive to including the auxiliary variables (except for ΔM2). This result holds whether the auxiliary variables are included separately or jointly. The lagged GDP growth rate allows for dynamic effects. The lagged inflation rate is a proxy for the quality of the policy framework—a high inflation rate reflects a poor policy framework and a weak growth rate after the crisis. The logarithm of PPP GDP in 2007 allows for economic convergence, in which initially poorer countries tend to grow faster. The ratio of trade to GDP captures the exposure of the economy to global shocks—more open economies were hit harder by the global crisis.

The final three columns show that these results are sensitive to inclusion of the only contemporaneous variable, ΔM2. This variable is meant to capture the response of macroeconomic policy to the crisis. Countries that responded to the slowdown with monetary expansion should have grown faster than others; the results support that view. However, there is almost surely a positive feedback from GDP growth onto M2 growth, so that the coefficients on M2 are probably biased. Including M2 in the regression reduces all of the mismatch coefficients, but they remain positive and the private NFCA coefficients remain statistically significant. One explanation of these results is that countries with large foreign exchange reserves and/or low foreign currency debts are better positioned to conduct countercyclical monetary policy.

V. A Symmetric Reserve Asset to Boost Local Currency Bond Markets

To accelerate the growth of local currency bond markets in developing countries, I propose that the IMF take two related actions: First, expand the special drawing right (SDR) basket to include the currencies of all countries that have sound macroeconomic policies and whose bond markets meet minimum standards of openness and supervision. Second, create synthetic SDR bonds backed by medium-term sovereign bonds denominated in the currencies of the SDR basket. IMF members would be expected to make these SDR assets their primary foreign exchange reserve asset.

Step One: Expand the SDR Basket

All currencies of countries with low and stable inflation, sound monetary, fiscal and supervisory policies, and open financial markets should be included in the SDR basket. There are two criteria for openness: First, there should be no quantitative restrictions on foreign purchases of a country's bonds. Second, any tax on capital flows should not exceed a moderate rate.

At present, it is likely that several dozen countries would qualify for inclusion in the SDR, including almost all advanced countries and a number of developing countries. The composition of the SDR basket should be revisited every few years, as is the current practice. The weights should be based on GDP at market prices and exchange rates, although other weighting schemes might be considered.

Two recent IMF staff reports (IMF 2011a, b) acknowledge the benefits of a broader SDR basket for reserve diversification and for financial development in emerging markets. However, they suggest that adding too many currencies with low weights would increase risks and transaction costs excessively. With respect to risks, this conclusion is not correct. Greater diversification reduces risks. Moreover, the selection criteria proposed here would exclude currencies that are particularly risky. With respect to transactions costs, as discussed in the following lines, having the IMF create SDR bonds for a broad pool of investors would give rise to considerable economies of scale, thereby minimizing the costs of having an inclusive SDR basket.

Step Two: Create SDR Bonds

The second part of the proposal is for the IMF to create synthetic SDR bonds that are backed by sovereign debt in the currencies of the SDR basket. Initially, the SDR bonds would focus on a 3-year maturity by limiting the underlying assets to bonds with remaining maturity of 2.5 to 3.5 years at the time of creation. The SDR bonds would be identified by vintage dates for the year and semester (or quarter) in which they are created. The range of maturities could be expanded over time based on market demand. Eventually, alternative instruments might be considered, such as GDP-linked bonds (Eichengreen 2011).

These SDR bonds would be similar to exchange-traded funds (ETFs) and could be traded among investors as ETFs are. In addition, the IMF would perform a role similar to an ETF manager in creating or liquidating the synthetic SDR bonds to keep their market value close to the net asset value of the underlying bonds. Purchases and redemptions would be conducted in any of the major international currencies, including at least the four largest currencies by trading volume: the US dollar, the euro, the yen, and the UK pound (BIS 2010). As is the practice with ETFs, the IMF would take a small slice of the returns on the underlying bonds to cover its costs. The IMF would not guarantee the performance of the SDR bonds, but the selection criteria and diversification would ensure that SDR bonds are very high-grade instruments.

This proposal should not be confused with that of the 'substitution account', which was proposed (but never adopted) in the 1970s to facilitate off-market swaps of dollars for SDRs that would have exposed the IMF to considerable exchange rate risk (Boughton 2001, chapter 18).

Advantages of SDR Bonds

The primary purchasers of SDR bonds, at least initially, are likely to be central banks and finance ministries. Indeed, Article VIII of the IMF Articles of Agreement obliges all members to 'collaborate with the Fund and with other members ... [in] making the special drawing right [SDR] the principal reserve asset in the international monetary system'.

SDR bonds would make the international monetary system more symmetric. They would provide investors, including central banks, with a standardized asset that provides both a high degree of diversification and a deep and liquid market. SDR bonds would reduce the distortions caused by excessive reliance on the US dollar as the main reserve asset. Replacing the current system, which is dominated by the dollar and the euro, would moderately reduce the exposure of reserve holders to developments in the US and euro area economies. It would also moderately reduce the US current account deficit because it would reduce the flow of official capital into the US and thus relieve upward pressure on the dollar.

Most importantly, SDR bonds would assist in the development of local currency bond markets in developing economies, thereby reducing the need to borrow in foreign currencies, which gives rise to dangerous currency mismatches. A new source of demand for developing economy government debt that is contingent on sound macroeconomic and financial policies would create an extra incentive for governments to adopt good policies.

SDR bonds would become the world's premier reserve asset, but this would not prevent central banks from holding a fraction of their reserves in specific currencies, as a hedge against liabilities denominated in those currencies or because a high share of their imports is priced in those currencies.

The IMF's Role Is Essential

In principle, central banks and institutional investors are already able to construct diversified portfolios that do not rely inordinately on one or two key currencies. In practice, the weight of precedent is heavy and the markets of the established key currencies have an enormous advantage in liquidity and transactions costs. No individual central bank or investor can hope to change these conditions. Moreover, any divergence of investment policies from prevailing norms exposes a central bank to criticism and confusion about its motives and its competence. We need to change the norms that prevail. A common global standard is necessary to develop a secondary market for synthetic SDR bonds.

Only the IMF, with the support of its members, can lead the world to a more symmetric system. No other institution has the expertise and the impartiality to choose the composition of the new SDR basket. The IMF is uniquely placed to assess its members' financial market conditions and macroeconomic policies—these are the focus of regular Article IV consultations with all member countries. In creating the primary reserve asset for most of the world's central banks, the IMF would benefit from unparalleled economies of scale and knowledge of its customers.

VI. Conclusions

More and more developing economies are able to borrow in their own currencies, a beneficial trend that is supported by improved macroeconomic policy frameworks. By reducing currency mismatches, local currency bond markets improve macroeconomic stability. Countries with stronger net foreign currency positions performed better in the aftermath of the global financial crisis and recession of 2008. The IMF should take the lead in accelerating the development of local currency bond markets by expanding the definition of the SDR and creating a synthetic SDR bond for global investors and central bank reserve managers.

References

Allen, Mark, Christopher Rosenberg, Christian Keller, Brad Setser, and Nouriel Roubini. 2002. 'A balance-sheet approach to financial crisis', *IMF Working Paper No. 02/210*, International Monetary Fund, Washington.

Australian Bureau of Statistics. 2009. 'Foreign Currency Exposure'.

BIS. 2010. *Triennial Central Bank Survey of Foreign Exchange and Derivatives Market Activity*. Basel: Bank for International Settlements.

Boughton, James. 2001. *Silent Revolution: The International Monetary Fund 1979-89*. Washington: International Monetary Fund.

Burger, John, Francis Warnock, and Veronica Warnock. 2012. 'Emerging local currency bond markets', *Financial Analysts Journal* 68 (4): 73–93.

Bussiere, Matthieu, Gong Cheng, Menzie Chinn, and Noemie Lisack. 2013. 'Capital controls and foreign reserve accumulation: Substitutes or complements in the global financial crisis?' Manuscript, Banque de France.

Eichengreen, Barry. 2011. 'What Can Replace the Dollar?' Essay on Project Syndicate website: https://www.project-syndicate.org/, 11 August.

Frankel, Jeffrey, and George Saravelos. 2010. 'Are leading indicators of financial crises useful for assessing country vulnerability? Evidence from the 2008-09 global crisis', Working Paper 16047, National Bureau of Economic Research, Cambridge, MA.

Gagnon, Joseph. 2010. 'Currency crashes in industrial countries: What determines good and bad outcomes?' *International Finance* 13 (2): 165–94.

Gagnon, Joseph and Marc Hinterschweiger. 2011. *Flexible Exchange Rates for a Stable World Economy*. Washington: Peterson Institute for International Economics.

Goldstein, Morris and Philip Turner. 2004. *Controlling Currency Mismatches in Emerging Markets*. Washington: Institute for International Economics.

IMF. 2011a. Enhancing international monetary stability—a role for the SDR? International Monetary Fund, Washington, 7 January.

———. 2011b. 'Criteria for broadening the SDR currency basket', International Monetary Fund, Washington, 23 September.

Truman, Edwin. 2012. 'John Williamson and the evolution of the international monetary system', Working Paper 12-13, Washington: Peterson Institute for International Economics.

CHALLENGES OF CAPITAL ACCOUNT MANAGEMENT

3

MICHAEL W. KLEIN

Capital Controls and Real Exchange Rates*

I. Introduction

One of the most vexing problems facing emerging market economies is currency appreciation in response to capital inflows. A strengthening currency damages exporters and import-competing firms. Capital inflows can fuel destabilizing asset price bubbles as foreign funds bid up the prices of real estate, equities, and other financial assets. An appreciation, in response to capital inflows, can also contribute indirectly to an asset price boom as the promise of cheap foreign-currency loans prompts domestic residents' borrowing. Booms are likely to end badly once the stream of inflows dries up and the appreciation reverses.

Standard monetary policy options offer little promise of effectively containing capital inflows or limiting their effects on the real exchange rate. Monetary policy is constrained because an effort to stem capital inflows and reduce the rate of nominal appreciation by lowering interest rates would result in inflationary pressures that contribute to a real appreciation. A contractionary fiscal policy could both lower appreciation and inflationary pressures, but it is unlikely that fiscal policy is nimble enough to respond in a timely fashion.

* I thank Patrick O'Halloran who provided excellent research assistance.

In the face of these challenges, attention has recently turned towards the use of capital controls. Some countries began to reintroduce controls on capital inflows in the early 2000s, reversing a trend towards capital account liberalization that began in the early 1990s. The pace of the reimposition of controls increased after the onset of the Great Recession, when capital inflows were imposed by both emerging markets and advanced countries, including Brazil, Iceland, Ireland, Peru, and Turkey. Additionally, there has been an evolving view that countries with long-standing controls on capital inflows, such as the People's Republic of China (PRC), performed relatively well during the Great Recession.[1]

This evolution of views on capital controls has occurred in Washington as well as in Sao Paolo. The so-called Washington Consensus of the 1990s favoured open capital accounts. But as early as 2002, Kenneth Rogoff, the then Chief Economist and Director of Research of the International Monetary Fund (IMF), wrote in the December issue of the IMF's publication, *Finance and Development*: 'These days, everyone agrees that a more eclectic approach to capital account liberalization is required.' More recently, the IMF staff published position papers that accept a role for capital controls.[2] While the current IMF position is that capital controls become an option only after other policy choices have been exhausted, another Washington institution, the Peterson Institute for International Economics, recently published a book whose authors argue that capital controls should not be merely a last resort but 'properly designed they might even be a regular instrument of economic policy' (Jeanne et al. 2012: 95)

This chapter analyses the relationship between controls on capital inflows and the dynamics of the real exchange rate for 43 countries over the period 2002–10. One challenge in any such exercise is to provide a

---

[1] Some argue that countries like the PRC and India, which had long-standing controls in place, were spared the financial upheavals that roiled more open economies, as mentioned in Ostry et al. (2010). In contrast, Kose et al. (2009) write: 'Capital account liberalization is believed to have played an important role in fomenting financial crises and has been indicted by some observers as the proximate cause for the crises experienced by emerging markets in recent decades. But there is little empirical evidence to support the view that capital account liberalization by itself increases vulnerabilities to crises.' (p. 27)

[2] See Ostry et al. (2010), Ostry et al. (2011b), and IMF Strategy, Policy and Review Department (2011).

context for the real exchange rate. In this chapter, we use the Balassa-Samuelson theory as a framework for the determination of the real exchange rate.[3] The estimates presented in this chapter find that, in line with the Balassa-Samuelson relationship, the bilateral real exchange rate with the US appreciates with an increase in income.

The central question of this chapter, however, is whether capital controls temper the appreciation of the real exchange rate. The strategy is to augment an empirical Balassa-Samuelson model with an indicator of capital controls. This presents a different type of challenge, since data on capital controls have been, until recently, quite blunt, not even distinguishing between controls on inflows and controls on outflows. The analysis uses a new data set that, unlike earlier cross-country capital control data, differentiates between controls on inflows and outflows, and also includes separate measures of inflow controls on six categories of assets.

The analysis in this chapter distinguishes between long-standing and episodic controls on capital flows, what are called in Klein (2012) 'walls' and 'gates', respectively. Countries such as the PRC have long-standing capital controls. Other countries, such as Brazil, impose controls episodically; for example, the Brazilian imposition of a 2 per cent tax on investment in existing Brazilian equities on 20 October 2009 (the Imposto sobre Operações Financeiras, known by its acronym IOF), which was a response to the 30 per cent appreciation of the real against the dollar from the beginning of that year.[4] At that time, the Brazilian finance minister, Guido Mantega, claimed that the appreciation of the real was the direct result of the US monetary policy, and represented the opening salvo in a 'currency war'.

The evidence presented in this chapter suggests that neither long-standing nor episodic controls are systematically associated with lower rates of real bilateral appreciation over the 2002–10 period, controlling for the Balassa-Samuelson effect. But there is evidence that appreciation was significantly lower in two countries with long-standing controls, the PRC and India, than what is consistent with the Balassa-Samuelson relationship. These two examples, however, do not constitute a case for

---

[3] Frankel (2004, 2006) used the Balassa-Samuelson framework in his empirical analysis of the real value of the renminbi.

[4] The IOF was raised to 4 per cent on 5 October 2010 and to 6 per cent less than two weeks after that.

the efficacious use of capital controls to stem appreciations, especially the use of episodic controls.

The next section of this chapter begins with a brief discussion of the capital controls data set used in the subsequent analysis, and presents the categorization of the 43 countries in the data set into three groups—those persistently open to inflows, those persistently closed to inflows, and those with episodically imposed controls on inflows. The Balassa-Samuelson analysis is presented in the following section. The final section offers some concluding remarks.

II. Capital Controls: Gates and Walls

Cross-country analyses of the effects of capital controls typically use data from the IMF's *Annual Report on Exchange Arrangements and Exchange Restrictions* (AREAER).[5] Before 1996, these data were quite blunt, and did not even distinguish between controls on inflows and outflows. Beginning in 1996 (which reports on conditions in 1995), the annual issues of the AREAER provided much greater detail than earlier issues, with indicators distinguishing between inflows and outflows, and across categories of assets. Schindler (2009) provides a method for using the information in these annual reports to create a data set for capital controls on inflows, and capital controls on outflows, for six categories of assets.[6] The data set he creates covers the period 1995 to 2005. We update this data using Schindler's method, and extend the data set to include the years 2006 to 2010.

One focus of this analysis is the distinction between long-standing controls on capital inflows and controls that are imposed episodically.

---

[5] Capital controls are rules, taxes, or fees associated with financial transactions that discriminate between domestic residents and those outside the country (OECD 2009).

[6] The six categories are money markets (debt instruments with an original maturity of one year or less), bonds (debt instruments with an original maturity of greater than one year), financial credits (which includes controls on banks), equities (shares of individual countries), collective investments (mutual funds or other investment trusts), and direct investment (investments that involve the participation in the management of the acquired entities).

Data on the experiences of each country with controls on inflows for five of the categories (all but direct investment) for the period 2002–10 enable us to divide the 43 countries into three groups—20 countries that were always open to inflows of all five categories of assets, 10 countries that were almost always closed to inflows of four or five of the five categories of assets, and 13 other countries that had some experience with capital controls but were not persistently closed to inflows across a wide range of categories of assets.[7] The list of members of each of these three groups is presented in Table 3.1.

Statistics presented in Table 3.1 show that there are sharp distinctions across these groups in terms of the imposition of controls. None of the country-year observations for the open category include an instance of a control on capital inflows, while 73 per cent of the country-year observations for the episodic countries and all of the country-year observations for the countries deemed 'closed' have some capital controls. The distinction between the episodic group and the closed group is shown by the statistic that 79 per cent of the annual observations for the closed category have controls on the five categories of assets (excluding direct investment) but this is true for only 6 per cent of the annual observations for countries in the episodic category. Thus, for the closed category, capital controls are both persistent and wide. Finally, the statistic on income per capita presented in Table 3.1 shows that annual geometric average of income per capita (in PPP constant 2005 US dollars) for the countries in the persistently closed group is one-fifth of that of the persistently open countries, and about one-third of that of the episodic group (note that the all the countries in the persistently closed group are emerging market nations and the preponderance of countries in the persistently open group are advanced economies).

---

[7] We do not consider controls on direct investment inflows in the subsequent analysis because these controls are typically imposed for reasons such as national security rather than, as with the other categories of controls, achieving short-run macroeconomic targets or promoting financial stability. Table A1 in the appendix presents a comprehensive listing of the experience with the controls on capital inflows, across the six categories of assets.

TABLE 3.1   Inflow Control Categories for 2002–10

Persistently open (20)	Persistently closed (10)	Episodic controls (13)
Austria (ADV)	People's Republic of China (EME)	Argentina (EME)
Belgium (ADV)	Colombia (EME)	Australia (ADV)
Canada (ADV)	India (EME)	Brazil (EME)
Czech Republic (EME)	Indonesia (EME)	Chile (EME)
Denmark (ADV)	Malaysia (EME)	Iceland (ADV)
Egypt (EME)	Morocco (EME)	Ireland (ADV)
Finland (ADV)	Philippines (EME)	Republic of Korea (EME)
France (ADV)	Russian Federation (EME)	Mexico (EME)
Germany (ADV)	South Africa (EME)	Peru (EME)
Greece (ADV)	Thailand (EME)	Poland (EME)
Hungary (EME)		Portugal (ADV)
Israel (ADV)		Sweden (ADV)
Italy (ADV)		Turkey (EME)
Japan (ADV)		
Netherlands (ADV)		
New Zealand (ADV)		
Norway (ADV)		
Spain (ADV)		
Switzerland (ADV)		
United Kingdom (ADV)		
Number of Country-Year Observations with Controls on Any Categories of Assets (DI Excluded)		
0 out of 180	90 out of 90	85 out of 117 (73%)
Number of Country-Year Observations with Controls on All Categories of Assets (DI Excluded)		
0 out of 180	71 out of 90 (79%)	7 out of 117 (6%)
Average GDP Per Capita, 2002–10 (in PPP-adjusted 2005 US Dollars); GDP Growth Rate		
$27,603; 1.76%	$5,540; 5.42%	$17,350; 3.37%

Source: International Monetary Fund (various issues) using the classification scheme described in Klein (2012).

III. Capital Controls and the Real Exchange Rate

The past decade has seen a general appreciation of currencies against the US dollar. This has raised concerns because of its effects on exports to the US, as well as because of the relative competitiveness of US exports in third-country markets. These concerns ratcheted up in the wake of expansionary monetary policy during the Great Recession. Efforts by the Federal Reserve to stem the slide of the US's economy prompted declarations of 'currency wars' and, in some countries, the imposition of controls on capital inflows.

Figure 3.1 shows the average real bilateral US dollar exchange rate of three sets of countries over the period 2002–10—the 10 countries with closed capital accounts, the 20 countries with open capital accounts, and the 13 countries that had episodic controls on capital inflows during this period. The average real bilateral exchange rates appreciated for each of these sets of countries, with the eight-year appreciation ranging from 28 per cent for the persistently open category to 44 per cent for the persistently closed category.

Of course, the fact that the rate of appreciation was higher for countries with persistent controls on capital inflows than for countries with open capital accounts does not imply that these controls failed to stem currency appreciation. Countries with persistent controls on capital inflows differ in many ways from other countries. As shown

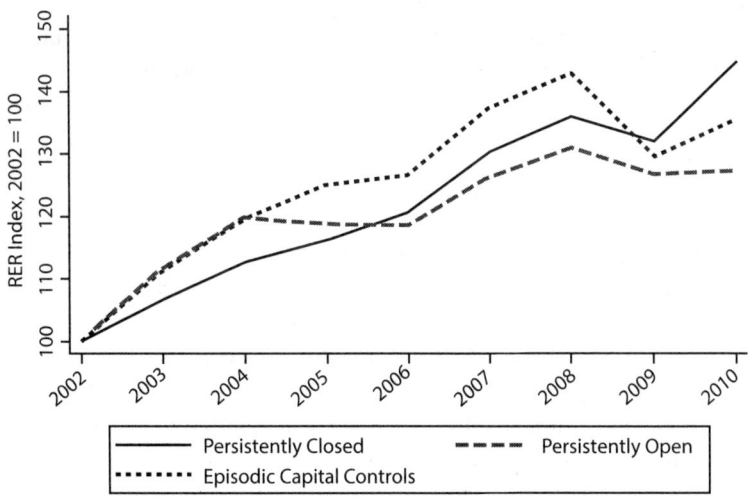

FIGURE 3.1   Bilateral Real US Dollar Exchange Rate Indices by Capital Control Category: Closed, Open, Episodic Controls
Source: Author's calculations based on data from IMF's *International Financial Statistics*.

in Table 3.1, these countries were poorer than the other countries in the sample and, consistent with convergence, GDP growth was higher for these countries. Fast-growing countries would be expected to have higher rates of appreciation, due to the Balassa-Samuelson effect.

The original papers by Balassa (1964) and Samuelson (1964) explained why price levels are higher in richer countries than in poorer countries. The theory posits that there is a bigger productivity difference between rich and poor countries in traded goods than in nontraded goods. This translates into higher wages in tradable goods in rich countries as compared to poor countries. International trade keeps the prices of traded goods relatively close across countries, but the lower wages in poor countries translates into lower prices of nontraded goods in those countries. The real exchange rate, representing the price of traded relative to nontraded goods, is, therefore, more overvalued in rich countries than in poor countries.

This cross-section insight can be used in a panel analysis if wages and prices of nontraded goods (such as real estate) rise more rapidly in fast-growing countries than in countries with slower growth.[8] Controls on capital inflows could mitigate this channel for exchange rate appreciation, at an annual frequency, if fast growth is associated with capital inflows that bid up prices and wages.

The analysis in this chapter is based on a regression that uses annual data for the 43 countries in the sample and takes the form:

$$\Delta \ln(\text{RER})_{i,t} = \beta_0 + \beta_1 \Delta \ln(\text{GDP})_{i,t-1} + \beta_2 \text{Peg}_{i,t-1} + \beta_3 \text{CL}_i + \beta_4 \text{EP}_{i,t-1}$$
$$+ \lambda_t + \varepsilon_{i,t}$$

where $\Delta \ln(\text{RER})_{i,t}$ is the percentage change in the real bilateral exchange rate with the United States (an increase represents an appreciation), $\Delta \ln(\text{GDP})_{i,t-1}$ is the lagged growth rate of GDP, $\text{Peg}_{i,t-1}$ is dummy variable that equals 1 if a country has a pegged exchange rate in year $t-1$, CL_i equals 1 for all years for the 10 countries with persistent controls on inflows, $\text{EP}_{i,t-1}$ equals 1 if there are controls any of the categories of inflows (other than direct investment) in year $t-1$

---

[8] Frankel (2004, 2006) uses this insight to gauge the changing undervaluation of the renminbi.

for any country not in the persistently closed category, and λ_t is a year fixed-effect variable.[9]

This approach has obvious limits in determining whether controls on capital inflows cause, rather than are just correlated with, lower rates of appreciation, conditional on income growth and whether a country has a pegged exchange rate. Countries with long-standing capital controls differ from the other countries in the sample along several dimensions. In an effort to isolate country-specific effects, regressions are also run in which the PRC, India, and the Russian Federation are represented by separate dummy variables, and the Closed dummy variable equals 1 for the remaining countries that had persistent controls on capital inflows. Similarly, another regression isolates episodic controls on inflows imposed by Brazil from episodic controls imposed by other countries.

Table 3.2 presents these estimates. The estimate reported in column I shows that lagged GDP growth is significantly correlated with a real exchange rate appreciation, with an additional growth of 1 percentage point associated with an appreciation of 0.4 percentage points. There is no significant partial correlation showing lower appreciation among the set of 10 countries with persistent controls on capital inflows, however. There is also no significant evidence that the 13 countries that imposed controls on inflows episodically saw an effect of these controls on their real exchange rates with the US.

The regression presented in column II separates the PRC from the other countries with persistent controls on capital inflows (so, in this case, Closed equals 1 for the nine other countries). There is a significant, and sizable, coefficient on the PRC dummy variable. The point estimate suggests that the real dollar/renminbi exchange rate appreciated by 6.3 per cent more per year than what would have been expected, given the growth rate of the Chinese economy. Removing the PRC from the set of countries in the Closed dummy variable causes its value to decrease (in absolute value) and its significance to decline (the p-value of the 10-country Closed variable is 0.31 in column I while the p-value for the nine-country Closed variable is 0.49 for the estimates reported in column II).

The estimates in column III takes this exercise one step further by including a separate dummy variable for India, as well as the PRC (and,

---

[9] It is not possible to control for country fixed effects in the panel estimates because Closed equals 1 in all years for the 10 countries with persistent controls on inflows.

TABLE 3.2   Change in Real Bilateral Dollar Exchange Rate Annual Data, 2002–10

	I	II	III	IV	V
Closed[†]	−0.010	−0.007	−0.006	−0.011	−0.010
(s.e.)	(0.010)	(0.010)	(0.010)	(0.009)	(0.010)
People's Republic of China		−0.063**	−0.065**	−0.065**	
(s.e.)		(0.017)	(0.018)	(0.018)	
India			−0.022**	−0.022**	
(s.e.)			(0.010)	(0.010)	
Russian Federation				0.032**	
(s.e.)				(0.008)	
Episodic	−0.014	−0.013	−0.013	−0.013	−0.018*
(s.e.)	(0.010)	(0.010)	(0.010	(0.010)	(0.010)
Brazil					0.027**
(s.e.)					(0.007)
d ln(GDP)	0.410**	0.532**	0.552**	0.545**	0.406**
(s.e.)	(0.178)	(0.201)	(0.213)	(0.213)	(0.173)
Peg	−0.005	0.001	0.001	0.002	−0.004
(s.e.)	(0.009)	(0.009)	(0.009)	(0.009)	(0.009)
Tests of Linear Combination of Coefficients					
People's Republic of China – Closed		−0.056**	−0.059**	−0.054**	
(s.e.)		(0.018)	(0.020)	(0.020)	
India – Closed			−0.017	−0.011	
(s.e.)			(0.011)	(0.010)	
People's Republic of China – India			−0.042**	−0.043**	
(s.e.)			(0.011)	(0.011)	
R^2	0.29	0.30	0.30	0.31	0.30
No. of Observations	386	386	386	386	386
[†]Closed includes	10 countries	9 countries	8 countries	7 countries	10 countries

(Cont'd)

TABLE 3.2   *(Cont'd)*

Source: Author's estimates based on data from IMF's *International Financial Statistics*.
Notes: Dependent variable: annual %Δ real bilateral US dollar exchange rate
(increase = appreciation)
Closed = 1 if Persistently Closed to Capital Inflows
$\Delta\ln(GDP_{t-1})$ = lag change in real GDP, Peg_{t-1} = 1 if Pegged Exchange Rate in Year
$t-1$
Year dummy variables in all regressions, standard errors clustered at country level
** = significant at the 95 per cent level of confidence or higher
* = significant at the 90 to 95 per cent level of confidence

in this case, Closed equals 1 only for the remaining eight countries with persistent controls on capital inflows). The coefficient on the India dummy variable of −0.022 is significantly different from zero (that is, it is significantly different from countries with open capital accounts), but is not significantly different from the coefficient on the dummy variable representing the other countries with persistent capital controls. The coefficient on the dummy variable for the PRC is significantly smaller than the coefficient on the dummy variable for India, with a difference of 4.2 percentage points.

The Russian Federation ruble significantly appreciated against the dollar during the sample period, partly because of the importance of oil in the Russian Federation economy. It is possible that the failure of the Closed dummy variable to show evidence of stemming appreciation is because of the experience of the Russian Federation. This possibility is examined in column IV, in which there are separate dummy variables for the Russian Federation, the PRC, and India. The estimates in this column show that, in fact, the ruble significantly appreciated against the dollar during this period, over and above what would be predicted by the Russian Federation's GDP growth, by an estimated rate of 3.1 per cent per year. But while the removal of the Russian Federation from the Closed category raises (in absolute value) the coefficient on this dummy variable, as well as its *p*-value, the coefficient on Closed remains statistically insignificant, and of a relatively minor magnitude of 1.1 per cent per year.

The final column of Table 3.2 examines whether the strong appreciation of the Brazilian real over this period is responsible for the failure of a significant coefficient on the episodic dummy variable. The dummy variable Brazil equals 1 in years in which Brazil imposed controls on capital inflows (and the lagged value of this is used in the regression). In this case, there is some evidence that the use of episodic controls by the other 12 countries tempered the appreciation of their currencies, albeit at the 92 per cent level of confidence. But, despite the significance of the coefficient on Episodic in this regression, the failure of episodic controls on capital inflows to temper the appreciation of the real provides a mixed message on the efficacy of these policies.

An illustration of these results is presented in Figure 3.2. This figure plots the deviations of the actual bilateral real dollar exchange rates (indexed to 100 in 2001) from the values predicted by a regression of the appreciation of the bilateral real dollar rate on lagged GDP growth and whether a country has a peg:

$$\Delta \ln \text{RER}_{i,t} = \beta_0 + \beta_1 \Delta \ln(\text{GDP})_{i,t-1} + \text{Peg}_{i,t-1} + \lambda_t + \varepsilon_{i,t}$$

where all variables are as defined in the preceding lines. Deviations are plotted for the PRC, India, the Russian Federation, and the average of the other seven countries with persistent controls on capital inflows.

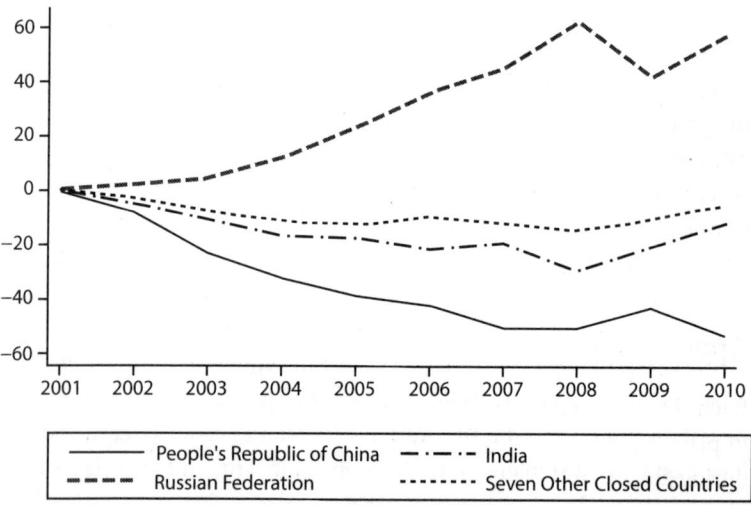

FIGURE 3.2   Real Exchange Rates: Deviations from Predicted
Source: Author's estimates and calculations based on data from IMF's *International Financial Statistics*.

This figure shows that the bilateral dollar–renminbi exchange rate depreciated over this period, and the magnitude of this is consistent with the finding of a significant, large negative coefficient on the PRC dummy variable in columns II–V of Table 3.2. The rupee also depreciated relative to its predicted value, although the magnitude of this was smaller than that of the renminbi. There is a much smaller (and, as we know from the results in Table 3.2, an insignificant) depreciation of the average values of the currencies of the other seven countries with persistent capital controls, excluding the Russian Federation which, as shown in this figure, had an appreciation relative to its predicted real exchange rate path.

IV. Conclusions

There has been increasing support for capital controls since before the onset of the Great Recession. This reflects, in part, the difficulty countries face when capital inflows contribute to currency appreciations, and the limited policy responses available to deal with this problem. But a central issue is the efficacy of capital controls. Research on particular episodes tends to find little support that capital controls temper appreciation or have other macroeconomic effects.[10] The cross-country empirical exercise presented in this chapter is consistent with these results. There is little systematic evidence presented here that capital controls, whether long-standing or episodic, affect the real bilateral appreciation of currencies. The evidence in this chapter shows that the real exchange rates of the PRC and, to a lesser extent, India have appreciated less than what would be predicted by GDP growth. But the source of this may not be controls on capital inflows alone, or, even if it is capital inflow controls, there is no evidence that this effect extends to other countries.

Appendix

Each cell of Table A1 reports the years in which a country had controls in place for the category of assets, with 'Open' signifying no controls during the entire 1995–2010 period and 'Closed' signifying controls in place in each part of the 1995–2010 period (1997–2010 for Bonds since data on this category was not available in 1995 or 1996).

---

[10] See, for example, DeGregorio et al. (2000).

TABLE A1   Years with Controls on Capital Inflows, by Category of Asset

	MM	BO	FC	EQ	CI	DI
Countries with Persistent Controls on Capital Inflows						
People's Republic of China	Closed	Closed	Closed	Closed	Closed	Closed
Colombia	Closed	Closed	Closed	Closed	'95–'99, '02–'10	'99–'10
India	Closed	'02–'10	Closed	Closed	Closed	Closed
Indonesia	Closed	Closed	'95–'02	Closed	Closed	Closed
Malaysia	Closed	Closed	Closed	Closed	Closed	Closed
Morocco	Closed	Closed	Closed	Closed	Closed	Open
Philippines	'95–'97, '03–'10	Closed	Closed	Closed	'95–'97, '03–'10	'03
Russian Federation	Closed	Closed	'95–'00, '02–'03, '05–'07	Closed	Closed	Closed
South Africa	Closed	Closed	Closed	Closed	'06–'10	Closed
Thailand	Closed	Closed	'01–'03, '05–'10	Closed	'95–'09	'95–'07
Countries with Episodic Controls on Capital Inflows						
Argentina	'03–'10	'03–'10	'03–'10	'06–'10	'04–'10	'98–'05
Australia	Open	Open	Open	'96–'10	Open	'95–'10
Brazil	'98–'01, '09–'10	'97–'01, '09–'10	'95–'01, '09–'10	Closed	'95–'02, '10	'95–'01, '06–'10
Chile	'95–'01	'97–'01	'95–'04	'95 – '02	'95–'03	'95–'01
Czech Rep.	'98–'00	'97–'00	Open	'96 – '97	'98–'99	Open
France	'95–'00	Open	Open	'95–'97	Open	Open
Germany	'95–'97	'97	Open	'95–'96	Open	Open
Hungary	'95–'00	'97–'00	'95–'00	Open	'95–'00	'10
Iceland	'08–'10	'05–'10	'08–'10	'95–'04, '06–'10	'08	'95, '04–'10
Ireland	'08–'10	Open	Open	Open	Open	'06–'10
Israel	'95–'97	'97	Open	'95–'97	'95–'97	Open
Republic of Korea	'95–'04	'97	'95–'04	'95–'97	'95–'03	'95–'96
Mexico	'95–'97	Open	'95–'97, '01–'10	'95	'95, '98–'10	'95–'99, '05–'10
Peru	'08–'09	Open	Open	Open	Open	Open

(Cont'd)

TABLE A1   *(Cont'd)*

	MM	BO	FC	EQ	CI	DI
Portugal	Open	'01–'10	Open	'01–'10	'04–'05	Open
Poland	Closed	'99–'10	'95–'06	Closed	'95–'01	Closed
Sweden	'03–'10	Open	Open	'03–'04	Open	Open
Turkey	'07–'10	Open	'09–'10	Open	Open	'95–'02

Source: International Monetary Fund (various issues) using the classification scheme described in Klein (2012).

Notes: Open All: Austria, Belgium, Denmark, Greece, Italy, Netherlands, Norway, Switzerland, the UK, and the US.

Only DI closed (years) : Canada ('95–'10), Egypt ('95), Finland ('05–'10), Japan ('98), New Zealand ('95–'10), and Spain ('95–'98).

MM: Money Market Debt Instruments (Maturity 1 year or less)

BO: Bonds (Maturity longer than 1 year)

FC: Financial Credits

EQ: Equities

CI: Collective Investments

DI: Direct Investments

Bibliography

Balassa, Bela. 1964. 'The purchasing power parity doctrine: A reappraisal', *Journal of Political Economy* 72 (December): 584–96.

De Gregorio, José, Sebastian Edwards, and Rodrigo Valdés. 2000. 'Controls on capital inflows do they work?' *Journal of Development Economics* 69: 59–83.

Frankel, Jeffrey. 2004. 'On the Renminbi: The Choice Between Adjustment Under a Fixed Exchange Rate and a Flexible Exchange Rate', Mimeo.

———. 2006. 'The Balassa-Samuelson Relationship and the Renminbi,' Mimeo.

International Monetary Fund. Annual Report on Exchange Arrangements and Exchange Restrictions, various issues.

IMF Strategy, Policy and Review Department. 2011. 'Recent Experiences in Managing Capital Inflows—Cross-Cutting Themes and Possible Policy Framework', International Monetary Fund.

Jeanne, Olivier, Arvind Subramanian, and John Williamson. 2012. *Who Needs to Open the Capital Account*. Peterson Institute for International Economics.

Klein, Michael W. 2012. 'Capital controls: Gates versus walls', *Brookings Papers on Economic Activity*, Fall.

Kose, M. Ayhan, Eswar Prasad, Kenneth Rogoff, and Shang-Jin Wei. 2009. 'Financial Globalization, A Reappraisal.' *IMF Staff Papers* 56, No. 1, April, pp. 8–62.

Organization for Economic Cooperation and Development (OECD). 2009. *Code of Liberalization of Capital Movements*. Paris.

Ostry, Jonathan, Atish Ghosh, Karl Habermeier, Marcos Chamon, Mahvash S. Qureshi, and Dennis B.S. Reinhardt. 2010. 'Capital Inflows: The Role of Controls.' *IMF Staff Position Note*, SPN/10/04.

Ostry, Jonathan, Atish Ghosh, Karl Habermeier, Luc Laeven, Marcos Chamon, Mahvash S. Qureshi, and Annamaria Kokenyne. 2011a. 'Managing Capital Inflows: What Tools to Use?' *IMF Staff Discussion Note*, SDN/11/06.

Ostry, Jonathan, Atish Ghosh, Marcos Chamon, and Mahvash S. Qureshi. 2011b. 'Capital Controls: When and Why.' *IMF Economic Review* 59(3).

———. 2012. 'Tools for managing financial-stability risks from capital inflows', *Journal of International Economics* 88(2): 407–21.

Rogoff, Kenneth S. 2002. 'Rethinking capital controls: When should we keep an open mind?', *Finance and Development*, December, 55–6.

Samuelson, Paul A. 1964. 'Theoretical notes on trade problems', *Review of Economics and Statistics* 46(May): 145–54.

Schindler, Martin. 2009. 'Measuring financial integration: A new data set', *IMF Staff Papers* 56(1): 222–38.

4

JONATHAN D. OSTRY

Capital Controls: When Are Multilateral Considerations of the Essence?*

I. Introduction

One of the main arguments against capital controls is that although they may be in an individual country's interest, they could be multilaterally destructive like tariffs on goods. A particular concern is that a country might impose controls to avoid necessary macroeconomic and external adjustment, in turn shifting the burden of adjustment onto other countries. A proliferation of capital controls across countries, moreover, might not only undercut warranted adjustments of exchange rates and imbalances across the globe, it could lead in the logical extreme to a situation of financial autarky or isolation the way that trade wars shrink the volume of world trade, seriously damaging global welfare. How should one view the multilateral aspects of deploying the capital controls instrument? When should multilateral concerns trump national interests?

---

* Views expressed are my own and should not be attributed to the IMF. This chapter draws on Ostry et al. (2010), Ostry et al. (2011), and Ostry et al. (2012a, 2012b, and 2012c).

These issues are not merely the ones that academicians are debating, but they are at the centre of global policy debates today. Pursuit of policies (in particular, capital controls, prudential regulations, and foreign exchange market intervention) to manage the risks from volatile capital flows has led to concerns that the spillovers from such policies may be detrimental and that some form of multilateral oversight and coordination of country-level policies is desirable. Some emerging market countries have voiced concerns about the spillovers from policies pursued by other recipient countries, and many have voiced concerns about the spillovers resulting from source-country policies, especially ultra-easy monetary policy which, while justified by domestic considerations, may have been the trigger for increased and increasingly risky and volatile capital flows to emerging market economies (EMEs). The G20, in its deliberations on managing capital flows, has urged that 'any country that has the potential to affect others through its national policy decisions should take the potential spillovers into account when setting national policies'.[1] The International Monetary Fund (IMF) has warned of the 'risk that capital flow management measures, were they to proliferate, could have escalating global costs' (2011). Rajan (2010) expresses worry that the use of foreign exchange market intervention may be forcing excessive and unwarranted external adjustment on other countries.

Of course, the background for all these debates is the proliferation of volatile cross-border financial flows as a defining feature of the global economy in recent decades, reflecting the ongoing financial integration that has proceeded alongside trade integration. While international asset trade has historically been dominated by the advanced economies, the emerging and frontier markets have increasingly become an important part of the landscape, especially when one considers the importance of net flows. No doubt this reflects the fact that capital account liberalization has been part of the development strategy of a number of EMEs. But many countries today are cognizant not only of the benefits that capital account openness can bring, but also of the risks that capital flow volatility necessarily confers.

The global financial crisis has reinforced the profound financial linkages across countries, and the resulting rise in volatility generated by

[1] Source: http://www.g20-g8.com/g8-g20/g20/english/for-the-press/news-releases/g20-leaders-summit-final-communique.1554.html. Accessed on 29 May 2014.

capital flows. Looking at the EMEs, with which this chapter is primarily concerned, inflows peaked at around $665 billion in 2007, plunged to less than $170 billion in 2008, surged again in 2009–10 as global economic recovery gathered some initial momentum, but dried up following the US sovereign debt downgrade in the third quarter of 2011, and have been bouncing around quite a bit ever since. Taking a longer view, the boom–bust cycles of net capital flows that have been part of the landscape for a number of decades seem, if anything, to be growing in intensity, as well as affecting a greater number of countries. Managing capital flow volatility is, thus, a challenge that seems to be gaining in importance.

EMEs have not stood idly by, but have tried to respond to these challenges, deploying a variety of policy tools. In using the instruments at their disposal, they have attempted to mitigate both the macroeconomic and the financial-stability challenges that volatile capital flows may bring. The macroeconomic challenges centre around the volatility of the exchange rate—sharp and excessive appreciations that can be followed by destructive depreciations when capital flows reverse. Financial-stability challenges centre around the excessive growth of credit—and especially worrisome in this context are short-term foreign-currency loans to unhedged domestic borrowers—that create negative externalities for the economy as a whole when a sudden stop occurs. Emerging market policymakers have deployed a variety of tools to manage these risks, including fiscal policy, monetary policy, exchange rate policy, foreign exchange market intervention, prudential regulations, and capital controls.

This chapter looks at the role of capital controls in mitigating the macroeconomic and financial-stability challenges posed by volatile capital flows. In section II, the role of capital controls as one element of a larger policy toolkit is examined, taking the rest of the world's actions as given. Section III examines how policies pursued at the country level add up multilaterally, and whether there should be multilateral rules of the road to guide policies at the country level. Section IV concludes the analysis.

II. The Role of Capital Controls within the Policy Toolkit

It is conceptually useful to think about capital flow volatility giving rise to two distinct types of risks: macroeconomic and financial stability. On the macroeconomic side, the concern is that a temporary surge will lead to an appreciation of the exchange rate and undermine competitiveness of the tradables sector—possibly causing lasting damage even when inflows abate or reverse. The main worry on the financial-stability side is that large inflows may lead to excessive foreign borrowing and foreign currency (FX) exposure, adding fuel to a domestic credit boom, an FX-denominated lending boom, and domestic asset price bubbles. How should capital controls be used alongside other instruments to manage these distinct risks?

Macroeconomic Risks

As was implicit in the foregoing, the response is likely to be multi-pronged, and depend on the specific circumstances facing the country:

External Adjustment

- To the degree that the *currency* is undervalued, and the current account balance exceeds its multilaterally warranted level, it is likely to be appropriate—both from the country's perspective and critically from a multilateral perspective—to allow the exchange rate to strengthen in response to inflows. This means that in these situations, the country would be expected to refrain from intervening in the foreign exchange market to contain appreciation. If the country's exchange rate regime were a peg, rather than a free or managed float, the country would be expected to allow the real exchange rate to appreciate in response to inflows, by not sterilizing whatever intervention it undertook in the FX market (necessary to respect the peg).
- When the exchange rate is overvalued (or close to being so), it is likely to be appropriate to moderate upward pressures on the currency through official purchases of foreign exchange. The *intervention* would likely over time be two-way since its purpose is to moderate the exchange rate volatility arising from capital flow volatility, rather than to achieve a specific target for the currency's value. How much intervention is appropriate for the country is likely to be guided by country-insurance perspectives. These, in turn, depend on a variety of considerations, including the volatility of different components

of the balance of payments, the openness of the economy to trade and foreign capital (especially short-term debt), and so on. The point is simply that accumulation of reserves is likely to be bounded given possible metrics for an appropriate level of the stock from a country-insurance perspective.

- It goes without saying that judgments about the appropriateness of the exchange rate's value or the level of reserves are complex—much more art than science. Methodologies exist to gauge misalignment or to benchmark adequacy of reserves, but they cannot function without the judgment of the policymaker and an assessment of country circumstances.

Domestic Adjustment

- Adjustment of domestic (macroeconomic) policies (monetary and fiscal policies) may well be useful in the context of managing capital flows, but it is important to bear in mind that macro policies are likely to have designated targets of their own. Monetary policy is likely to be targeted at achieving low and stable inflation, and thereby helping to stabilize the cyclical position of the economy. Fiscal policy may also have a role in offsetting cyclical fluctuations but it is also likely to be geared to securing sustainability of the public debt over the medium term. As long as adjustments in the policy settings do not move the economy away from the primary targets of the policies, they can and should be used to help manage capital flows. For instance, in response to a surge in inflows, fiscal policy could be tightened and monetary policy loosened, provided this does not go against the achievement of the those policies' primary targets.
- It is sometimes argued that there is a pecking order in respect of the use of different policies to manage the macroeconomic risks from capital flows, and it is sometimes alleged that capital controls should be imposed as a last resort. After all the other policies have been tried and residual risks remain. What is clear is that it is both in the unilateral interest of the country, as well as on the multilateral interest (on this, more in the following lines), that capital controls should not be used before the exchange rate has been allowed to rise to its multilaterally consistent level (undervaluation being in neither the country's

nor the rest of the world's interest).[2] It is also clear that domestic macroeconomic policies should be set at levels consistent with their primary targets and that, to the degree that adjustments in those policies would aid also in the goal of managing capital flows without compromising domestic targets, it would seem sensible to use those tools. The inference I draw is that capital controls are probably best left until external and macroeconomic adjustments have taken place because these adjustments will probably be helpful in dealing with the inflow problem efficaciously.[3] I infer also that controls pursued for the purpose of thwarting or avoiding those adjustments are likely to be undesirable. Finally, I infer that controls used to manage the macroeconomic risks associated with inflow surges are likely to be temporary, since in all likelihood a permanent inflow is likely to require a permanent adjustment in the exchange rate. Thus, controls used for macroeconomic reasons would likely be reduced/removed once the inflow surge abated.

Financial Fragility

Beyond their macroeconomic effects, capital inflows—especially certain types of liabilities—can make the country more vulnerable to financial crisis. The risks stem from two sources: direct lending from abroad (or that otherwise bypasses the regulated financial sector in the recipient country) and flows that are intermediated by domestic banks.

An obvious example of the former is debt versus equity flows, because equity allows for greater risk sharing between creditor and borrower. More generally, it is not implausible that herd behaviour and excessive optimism on the part of foreign lenders, coupled with myopic borrowers who underestimate foreign exchange and liquidity risks, can lead to foreign borrowing that is excessive from a financial-fragility perspective. Based on these considerations, the theoretical literature yields a pecking order of capital inflows, in decreasing order of riskiness, with short-term instruments more risky than long-term ones within each category:

---

[2] I assume for the moment that there are no domestic distortions to which undervaluation would be the appropriate policy response.

[3] Controls, however, might be useful to cope with the time lags involved in implementing macro policies or in making those policies effective.

- foreign-currency debt;
- consumer price–indexed local currency debt;
- local currency debt;
- portfolio equity investment; and
- foreign direct investment.

Capital inflows that are intermediated through the banking system might also fuel domestic lending booms, including foreign exchange–denominated credit, which may be especially dangerous—to both the bank and to the end-borrower—if extended to borrowers lacking a natural hedge (for example, households rather than exporters).

For flows that are intermediated by domestic banks, both prudential regulation and capital controls (on the financial sector) are potential instruments. Which to choose depends on the nature of the risks and, indeed, the distinction between prudential regulations and capital controls may be blurred in practice. For instance, a regulation prohibiting banks from extending FX-denominated loans to unhedged borrowers is a prudential measure; yet, in the context of capital inflows, it might act as a capital control if most of the loans being extended in FX by domestic banks correspond to their own foreign borrowing (with the prohibition reducing banks' foreign borrowing because they face limits on their open FX positions). In general, the instrument employed should target the relevant risk. Therefore, if the concern is FX-denominated lending, then prudential regulation of bank lending (for example, prohibiting loans to unhedged borrowers, or requiring higher capital charges against these loans) is indicated. But if the risk pertains mainly to the nature of external borrowing by banks (for example, excessive reliance on short-term wholesale funding from abroad), then financial sector or economy-wide capital controls may be called for.

When flows bypass the domestic banks (either direct lending from abroad or intermediated through finance companies or other unregulated segments of the domestic financial system), then by definition prudential tools will have little traction, and capital controls may be required. For example, unremunerated reserve requirements on foreign currency debt can be used to reduce external foreign currency–denominated borrowing, and even if this encourages substitution in to other forms of external debt, the risks are reduced. Inflow taxes on short-term debt reduce the price differential between short- and long-term debt and induce longer maturities. The optimal size of the tax depends on the risk of liquidity panics, the size and social cost of the associated fiscal adjustment, and the elasticity of substitution between debt of different maturities. Financial transaction taxes are relatively more costly for short-term carry trades and may deter such flows. Minimum-stay requirements are a direct method of lengthening the maturity of liabilities.

As discussed, capital controls should only be imposed in response to macroeconomic concerns when the flows are expected to be temporary (because the economy should adjust to permanent shocks). An important difference when controls are contemplated for financial-stability reasons is that they can be imposed on flows that are expected to be more persistent. Indeed, persistent flows are more likely to fuel credit booms and asset price bubbles, making the case for policy intervention stronger. Since no capital inflow surge will truly be permanent, the prudential and capital controls measures can be reduced when the inflow abates (with the administrative apparatus for these measures kept in place for when they are next required).

Synthesis

The discussion so far is synthesized in figures 4.1–4.3. Figure 4.1 portrays the policy toolkit available to deal with macroeconomic and financial-stability risks (portrayed along the left and right arms of the figure, respectively). Along the left arm, the logic is that capital controls should not substitute for external adjustment or warranted macroeconomic adjustment, so logically the use of capital controls comes after such adjustments. Along the financial-stability arm, however, prudential policies and capital controls could be used simultaneously to deal with particular types of risk, the former more intensively to deal with risks created by flows intermediated through the regulated financial system, the latter for flows not intermediated through the regulated financial system.

Figures 4.2 and 4.3 go into more detail about the toolkit available to deal with the financial-stability risks. Each figure argues that prudential measures and capital control tools can be tailored to the specific risks that need to be addressed—maturity risk, credit risk, currency risk, risk of asset price bubbles, and so on. Figure 4.2 deals with the case of flows

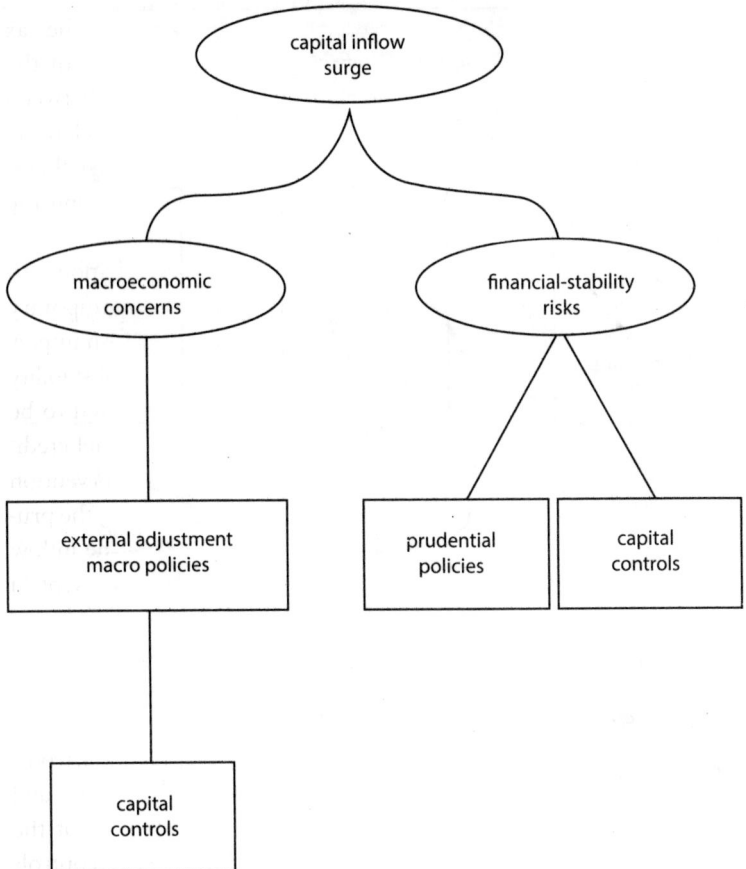

FIGURE 4.1   Policy Responses to Manage Inflow Surges
Source: Adapted from Ostry et al. (2011).

intermediated through the regulated financial sector, while Figure 4.3 deals with the case of direct borrowing and thus beyond the reach of the prudential regulator.

III. Multilateral Considerations

It is no surprise that the expansion of the toolkit to include policies outside the standard macroeconomic measures (fiscal and monetary measures) has raised a host of multilateral issues. There seem to be

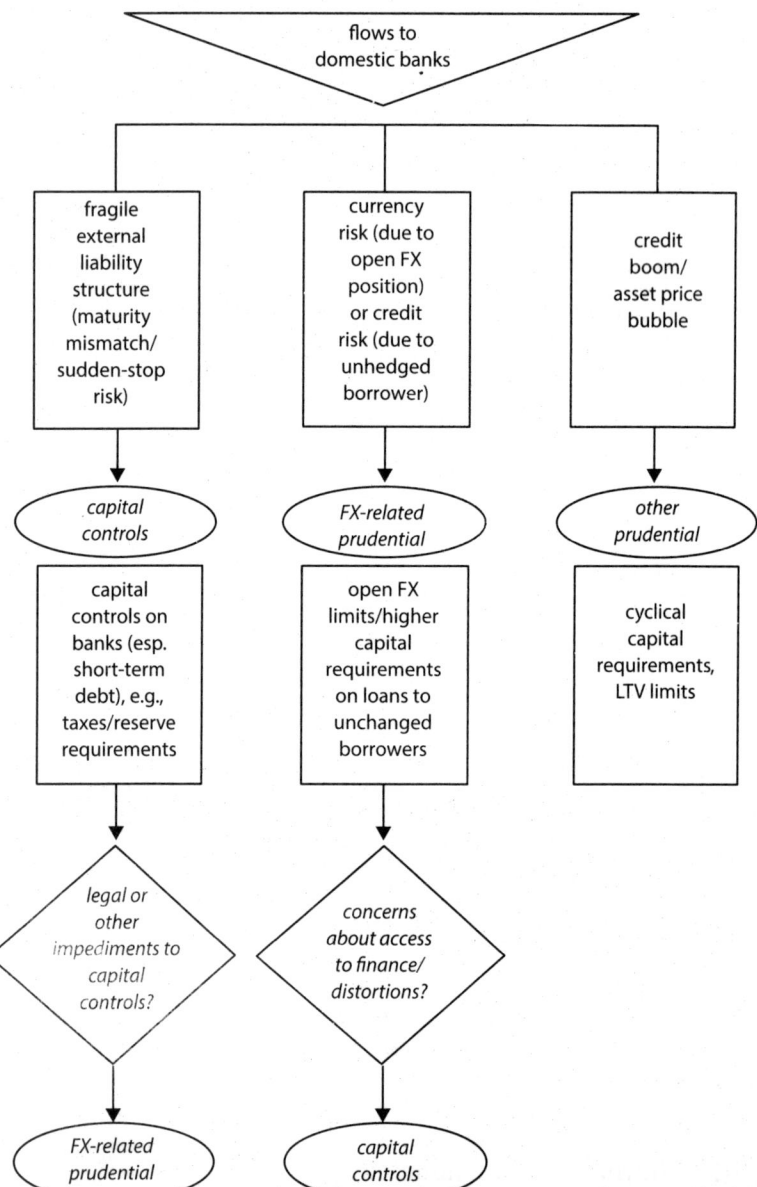

FIGURE 4.2   Choice of Instruments: Flows Intermediated through the
Financial Sector
Source: Ostry et al. (2011).

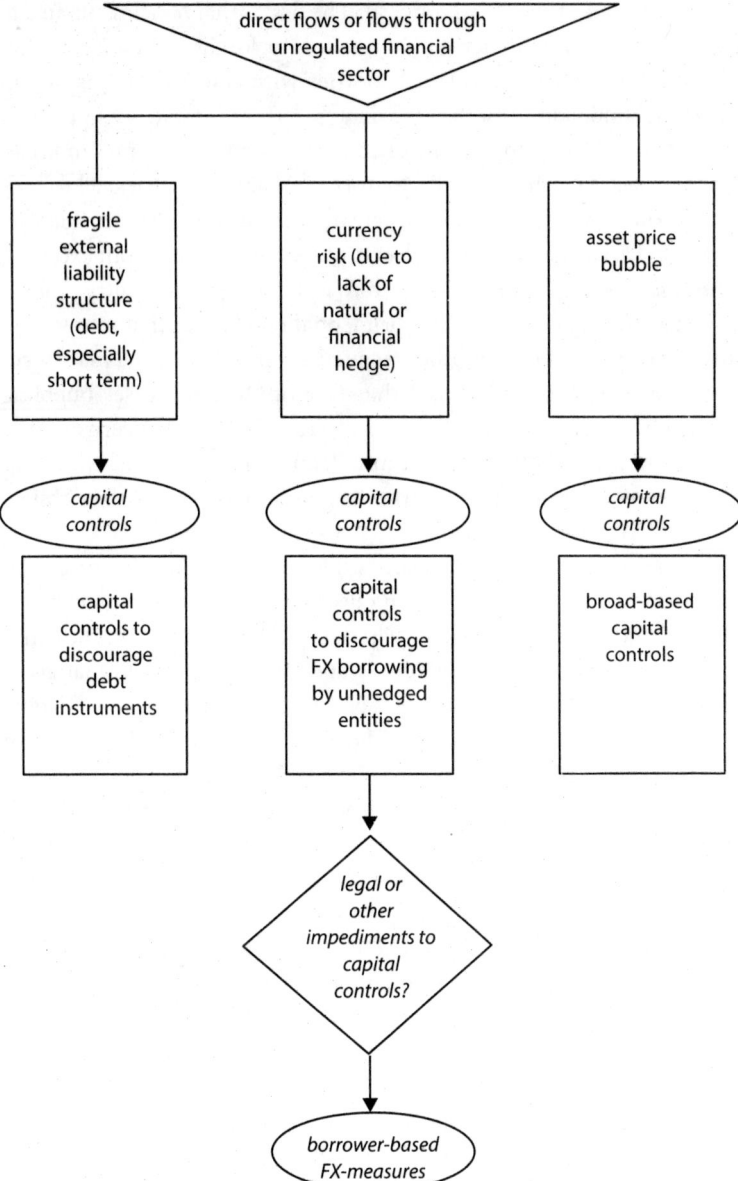

FIGURE 4.3 Choice of Instruments: Flows Not Intermediated through the Financial Sector

Source: Ostry et al. (2011).

several areas of multilateral concern. The first is that policies pursued at the country level (whether capital controls or foreign exchange market intervention) may saddle other countries with adjustments that are in neither the individual nor the global interest (for example, when policies in one country sustain currencies that are misaligned from a multilateral perspective). The second is that source-country policies fail to take into account the externalities they create through cross-border financial flows, and accordingly lead to adverse outward spillovers from excessive or excessively-risky outflows. The third is that recipient-country policies (for example, capital controls or prudential regulations that mimic controls) may deflect flows to other recipients, exacerbating the macroeconomic or financial-stability risks they face [in the latter case, 'bubbling thy neighbor' as argued by Forbes et al. (2012)]. These concerns lead to the question of whether, from a multilateral perspective, discretion to pursue policies should be circumscribed and, relatedly, on the possible gains from coordinating policies.

It bears noting that worries about the multilateral aspects of capital flow management have a very long history, and were a prime concern of the founding fathers of the IMF in their deliberations about the IMF's Articles of Agreement. Both Keynes and White considered that coordination was desirable to achieve appropriate management of capital flows, highlighting that 'control will be more difficult by unilateral action than if movements of capital can be controlled at both ends' (Keynes) and that 'without the cooperation of other countries, such control is difficult, expensive, and subject to considerable evasion' (White) (Helleiner 1995). The desirability of coordination has been reinforced lately, with statements by several emerging market policymakers (for example, Brazil and the Republic of Korea) to the effect that excess global liquidity is severely complicating management of capital inflows and running the risk of currency wars and proliferation of capital control measures.[4]

The state of empirical knowledge about the unilateral effects of capital controls and the nature and size of spillovers is as yet insufficient to serve as a persuasive guide for policy. To begin, there is considerable uncertainty about the unilateral effects of capital controls, with

---

[4] Sources: http://www.ft.com/cms/s/0/69c0b800-032c-11e2-a484-00144 feabdc0.html; http://www.koreatimes.co.kr/www/news/biz/2012/09/182_ 120013.html; http://online.wsj.com/article/SB10000872396390444165804578 006513150635592.html. Accessed on 29 May 2014.

more persuasive evidence that such controls alter the composition of flows than the aggregate level (Magud et al. 2011; Ostry et al. 2012c; and Table 4.1). Of course, to the degree that controls are ineffective at the country level in altering aggregate flows, there would be no multilateral impact either, and accordingly no multilateral reason to proscribe their use. Direct evidence on the size of cross-border spillovers is also remarkably scant, with Forbes et al. (2012) finding some evidence at the level of portfolio flows but not aggregate flows. Jeanne (2012) draws some persuasive connections between the use of capital controls and the pursuit of exchange rate and external objectives. There is a much older, and well-established (and convincing) literature on the nature and size of spillovers from source-country policies (especially monetary policy) to recipient countries [for example, Calvo et al. (1993), Reinhart and Reinhart (2008), and Ghosh et al. (2014)]. The experience of Sweden and Latvia, for example, during the recent crisis, also serves to underscore the importance of spillovers from regulatory and supervisory policies in source countries for recipient countries. The mixed nature of the overall evidence on spillovers, however, means that economic logic, rather than empirical evidence, is likely to be the more important driver of advice to policymakers.

The policy debate on the multilateral aspects of capital flow management seems to gravitate around four cases. The first is the use of capital controls as a substitute for warranted external adjustment, where the constructive intent of the policy is to sustain, for example, an undervalued currency. If there is no underlying distortion (for example, a production externality) that might justify the undervaluation policy, it is clear that this use of capital controls is not in the self-interest of the country. This is why, in the left-hand arm of Figure 4.1, capital controls lies below external adjustment. More relevant for the discussion in this section, however, is that using capital controls as the vehicle to sustain undervaluation is also multilaterally undesirable, since it implies that the rest of the world must sustain external balances and currencies that are also multilaterally undesirable, and as such the warranted adjustment of global imbalances towards their equilibrium is frustrated. This case, thus, seems reasonably straightforward. Capital controls should never substitute for warranted external adjustment.

A second case relates to terms of trade manipulation. The reason for thinking about terms of trade manipulation clearly stems from the case

TABLE 4.1 Selected Cases of Control Measures on Capital Inflows

Country	Year	Controls	Study	Did controls on inflows:		
				Reduce the volume of net flows	Alter the composition	Reduce real exchange rate pressures
Brazil	1993–7	– Explicit tax on capital flows on stock market investments, foreign loans, and certain foreign exchange transactions – Administrative controls (outright prohibitions against, or minimum maturity requirements for, certain types of inflows)	Cardoso and Goldfajn (1998)	Yes (ST)	Yes (ST)	
			Reinhart and Smith (1998)	Yes (ST)	Yes (ST)	
			Ariyoshi and others (2000)	No	No	No
			Edison and Reinhart (2001)			No
			Carvalho and Garcia (2008)	Yes (ST)		
Chile	1991–8	– Introduced URR on foreign borrowing, later extended to cover nondebt flows, American Depository Receipts, and potentially speculative FDI – Raised the discount rate	Valdes-Prieto and Soto (1998)	No	Yes	No
			Le Fort and Budnevich (1997)	No	Yes	Yes
			Larrain, Laban, and Chumacero (1997)	No	Yes	
			Cardoso and Laurens (1998)	Yes (ST)	Yes (ST)	No
			Reinhart and Smith (1998)	Yes (ST)	Yes	
			Edwards (1999)	No	Yes (ST)	No
				Yes (ST)	No	No

Country	Period	Measure	Reference			
Colombia	1993–8	– Introduced URR on external borrowing (limited to loans with maturities up to 18 months) and later extended to cover certain trade credits	Gallego and Schmidt-Hebbel (1999)	No	Yes	No
			Ariyoshi et al. (2000)	No		Yes (ST)
			De Gregorio, Edwards, and Valdes (2000)			Yes
			Edwards and Rigobon (2009)			
			Le Fort and Budnevich (1997)	Yes (ST)	Yes	Yes
			Cardenas and Barrera (1997)	No	Yes	
			Reinhart and Smith (1998)	No	No	
			Ariyoshi and others (2000)	No	No	No
	2007–8	– Introduced URR of 40 per cent on foreign borrowing and portfolio inflows – Imposed limits on the currency derivative positions of banks (500 per cent of capital)	Concha and Galindo (2008)	No	Yes	No
			Cardenas (2007)	No	Yes (ST)	
			Clements and Kamil (2009)	No	Yes	
Croatia	2004–8	– Introduced prudential marginal reserve requirements on bank foreign financing	Jankov (2009)		Yes	

(Cont'd)

TABLE 4.1 (Cont'd)

Country	Year	Controls	Study	Did controls on inflows:		
				Reduce the volume of net flows	Alter the composition	Reduce real exchange rate pressures
Malaysia	1994	– Prohibition against sale of short-term debt securities and money market instruments to nonresidents, and against commercial banks' engagement in nontrade-related swaps or forward transactions with nonresidents – Ceilings on banks' net liability position. – Noninterest-bearing deposit requirement for commercial banks against ringgit funds of foreign banks	Ariyoshi et al. (2000) Tamirisa (2004)	Yes	Yes	Yes (ST) No

				Ariyoshi and others (2000)			
Thailand	1995–6	– URR imposed on banks' nonresident baht accounts – Introduced asymmetric open-position limits to discourage foreign borrowing. – Imposed reporting requirements for banks on risk-control measures in foreign exchange and derivatives trading		Yes	Yes	Yes	Yes
	2006–8	– URR of 30 per cent imposed on foreign currencies sold or exchanged against baht with authorized financial institutions (except for FDI and amounts not exceeding $20,000). Equity investments in companies listed on the stock exchange were made exempt from the URR					

(Cont'd)

TABLE 4.1 (*Cont'd*)

Country	Year	Controls	Study	Did controls on inflows:		
				Reduce the volume of net flows	Alter the composition	Reduce real exchange rate pressures
Cross-country evidence			Reinhart and Smith (1998)	Yes (ST)	Yes (ST)	
			Montiel and Reinhart (1999)	No	Yes (ST)	
			Edison and Reinhart (2001)			No
			Binici et al. (2009)	No	No	

Sources: Ostry et al. (2010) Magud et al. (2011).

Note: A blank entry refers to the cases where the study in question did not analyze the particular relationship. (ST) refers to cases where only short-term effects were detected.

of goods trade, where we worry about the exploitation of monopoly / monopsony power. There is at a conceptual level a perfect analogy with intertemporal asset trade, where large players in global capital markets can restrict the supply of or demand for capital and thereby alter the intertemporal terms of trade, the world interest rate. Creditors would have an interest in supplying less capital to boost their terms of trade and debtors would have an interest in demanding less capital (for example, by putting on inflow controls). From the point of view of an arbitrary net debtor in global markets, the best case scenario is where another debtor imposes inflow controls, lowering the world interest rate, and allowing the country to borrow the same volume of inflows at a lower cost (and vice versa for a net creditor supplying capital to the markets). Since there is no underlying distortion, the reduction in the volume of intertemporal trade is a deadweight loss for the system as a whole, and is, thus, multilaterally inefficient and objectionable (in the same way as use of tariffs to manipulate global trade in goods is objectionable). One may think that the above scenario is far-fetched in that countries do not typically use capital controls to manipulate world interest rates. However, before dismissing the issue altogether, one may wish to consider whether other policies do not occasionally have the effect of moving the world interest rate in a direction consistent with the terms of trade manipulation scenario: for example, whether there are cases where large debtors pursue policies that lower world interest rates (for example, monetary policy), or large creditors maintain restrictions on capital outflows that raise world interest rates.

A third case relates to financial-stability externalities. The issue here is that there is a domestic externality that results in excessive foreign borrowing in risky forms (short-term, foreign-currency debt). The national welfare perspective may, therefore, call for some form of tax on foreign borrowing, particularly on the more risky instruments (Korinek 2011). The capital control in such a case incentivizes the private sector to internalize the financial-stability externality generated by its borrowing. While there will be spillovers from the imposition of the capital control, whether they are a problem from a global efficiency perspective is not obvious. It should be remembered that from a domestic standpoint, the imposition of controls is justified to offset a distortion; if the diversion of flows to other countries exacerbates distortions in those other countries (say, because they too suffer from a financial-stability externality), the answer may simply be for those other countries to impose controls of their own. A 'capital control war' in which each country gradually works towards a level of controls and tolerance of financial-stability risk that suits its domestic needs may even be optimal. Whether it is or not depends upon whether offsetting the domestic distortion with capital controls itself does damage or creates costs (the costs may be standard bureaucratic costs or more likely costs from imperfect targeting of the riskiest flows—collateral damage). When using controls is costly, then in general there will be a benefit to coordination. Intuitively, the decentralized Nash equilibrium will no longer be efficient because each country now has two targets (the domestic distortion and the cost of using the capital control instrument) but only one instrument (what is going on at the country level is that each country overestimates the financial-stability benefit from controls because it fails to take account of the mutual deflection of flows that occurs in the Nash equilibrium). Interestingly, if the costs associated from imposing the capital control are convex, the globally efficient outcome will require coordination between source and recipient countries (what Keynes referred to as 'operating at both ends of the transaction'). The incentive of source countries to engage in coordination is far from clear, however—a thorny problem when putting coordination into practice.

The fourth and final case concerns production externalities. Here, the situation is that production of exportables is associated with, for example, a learning-by-doing externality (external to the firm) that results in underproduction of exportables. The optimal policy in such a situation would be a production subsidy. However, there may be constraints so that the first best policy is not feasible, for example budgetary resources to fund the subsidy are unavailable, or alternative tax policies (for example, taxing production of nontradables) are also infeasible, say, because the relevant sectors are informal and, thus, would escape the tax net. In such a situation, the country may opt for a policy of undervaluation supported by capital controls. Like the other cases considered previously, there will be spillovers associated with this policy, as the undervalued currency will force other countries to run larger trade deficits than they would otherwise run. Is this multilaterally problematic? This is clearly a judgment call, but note that because the policy of undervaluation chosen by the country is not the first best means to address its domestic distortion (since the policy distorts consumption decisions as well as production decisions, but only the latter are affected by the externality), and because it has stronger negative spillovers for the rest of the world than the first best policy, it is likely that the use of capital controls in such a case would invite multilateral scrutiny. In any case, given the likelihood that countries could disguise the true intent of the policy, the bar should be set quite high in condoning the possible use of capital controls as a response to production externalities.

IV. Conclusion

This chapter has examined the use of capital controls within the overall policy toolkit to manage capital flow volatility. It has been argued that there is no sure-fire, one-size-fits-all way to deal with the impact of potentially destabilizing short-term flows. From an individual country point of view, the usual elements of the toolkit include allowing the exchange rate to adjust, using foreign exchange market intervention when currency values deviate significantly from fundamentals, adjusting the domestic macroeconomic policy mix, and strengthening the prudential framework. In some circumstances, however, the usual macro policy remedies will not be appropriate (for example, since inflation is a concern, so lowering domestic policy rates would be ill advised, the currency is already too strong, or reserves are more than adequate). In others, it may not be possible to address financial-fragility concerns through the domestic prudential framework alone. For both macroeconomic and financial-stability reasons, therefore, there may be circumstances in which capital controls are a legitimate component of the policy response to surges in capital inflows.

Multilateral dimensions, however, are integral to a balanced perspective on the appropriateness of using capital controls to manage inflows. While controls can be helpful to individual countries under certain conditions, their widespread use could have deleterious effects on the efficient allocation of investment across countries, and harm prospects for global recovery and growth. Greater use of controls could also lead to crowding out of less distortionary policies to manage inflows, and contribute to contagion, with countries whose individual circumstances do not justify the use of controls choosing to adopt restrictions on inflows. Widespread adoption of controls could also contribute to widening of global imbalances, especially if restrictions were implemented

by countries with undervalued currencies as a means to resist appreciation. A multilateral framework governing the re-imposition of controls,
balancing the various considerations, could be helpful in managing possible cross-country spillovers.

The chapter has argued that the use of capital controls is multilaterally problematic when their purpose is to short-circuit external
adjustment, engage in terms of trade manipulation, or offset domestic
production externalities when other policies can get the job done at
lower cost. When the goal of capital controls is to offset domestic
financial-stability externalities, the existence of spillovers does not per
se mean that the controls are multilaterally problematic. Spillovers
are an inherent part of how market systems function and their existence does not mean that the policy that gives rise to the spillover is
multilaterally problematic. However, when the use of capital controls
itself creates costs for the country (for example, bureaucratic cost or
the collateral damage from imperfect targeting of the risky flows),
then there may well be a need for policy coordination to achieve a
globally efficient outcome. If costs are convex, the coordination is
likely to require involvement of both source and recipient countries,
what Keynes referred to as 'operating at both ends of the transaction'.
The right answer is not that countries should choose policies that run
counter to the domestic interest. It is rather that they should choose
from among the policies that support domestic objective those policies
that have less damaging outward spillovers, in consonance with the
philosophy underlying the 'integrated surveillance decision' adopted
by the IMF's membership late last year (IMF 2012).

References

Ariyoshi, A., K. Habermeier, B. Laurens, I. Okter-Robe, J. Canales-Kriljenko,
and A. Kirilenko. 2000. 'Capital controls: Country experiences with their use
and liberalization', *IMF Occasional Paper 190*, International Monetary Fund,
Washington DC.

Binici, M., M. Hutchison, and M. Schindler. 2009. 'Controlling capital? Legal
restrictions and the asset composition of international financial flows', *IMF
Working Paper 09/208*, International Monetary Fund, Washington DC.

Calvo, G., L. Leiderman, and C. Reinhart. 1993. 'Capital inflows and real
exchange rate appreciation in Latin America: The role of external factors',
IMF Staff Papers 40(1): 108–51.

Cardenas, M. 2007. 'Controle de capitales en Colombia: Funcionan o no? *Debate de Coyuntura Económica*, December, Colombia, Fedesarollo, Bogotá.

Cardenas, M., and Felipe Barrera. 1997. 'On the Effectiveness of Capital Controls: The Experience of Colombia during the 1990s', *Journal of Development Economics* 54 (1): 27–57.

Cardoso, E., and I. Goldfajn. 1998. 'Capital flows to Brazil: The endogeneity of capital controls', *IMF Staff Papers* 45 (1): 161–202.

Cardoso, J., and B. Laurens. 1998. 'Managing capital flows—Lessons from the experience of Chile', *IMF Working Paper 98/168*, International Monetary Fund Washington DC.

Carvalho, B., and M. Garcia. 2008. 'Ineffective controls on capital inflows under sophisticated financial markets: Brazil in the nineties, in *Financial Markets Volatility and Performance in Emerging Markets*, S. Edwards and M. Garcia (eds). Cambridge, MA: National Bureau of Economic Research.

Clements, B., and H. Kamil. 2009. 'Are capital controls effective in the 21st century? The recent experience of Colombia', IMF Working Paper 09/30, International Monetary Fund, Washington DC.

Concha, A., and A. Galindo. 2008. 'An assessment of another decade of capital controls in Colombia: 1998–2008', *Paper for XIII LACEA Meeting*, Rio de Janeiro, Brazil.

De Gregorio, J., S. Edwards, and R. Valdes. 2000. 'Controls on capital inflows: Do they work? *Journal of Development Economics* 3 (1): 59–83.

Edison, H., and C. Reinhart. 2001. 'Stopping hot money: On the use of capital controls during financial crises', *Journal of Development Economics* 66 (2): 533–53.

Edwards, S. 1999. 'How effective are capital controls?' *Journal of Economic Perspectives* 13 (4): 65–84.

Edwards, S., and R. Rigobon. 2009. 'Capital controls on inflows, exchange rate volatility and external vulnerability', *Journal of International Economics* 78 (2): 256–67.

Forbes, K., M. Fratzscher, T. Kostka, and R. Straub. 2012. 'Bubble thy neighbor: Portfolio effects and externalities from capital controls', *NBER Working Paper 18052*, National Bureau of Economic Research, Cambridge, MA.

Gallego, F., and K. Schmidt-Hebbel. 1999. 'Capital controls in Chile: Effective? Efficient?' *Central Bank of Chile Working Paper 59*, Banco Central de Chile, Santiago.

Ghosh, A., M. Qureshi, J. Kim, and J. Zalduendo. 2014. 'Surges', *Journal of International Economics* 92 (2): 266–85.

Helleiner, E. 1995. *States and the Reemergence of Global Finance: From Bretton Woods to the 1990s*. Ithaca, NY: Cornell University Press.

IMF. 2011. *The Multilateral Aspects of Policies Affecting Capital Flows*, Washington DC: International Monetary Fund.

IMF. 2012. *Modernizing the Legal Framework for Surveillance–An Integrated Surveillance Decision.* Washington DC: International Monetary Fund. Available online at: www.imf.org/external/np/pp/eng/2012/062612.pdf. Accessed on 29 May 2014.

Jankov, L. 2009. 'Spillovers of the crisis: How different is Croatia?" *Paper presented at Recent Developments in the Baltic Countries—What Are the Lessons for Southeastern Europe?* 23 March, Oesterreichische Nationalbank, Vienna.

Jeanne, O. 2012. 'Capital account policies and the real exchange rate', *NBER Working Paper 18404*, National Bureau of Economic Research, Cambridge, MA.

Korinek, A. 2011. 'The new economics of prudential capital controls', *IMF Economic Review*, 59 (3): 523–61.

Larraín, F., R. Laban, and R. Chumacero. 1997. 'What determines capital inflows? An empirical analysis for Chile', *John F. Kennedy School of Government Faculty Research Working Paper R97-09*, Harvard University, Cambridge, MA.

Le Fort, G., and C. Budnevich. 1997. 'Capital account regulations and macroeconomic policy: Two Latin experiences', *Central Bank of Chile WP 06*, Banco Central de Chile, Santiago.

Magud, N., C. Reinhart, and K. Rogoff. 2011. 'Capital controls: myth and reality—A portfolio balance approach', *NBER Working Paper No. 16805*, National Bureau of Economic Research, Cambridge, MA.

Mohanty, M., and M. Klau. 2005. 'Monetary policy rules in emerging market economies', in R.J. Langhammer and L.V. de Souza (eds), *Monetary Policy and Macroeconomic Stabilization in Latin America*, pp. 205–45. Springer: Berlin Heidelberg.

Montiel, P., and C. Reinhart. 1999. 'Do capital controls and macroeconomic policies influence the volume and composition of capital flows? Evidence from the 1990's', *Journal of International Money and Finance* 18 (4): 619–35.

Ostry, J.D., A.R. Ghosh, K. Habermeier, M. Chamon, M.S. Qureshi, and D.B.S. Reinhardt. 2010. 'Capital inflows: The role of controls', *IMF Staff Position Note 10/04*, International Monetary Fund, Washington, DC.

Ostry, J.D., A.R. Ghosh, K. Habermeier, M. Chamon, M.S. Qureshi, L. Laeven, and A. Kokenyne. 2011. 'Managing capital inflows: What tools to use?' *IMF Staff Discussion Note 11/06*, International Monetary Fund, Washington, DC.

Ostry, J.D., A.R. Ghosh, and M. Chamon. 2012a. 'Two targets, two instruments: Monetary and exchange rate policies in emerging market economies', *IMF Staff Discussion Note 12/01*, International Monetary Fund, Washington, DC.

Ostry, J.D., A.R. Ghosh, and A. Korinek. 2012b. 'Multilateral aspects of managing the capital account', *IMF Staff Discussion Note 12/10*, International Monetary Fund, Washington, DC.

Ostry, J.D., A.R. Ghosh, M. Chamon, and M.S. Qureshi. 2012c. 'Tools for managing financial-stability risks from capital inflows', *Journal of International Economics* 88 (2): 407–21.

Rajan, R. 2010. 'Beggaring the world economy', *Project Syndicate*, 7 October. Available online at http://www.project-syndicate.org/commentary/beggaring-the-world-economy. Accessed on 29 May 2014.

———. 2008. 'Capital flow bonanzas: An encompassing view of the past and present', *NBER Working Paper 14321*, National Bureau of Economic Research, Cambridge, MA.

Reinhart, C., and T. Smith. 1998. 'Too much of a good thing: The macroeconomic effects of taxing capital inflows', in *Managing Capital Flows and Exchange Rates: Perspectives from the Pacific Basin*, R. Glick (ed.), pp. 436–64. Cambridge: Cambridge University Press.

Reinhart, C., and V. Reinhart. 1999. 'On the use of reserve requirements in dealing with the capital-flow problem', *International Journal of Finance and Economics* 4 (1): 27–54.

Tamirisia, N. 2004. 'Do macroeconomic effects of capital controls vary by their type? Evidence from Malaysia', *IMF Working Paper 04/3*, International Monetary Fund, Washington DC.

Valdes-Prieto, S., and M. Soto. 1998. 'The effectiveness of capital controls: Theory and evidence from Chile', *Empirica* 25 (2): 133–64.

SELECT COUNTRY EXPERIENCES

5

SUBIR GOKARN AND BHUPAL SINGH

Costs and Benefits of Capital Account Management in India

A Practitioner's Perspective*

I. Introduction

This chapter attempts to make an assessment about the cross-border capital flows, their relative volatility / stability and implications as they have for financing the current account gap, exchange rate volatility, and domestic liquidity—essentially from the perspective of an emerging market economy (EME). As financial flows, by their very nature, are footloose, unlike the trade flows, which are bound by underlying real sector transactions, capital flows to emerging markets (both inflow and outflows) are marked by inherent volatility and risk aversion. There is no denying the fact that capital flows have played an important role in overcoming the financing constraint of the EMEs and boosted investment and growth. They have also imposed significant costs in terms of stability of the financial system

* The views expressed are authors' personal views. The paper was presented at the RBI–ADB Conference on Managing Capital Flows, 19–20 December 2012, Mumbai. Authors gratefully acknowledge the valuable comments offered by Sugata Marjit of the Centre for Studies in Social Sciences, Kolkata, on the paper as the discussant.

and spillovers to real economy. It is well recognized now that although global capital flows have a potential for improving efficiency and growth prospects, they also can trigger instability due to a variety of reasons (Reddy 2000).[1] The traditional impossible trinity (open capital account-fixed exchange rate-independent monetary policy) has now been relooked from the perspective of stability of financial markets and institutions. The EME perspective seems to be guided by this basic philosophy and the policy perspective seems to be motivated by managing the trinity—in essence striking a balance between these seemingly conflicting objectives. Capital flows, given their very nature, are assessed from the perspective of their role in providing short-term liquidity and market development versus the longer-term role of augmenting capital stock.

The conduct of exchange rate policy has also become increasingly complex for the EMEs, especially in the presence of increased volatility in international capital flows that has resulted from integrated global financial markets. Increased capital mobility, greater exposure to exchange rate risk, increased openness to international trade, and shift in the composition of exports from primary products towards manufactures and services are the major features witnessed in the EMEs in the past decade. Emergence of new financial institutions and products acts as a source of additional vulnerability for EMEs with weak financial infrastructure (Hoe Ee 2001).

This chapter first sets out the basic theory/principles guiding the capital controls and capital account management. Second, it also attempts to summarize the new learning for the EMEs over the period of time in dealing with volatility in capital flows. Third, as the exchange rates seem to move in lockstep with capital flows, we also try to analyse the Indian experience with the recent ebbs and surges in capital flows and movement in exchange rates. Fourth, the policy responses in dealing with capital flows are not always free of costs. In other words, as there are visible benefits to capital account management measures for the EMEs,

---

[1] Financial and banking crisis in a number of EMEs during the 1990s and 2000s, such as Mexico, the Republic of Korea, South East Asia, and Argentina, have not only forced analysts and policymakers to continuously reassess the role of capital flows in domestic economy but also brought a significant change in thinking about the conventional theoretical framework and the issues of capital flows—their macroeconomic implications and framework for managing such flows.

these also entail explicit or implicit cost or unintended consequences in terms of forming market expectations, development of market, and impact on certain categories of stakeholders. Thus, an assessment of costs and benefits of such policy responses and their evaluation on an ongoing basis becomes critical. This section makes an assessment of the administrative-, price- and market-based measures taken during the post-global financial crisis (GFC) period. Section V concludes by drawing important lessons for India and the EMEs.

II. Principles of Capital Controls

Although capital controls were dismantled in developing countries in the 1980s and the 1990s, a series of financial crises in EMEs forced many countries to resume capital controls in various forms and varying degrees. Though the debate on the effectiveness of such controls to fight the pressures on exchange rates or the financial stability is still inconclusive, a range of instruments/methods were deployed to counter/pre-empt the pressure on exchange rate and the financial markets.

(i) Administrative vs Market-based Controls

While the exchange controls are a form of limited capital controls, they are neither necessary to restrict capital movement nor are they necessarily intended to control capital account transactions. Capital controls are recognized to take the form of taxes, price, or quantity controls or outright prohibitions on international trade in assets. Thus, broad forms of capital controls are: (a) direct or administrative controls, and (b) indirect or market-based controls. Direct controls, also known as quantity controls, restrict capital transactions and associated payments and transfer of funds through outright prohibitions, explicit quantitative limits, or an approval procedure. Direct/administrative controls seek to directly affect the volume of cross-border capital transactions. These are generally associated with administrative obligation on the banking system to control flows. Quantity restrictions on capital flows may include rules mandating ceilings or requiring special authorization for new or existing borrowing from foreign residents. Administrative controls may also take the form of a government agency approving transactions for certain types of investment. Access to certain types of investment may be out rightly restricted.

Indirect or market-based controls discourage capital flows by varying the cost of capital. Such controls may again assume various forms: dual or multiple exchange rate system, explicit or implicit taxation of cross-border financial flows (for example, Tobin tax), and various price-based measures. Depending on the specific type, market-based controls may affect only the price or both the price and the volume of a given transaction. Theoretically speaking, price-/market-based measures of capital controls are recognized to be superior over the administrative/quantitative measures. However, in practice, the relative effectiveness of each of the measures may vary depending on the country-specific conditions.[2]

(ii) Controls on Inflows versus Outflows

Capital controls are imposed to limit short-term inflows in response to concerns about macroeconomic situation characterized by increasing volatility impacting monetary stability. Short-term inflows often reflected high domestic interest rate differentials in the context of pegged or heavily managed exchange rate regimes, which had often given markets a false sense of security (Ariyoshi et al. 2000). Another important reason for imposing controls is to limit sterilization and associated quasi-fiscal costs of a central bank. Persistent sterilization operations may increase interest rates, which again encourage inflows. As inflows increase, they lead to real appreciation of the domestic currency. which in turn reduces the export competitiveness and turns the balance of payments (BOP) vulnerable. Capital controls are also imposed to alter the composition of capital inflows and create a hierarchy of flows as short-term inflows are found to be more prone to crisis.

The need to limit downside pressure on currencies has also led the authorities to impose controls on capital outflows. The country

---

[2] In most countries, controls were imposed in the backdrop of amply liberalized exchange regime. It has been observed that in most cases, the instruments of controls were aimed at the activities of the nonresidents by restricting their access to domestic currency funds used to take speculative positions (Ariyoshi et al. 2000). An important focus of the controls was to delink the onshore market from its offshore counterpart with a mix of direct and price-based measures to alleviate downward pressure on the domestic currency. Secondly, the focus of the instruments of controls was to limit the nontrade-related transactions with nonresidents in both the spot and the forward/swap markets.

experiences indicate that such restrictions have mainly been applied to short-term capital transactions to counter volatile speculative flows that threatened to undermine the stability of the exchange rate and deplete foreign exchange reserves (Ariyoshi et al. 2000). These restrictions, used for short-term capital transactions, are stated to serve the authorities to 'buy time' and insulate the real economy from volatility in the international financial markets (Ariyoshi et al. 2000; Bakker 1996).

(iii) Trinity and New Learning from an Emerging Market Perspective

A corollary of the Fleming and Mundell model, which laid out the requirement of balance in the external sector of an economy for achieving equilibrium, has come to be known as the 'impossible trinity'—the idea that free capital mobility, fixed exchange rates, and independence in monetary policy cannot coexist (Mundell 1963). Sterilization in various degrees and a managed float, however, are two instruments which allow policymakers a certain degree of manoeuvrability in this respect. The third way out of the trilemma is offered by regulating the extent of capital mobility through the use of capital controls (see Figure 5.1). The debate on capital account liberalization, however, extends much beyond the impossible trinity as free capital flows have numerous direct and indirect effects not captured within any single model.

The intervention by central banks in foreign exchange markets assumes significance from the viewpoint of evolving role of capital

Containing exchange rate volatility

Monetary management— active market operations

Capital controls/capital account management

FIGURE 5.1 The Trilemma
Source: Adapted from Frankel (1999).

flows in determining exchange rate movements as against traditional factors such as trade deficits and economic growth. Second, unlike trade flows, capital flows in 'gross' terms, which affect exchange rate, can be several times higher than net flows on any day. Therefore, herding becomes unavoidable (Jalan 2003). Thus, capital movements have rendered exchange rates significantly more volatile than before (Mohan 2003).[3] Instead of the real factors underlying trade competitiveness, it is expectations and reactions to news which drive capital flows and exchange rates, often away from the fundamentals.[4] For the majority of developing countries which continue to depend on exports as key to the health of their BOP, exchange rate volatility has had significant real effects in terms of fluctuations in employment and output and the distribution of activity between tradables and nontradables. In the highly competitive trading environment, where countries seek to expand market shares aggressively by paring down margins, even a small change in exchange rates can develop into significant and persistent real effects. It needs to be mentioned that the impact of greater exchange rate volatility has been significantly different for reserve currency countries than developing countries. For the former, mature and well-developed financial markets tend to absorb the shocks/risks associated with large exchange-rate fluctuations with limited spillover to real economic activity. Thus, central bank does not have to take care of such risks through its monetary policy operations.

[3] The volatility in capital flows was again highlighted during the East Asian crisis and the recent GFC. Since the 1980s, vicissitudes of capital movements have shown up in volatility in exchange rate movements with major currencies moving far out of alignment of underlying purchasing power parities. Of late, it is capital flows that seem to move exchange rates and account for much of their volatility.

[4] Capital flows have been observed to cause overshooting of exchange rates as market participants act in concert while pricing information. In this context, it would be desirable to take note of the balance sheet approach, which identifies financial interlinkages, imbalances, vulnerabilities, and risks in the economy. It focuses on the risks created by maturity, currency, and capital structure mismatches. This framework draws attention to the vulnerabilities created by debt among residents, particularly those denominated in foreign currency, and it helps to explain how problems in one sector can spill over into other sectors eventually triggering BOP crisis.

On the other hand, for the majority of developing countries, which are labour-intensive exporters, exchange rate volatility has had significant employment, output, and distributional consequences, which can be large and persistent (Mohan 2003).

Most EMEs have smaller and localized foreign exchange markets where nominal domestic currency values are generally expected to show a depreciating trend, since relative inflation rates are generally higher than those of major industrial countries. In this situation, there is a common tendency among market participants to hold long positions in foreign currencies and to hold back sales when expectations are adverse and currencies are depreciating. Another feature, very common to the EMEs, is the tendency of importers/exporters and other end-users to look at exchange rate movements as a source of return without appropriate risk-management strategies. Short-term exchange rate movements are not aligned with the so-called fundamentals or country's capacity to meet its payments obligations, including debt service. This leads to adverse expectations, which tend to be self-fulfilling in nature, given their effect on leads and lags in payments and receipts.[5] The consequent volatility that sets in may not be in tune with the fundamentals. Given the herd behaviour of market participants, the situation can lead to further buying or hedging activity among nonbank participants. In thin and underdeveloped markets, dominated by a few leading operators, there is a natural tendency to do what everyone else is doing in the event of an adverse development rather than taking a contra position. Such situation calls for a quick policy response by the authorities.

III. Exchange Rate Volatility: Role of Capital Flows

The ebbs and surges is capital flows are reflected in the adjustment of exchange rate in India. These are mirrored in the significant two-way movements of the rupee during the last few years (Figure 5.2). The two-way movement is a clear demarcation of India's flexible exchange rate policy—without a fixed target or a pre-announced target or a band, while allowing the underlying demand and supply conditions to

---

[5] A self-sustaining triangle develops comprising the supply–demand mismatch, increased inter-bank activity led by excessive arbitrage activities, and accentuated volatility triggered by negative sentiments.

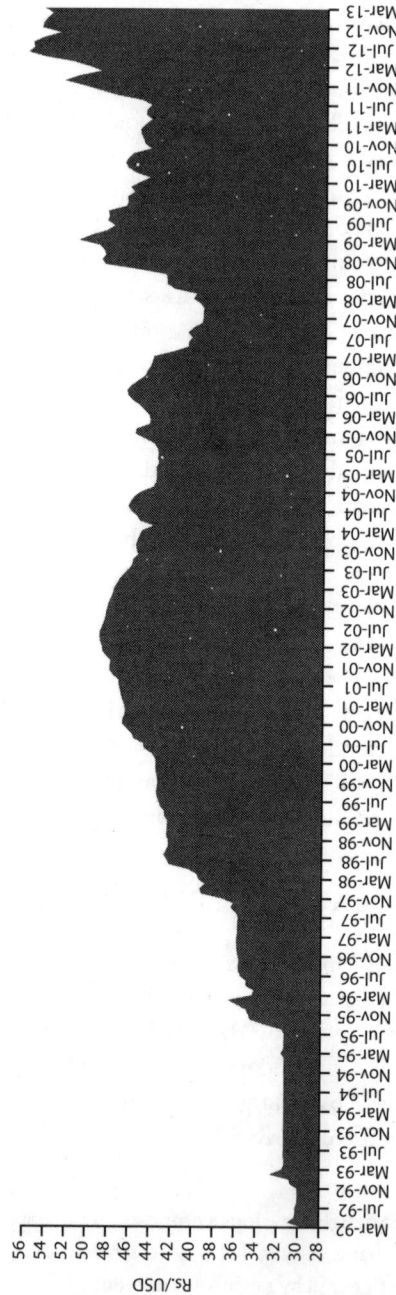

FIGURE 5.2   Two-way Movement in Rupee-Dollar Exchange Rate (Rs/USD)

Source: Database on Indian Economy, Reserve Bank of India

determine the exchange rate movements over a period in an orderly way. Subject to this predominant objective, the exchange rate policy is guided by the need to reduce excess volatility.

Looking at the episodes of exchange rate volatility in the post-2008 GFC period, particularly the volatility triggered by the US rating downgrade in August 2011, risk aversion among global investors in the wake of persistent uncertainty in the euro area led to flight of capital to safe haven assets and imparted greater volatility in exchange rates. There has been added pressure on the exchange rates of EMEs, particularly those running a current account deficit (CAD) like India (Figure 5.3). In the case of India, the recent movements in the exchange rate were significantly driven by strength of the US dollar against other major currencies, weakness of Asian currencies, and vulnerability in the domestic equity market. Some of the domestic factors that have also contributed to a sharp depreciation of the Indian rupee during recent times, inter alia, include the deterioration in the fiscal situation, slow-down in economic and industrial activity, and widening trade deficit. The global uncertainty and deleveraging process posed additional difficulties for development and trade finance. The key characteristics of the recent currency dynamics has been currency volatility with one-way bias:

1. The domestic forex market has witnessed a prolonged period of volatility characterized by one-way depreciation bias.
2. As compared with an appreciation of 1.1 per cent during 2010–11, the Indian rupee fell by more than 12 per cent during 2011–12. Between August 2011 and August 2012, the Indian rupee has depreciated by nearly 19 per cent.
3. In the period prior to August 2011, rupee was relatively stable with daily volatility of up to 5 per cent on an annualized basis. September 2011 onwards, however, the level of volatility doubled to more than 10 per cent, which moderated to a certain extent, immediately reflecting the impact of measures of December 2011.
4. A comparison across EMEs clearly reveals that the economies with CAD were characterized by higher depreciation of currencies as the risk aversion impacted significantly on their financing ability (Figure 5.3). Such economies also seem to be characterized by relatively higher currency volatility.

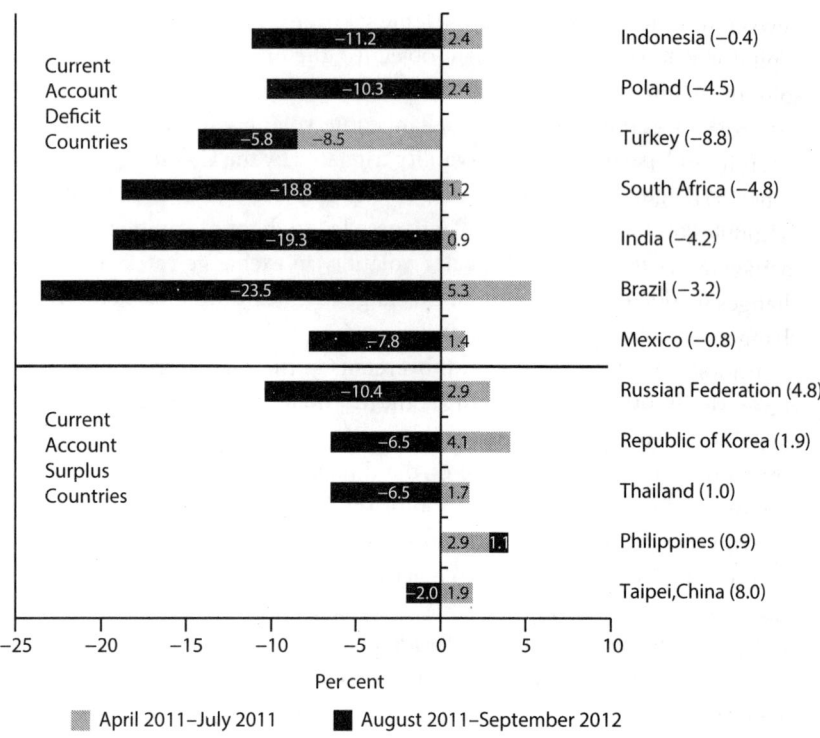

FIGURE 5.3   Major EME Currency Movements vis-à-vis US Dollar
Source: International Financial Statistics, IMF.
Note: Since Q4 of 2011 Indonesia has turned into a current account deficit country. Figures in brackets are current account balances-GDP ratios.

(i) Key Drivers of Exchange Rate Volatility

Unlike in the decades of the 1980s and the 1990s, when current account transactions dominated the foreign exchange market, sources of supply and demand have changed significantly during last few years with large transactions emanating from the capital account. The behaviour as well as the incentive structure of the participants who use the foreign exchange market for current account transactions differs significantly from those who use it for capital account transactions. Shift in these traditional determinants has also been reflected in enhanced volatility in currency markets. On many occasions, the pressure on exchange rate through increase in demand emanates from news-based expectations.[6] However, there are occasions when large capital inflows as also huge lumpiness in demand do take place, in spite of adhering to all the tools of management of capital account. The role of the Reserve Bank comes into focus during such times when it has to prevent the emergence of such destabilizing expectations. In such cases, recourse is undertaken to direct purchase and sale of foreign currencies, sterilization through open market operations, management of liquidity under liquidity adjustment facility (LAF), changes in reserve requirements, and signalling through interest rate changes.

Among the recent drivers of the volatility in the exchange rate of rupee, the global drivers could be summarized as: volatility in global capital flows to EMEs after August 2011 due to general risk aversion; euro concerns intensifying; long-term refinancing operations (LTRO), quantitative easing (QE), outright monetary transactions (OMTs), and the role of liquidity; liquidity and fundamentals in euro zone; commodity prices. The key domestic drivers of exchange rate volatility could be identified as widening CAD accompanied by a slowdown in capital flows, large fiscal deficit, growth slowdown, and uncertainties in domestic policy environment. As the global and domestic developments unfolded, there emerged clear phases of movement in nominal exchange rate as follows (see Figure 5.4).

Phase I: Post-US Downgrade—August to October 2011

After being largely range-bound, the rupee in nominal terms persistently depreciated against US dollar since August 2011. The rupee traded with a depreciating bias and depreciated by around 10 per cent against the US dollar during this period. The downgrade of US's sovereign rating by Standard & Poor from AAA to AA+ dampened investors' sentiments and led to heightened risk aversion on the part of global investors and a selloff of assets in EMEs. During the period, the rupee depreciated in tandem with other EME currencies on global concerns.

---

[6] Sometimes, such expectations are destabilizing and often give rise to self-fulfilling speculative activities. Recognizing this, increased emphasis is being laid on the management of capital account through management of foreign direct investment, portfolio investment, overseas commercial borrowings, nonresident deposits, and capital outflows.

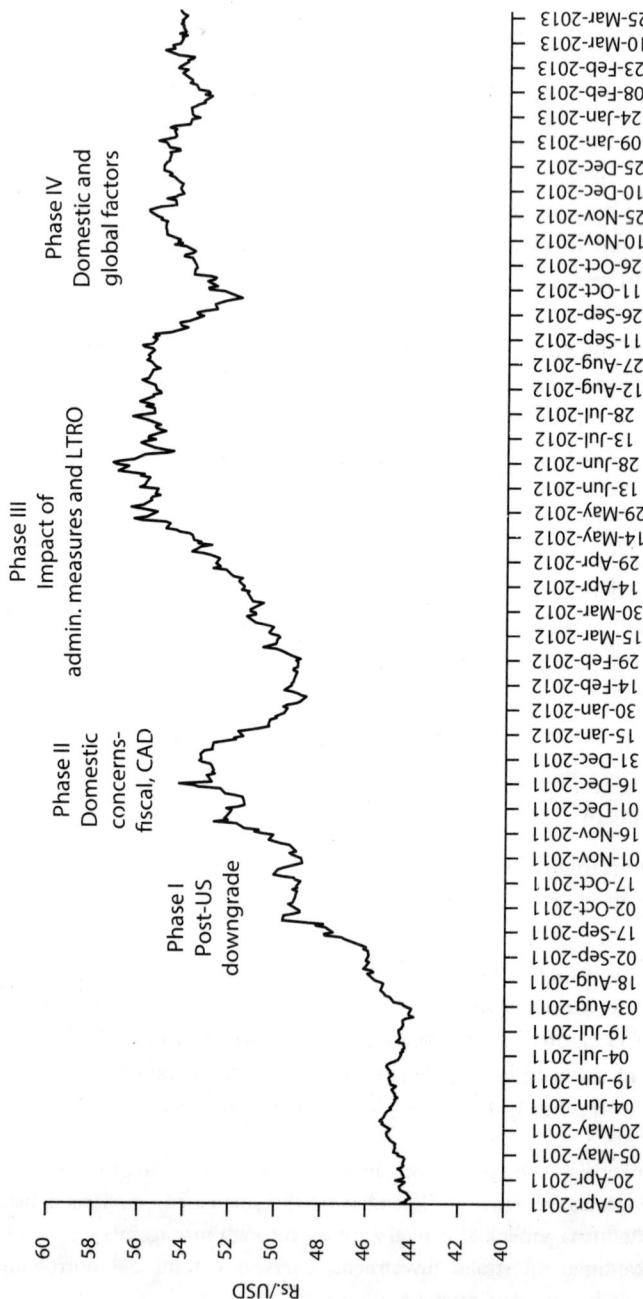

FIGURE 5.4 Nominal Exchange Rate of Indian Rupee—Recent Developments

Source: Databank on Indian Economy, Reserve Bank of India.

Phase II: Domestic Policy Concerns and LTRO— November 2011 to April 2012

The depreciating trend of the rupee continued during this period. However, unlike the previous period when the rupee along with most other EME currencies depreciated on global concerns, this period was marked by rupee decoupling from other EME currencies and depreciating sharply by around 8.2 per cent (from 49.08 to 54.3 per US dollar) on the back of domestic concerns pertaining to India's rising fiscal deficit and CAD. However, from January to February 2012, the rupee traded with an appreciating bias on the back of factors, such as (a) impact of the measures taken by the RBI in November and December 2011 to curb speculation and attract forex inflows and (b) positive global sentiment after fund infusions by the European Central Bank through the LTRO, which led to a rally in the asset-classes of emerging markets. The rupee moved in a narrow range from the last week of January 2012 till the beginning of April 2012.

Phase III: Trade Deficit, GAAR, and Greexit—April 2012 to June 2012

The emergence of the weakening of the rupee from the beginning of April 2012 can be attributed to a set of factors: (a) widening of India's trade deficit due to deceleration in exports coupled with higher imports; (b) drying up of capital flows particularly FII flows, inter alia, due to policy uncertainty on General Anti-Avoidance Rules (GAAR); and (c) sharp worsening of economic situation in the euro area with growing apprehension about the exit of Greece. In order to improve the inflows as also to reduce the volatility in the rupee, the RBI undertook additional measures in May 2012.

Phase IV: See-Saw—Domestic Policy and Re-emergence of Euro Area Concerns—after July 2012

The rupee appreciated by 5.2 per cent in the month of September 2012 alone, driven by both global developments and reform measures announced by the government that led to improved investor sentiment. RBI also undertook additional policy measures in September 2012 to facilitate capital inflows. These include enhancing the maximum permissible external commercial borrowings (ECBs) for repayment of rupee loans and fresh rupee capital expenditure, permitting infrastructure companies to avail of trade credit up to a maximum period of five years for import of capital goods, and rationalizing overseas direct investment by Indian entities in respect of annual performance returns. However, since the second week of October 2012, the rupee weakened due to demand for dollar by oil importing companies, re-emergence of the euro area concerns, and apprehensions about the implementation of domestic policy announcements.

(ii) Real Exchange Rate Dynamics

Although nominal exchange rates are often the focus of market analysts, it is equally important to gauge the real exchange rate which is considered an important measure of the external competitiveness of an economy.[7] The relative prices, reflecting the relative cost of production of domestic goods vis-à-vis foreign goods is the key determinant of real exchange rate. It is evident from Figure 5.5 that there seemed to be considerable competitive advantage for India during the 1990s in relation to the rest of the world as the inflation differentials remained largely negative. This seems to have contributed to the sharp depreciation of real exchange rate in the 1990s and improved trade competitiveness (Figure 5.6). There seems to be some loss of competitiveness during the 1990s as the inflation rate in India remained higher than the global inflation rate; although there has been moderation in domestic inflation rate, the global inflation rate has moderated at a significantly faster pace.

It is now generally acknowledged that trade and capital flows influence the exchange rate. A surge in capital flow leads to an increase in consumption demand for both traded and nontraded goods. In case

---

[7] From the viewpoint of external competitiveness, variables such as remuneration of factors of production, exchange rate, productivity—through the use of better technical skills and human resource development, as also economies of scale have a large influence on the extent of competitiveness. Institutional and policy mechanisms that impart flexibility to the economy in shifting the resources to their most productive uses also play a pivotal role in enhancing the competitiveness.

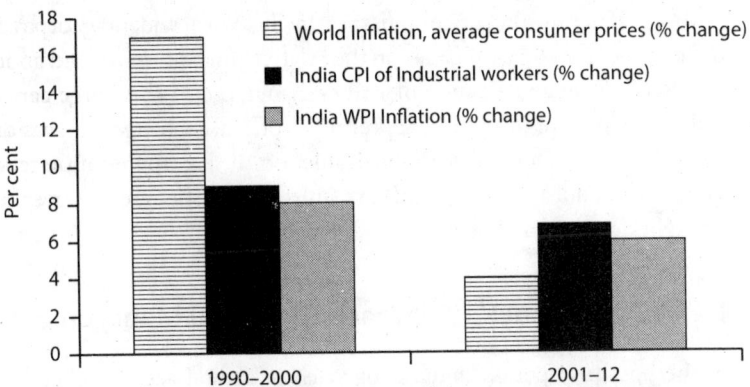

FIGURE 5.5 Inflation Differential between India (WPI) and World (CPI)
Source: Computation based on the data from Database on Indian Economy,
Reserve Bank of India and International Financial Statistics, IMF.

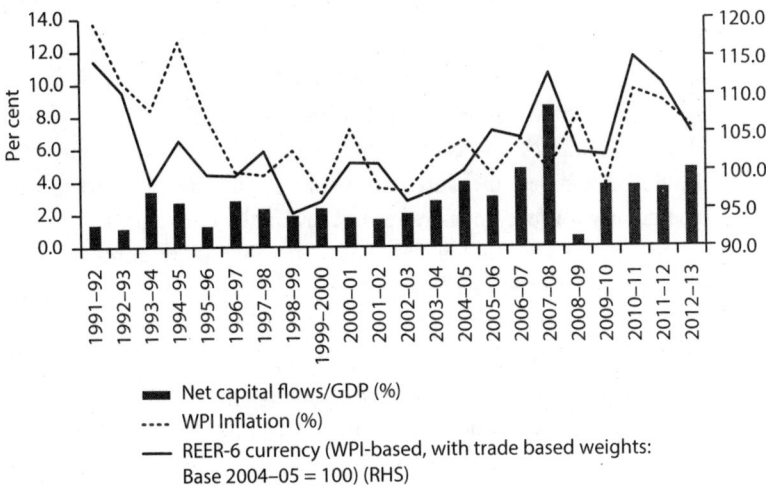

FIGURE 5.6 Role of Inflation and Capital Flows in Driving Real Exchange Rate
Source: Reserve Bank of India.

of nontraded goods, excess demand generated by capital flows is not
proportionately matched by a rise in supply and hence, results in a rise
in the price of nontraded goods to reach to equilibrium. On the other
hand, elevated demand for traded goods is met with imported goods

without affecting the price and thereby leads to widening of trade deficit. Accordingly, an increase in the relative price of nontraded goods would entail an appreciation of real exchange rate. When large capital inflows themselves lead to an appreciation of real exchange rate, it leads to the so-called Dutch disease phenomenon. If real appreciation takes place, it could lead to larger inflows unless domestic interest rates are brought down commensurately.

IV. A Practitioner's Approach to Capital Management

In the post-1991 period, India's approach to capital account liberalization has been to facilitate both inward and outward capital flows in a cautious manner. The policy approach in India to the issue of capital flows has evolved from the broader objective of maintaining financial and macroeconomic stability. The salient elements of this framework have been:

1. An explicitly stated active capital account management framework, based on the policy stance of encouraging nondebt creating and long-term capital inflows and discouraging debt flows
2. Having the policy space to use multiple instruments—quantitative limits, price-based measures, as well as administrative measures, particularly for foreign currency borrowing by corporates
3. Avoiding excessive foreign currency borrowings by domestic entities, particularly the sovereign
4. Prudential regulations to prevent excessive dollarization of balance sheets of financial sector intermediaries, particularly banks
5. Cautious approach to liability dollarization by domestic entities
6. Significant liberalization of permissible avenues for outward investments for domestic entities

Thus, while till the 1980s capital inflows were barely adequate to finance the CAD, a paradigm shift occurred in the 1990s with the capital flows far exceeding the CAD, turning the BOP into capital surplus from a prolonged phase of capital scarcity (Figure 5.7). The net capital flows as a ratio to GDP rose to 3.7 per cent of GDP during the 2000s from 2.2 per cent in the 1990s and 1.2 per cent during the period 1950–80. This voluminous increase was a reflection of a shift from the controlled capital account to a progressively liberalized regime.

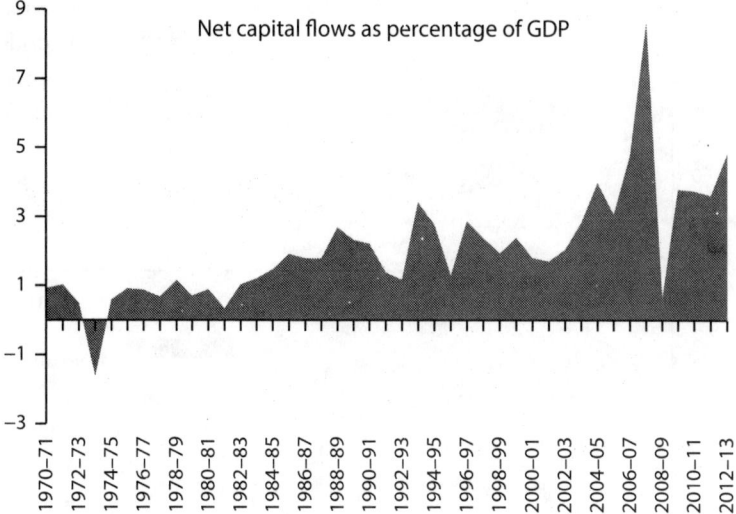

FIGURE 5.7   Net Capital Flows to India
Source: *Handbook of Statistics on Indian Economy*, Reserve Bank of India.

The capital account was also characterized by significant compositional shifts from debt and external aid to the nondebt foreign investment inflows (Figure 5.8). Over the years, the decline in debt flows reflected the policy-induced changes in the composition of the capital account in favour of nondebt flows. Both Foreign Direct Investment (FDI) and portfolio equity flows have also surpassed the debt flows, reflecting the long-term growth, stability, and the lower risk perception of the economy.

The anatomy of instruments of controls reveals that controls on capital inflows are both quantity and price based, taking into consideration the hierarchy of capital flows. As against this, the controls on outflows have been mainly quantity based (Table 5.1). The controls have been broadly successful in achieving desirable objectives.

The adequacy of capital controls cannot be generalized. The effectiveness of capital controls are time and situation specific. The design of capital controls seems to be motivated by the inherent volatility in capital flows, giving rise to the so-called hierarchy in capital flows as evidenced in the Indian context (Table 5.2). Capital inflows can reverse quickly, leaving the country exposed to a liquidity crisis. In this context,

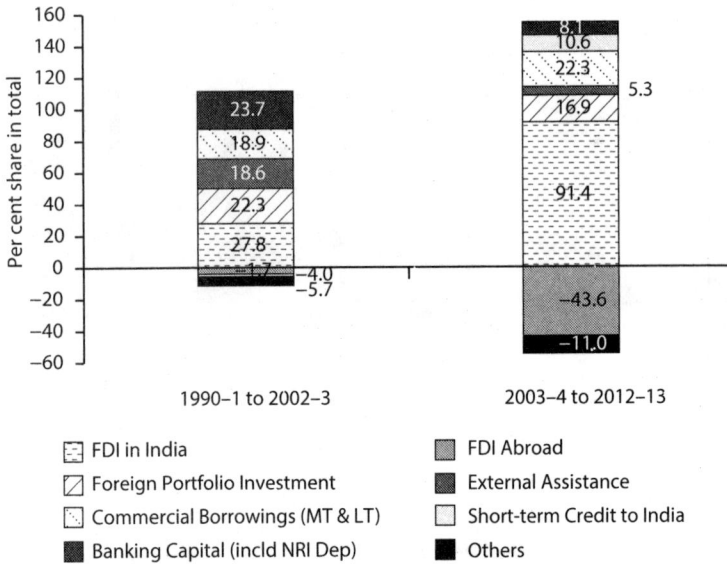

FIGURE 5.8 Shifts in the Composition of Capital Flows to India
Source: Handbook of Statistics on Indian Economy, Reserve Bank of India.

the distinction between push and pull factors becomes important.[8] According to Calvo et al. (1993), low US interest rates—hence, push factors—were dominant in explaining capital flows to Latin America in the early 1990s. Similarly, in the most recent episode of capital flows to the EMEs since early 2000, push factors appear to be playing a key role.[9]

To conclude, the instruments of capital controls and their application to control inflows and outflows in select EMEs provide some conjectures for policy purposes. These are summarized in the following points.

---

[8] While 'push' factors attribute capital flows to conditions in creditor countries, the 'pull' factors refer to conditions in debtor (recipient) countries. The former help explain the timing and magnitude of capital inflows and the latter explain the geographic distribution of capital inflows.

[9] According to estimates by Ferruci et al. (2004), almost two-thirds of the compression in bond spreads between October 2002 and early 2004 can be attributed to push factors alone—in particular, the fall in the US short-term interest rates since 2001. This implies a need for caution by EMEs in borrowing too heavily during times of benign external financing environment, as a reversal in credit conditions is more often than not beyond the control of the borrower.

TABLE 5.1   Types of Capital Controls on Inflows and Outflows in India

Items	Administrative/ Quantity based	Price/Market based
FDI, in India	Sectoral caps and a negative list of the sectors of strategic national importance where FDI is not permitted.	
Indian Overseas Investment	400 per cent of net worth of the company	
Portfolio Investment in India—Equity	Sectoral caps, FII holdings ceiling at 24 per cent of the paid-up capital	It can be raised up to the sectoral cap set for FDI provided it is passed in the AGM and approved by Board of Directors.
ADRs/GDRs	Fall under overall FDI sectoral caps	Automatic route, subject to specified guidelines and reporting requirements
Portfolio Investment in India—Debt	Quantitative Limits, corporate debt—$51 billion and government securities— $30 billion.	
External Commercial Borrowings/ FCCBs Short-term trade credit to India	End-use based and borrower category-specific restrictions	Indicative ceiling on overall annual borrowing. Ceiling on interest rate linked to LIBOR Ceiling on interest rate linked to LIBOR
Overseas Borrowings by Banks	Linked to Tier-I capital of banks (100%)	
NRI Deposits		Interest rates on Rupee-denominated deposits should be at par with the interest on domestic deposits of comparable maturities. Interest rate ceiling on foreign currency deposits linked to LIBOR

Source: Reserve Bank of India.

TABLE 5.2 Volatility of Private Capital Flows to India (Coefficient of Variation—2000: Q2 to 2012: Q3)

Components	CV (Percentage)
FDI in India	80.3
Portfolio Investment in India (FIIs)	257.3
Commercial Borrowings to India	152.4
Short-term Credit to India	152.8
Nonresident Deposits of Commercial Banks	129.5
Overall Capital Account	90.1

Source: Authors' calculation.

1. While the controls on capital inflows seem to have proved somewhat effective in containing exchange market pressures, the experiments with controls on outflows by the EMEs, particularly in crisis situations, did not help in alleviating the exchange market pressures.

2. While the controls on inflows provided a mix of both administrative and price-based instruments, the instruments of control on outflows were dominated by severe direct/administrative measures as the latter were mostly associated with crisis situations.

3. In case of pressures arising out of capital outflows, the controls in the form of numerous restrictions on the banks for external transactions were not fully effective as they were circumvented in many instances.

4. Moreover, various instruments of controls provided only the temporary relief or contained the initial pressures on forex markets in the presence of internal or external imbalances (that is, high fiscal deficit, weaknesses in the financial sector, high CAD).[10]

5. Offshore markets in the domestic currency (for example, NDF markets) proved to be an import source of speculation and in some instances control measures could not succeed.

6. In case of crises-hit countries, the instruments deployed to control outflows were ultimately replaced by the abandonment of exchange rate band/peg in favour of float.

[10] Pressure of current account due to excessive expenditure and natural depreciation of currency induced by high inflation, which gets delayed through favourable flows, can accentuate the depreciation problem when flows dry out. Sharp movements are consequence of deferred adjustments.

7. While controls to limit short-term inflows could be helpful in specific circumstances, controls entailed longer term costs. However, temporary uses of controls are more effective and can even improve the financial environment.

8. Controls during crisis are not very effective and can divert the attention of the government from their prime aim in strengthening the financial and macroeconomic environment.

(i) Understanding the Market Behaviour

The policy responses of the central bank to volatile exchange rates and capital flows are designed to contain herd behaviour in the market, anchor expectations, and rein in self-fulfilling expectations that may cause market distortions. The commercial banks, as major players in the domestic foreign exchange market in India, are expected to show caution while offering foreign exchange derivative products to corporates, as the latter enter into such transactions without much understanding of the downside implications. If the market moves adversely, it can result in enormous problems not only for the banks but also for corporates. Therefore, the RBI has been emphasizing that banks should insist on board-approved policy covering unhedged foreign exchange exposure of all the clients including SMEs, while extending fund and nonfund based credit facilities to corporates, rigorously evaluate the risks arising out of unhedged foreign currency exposures of the corporates and price them in the credit risk premium.[11]

On occasions, the flexibility provided to corporates in terms of cancellation and rebooking forward contracts and booking of forward contracts under past performance route, were being utilized for speculative purposes. It has been observed that sometimes corporates have used derivatives for generation of profit from noncore activities instead of using them for risk mitigation, thereby accentuating market instability. Such speculative forces were proving to be self-reinforcing and resulting in a situation where exporters kept on deferring their receipts and importers rushed in to buy forwards, thus aggravating the problems of leads and lags exerting further pressure on rupee. This is

---

[11] There still does not seem to be clear evidence whether lack of hedging is due to the unavailability of instruments or other factors.

typical behaviour on part of the exporters and importers, which comes into play during the spells of sharp move in the rupee, particularly during the depreciation phase. Further, there is a tendency of some corporates to leave their foreign exchange exposure unhedged to benefit from the movement of currency in their favour and also save the hedging cost. From the viewpoint of minimizing risks and maintaining overall stability, it needs to be emphasized that corporates should be focusing more on their core businesses to generate returns rather than looking to generate alpha from diversifying into trading in foreign exchange markets.

(ii) A Cost–Benefit Analysis

The literature on cross border capital flows reveals that rapid increase in the mobility of capital flows has been associated with various benefits and costs. Literature broadly focuses on two major implications of volatile capital flows, that is, macroeconomic stability and financial stability. Short-term volatile capital flows have a significant influence on the asset prices, exchange rate, and the interest rate arithmetic of the financial markets and monetary conditions, consumption, investment, trade, and thus, the aggregate demand, rendering some of the earlier anchors of the monetary policy formulation perhaps obsolete. The aggregate demand in turn affects output and prices, the two most important policy objectives for most policy authorities.

The GFC of 2008 led to sudden stop of capital inflows to most EMEs, exerting severe financing problems for the international trade and causing wide swings in exchange rates. The post GFC period has once again exhibited surges and ebbs of capital flows—with relatively short-lived alternating phases of inflows and outflows. The responses have been guided by the country-specific situations from explicit administrative controls to Tobin-type taxes to varied intervention strategies in foreign exchange markets. However, the rate of success of such policy responses varied and was largely conditioned by the overall global risk aversion and domestic macroeconomic conditions. The key principles driving the policy response can be classified as follows.

First, the choice between rate targeting and volatility management is generally motivated by the following underlying factors: prevailing policy position, intensity and persistence of pressures, and lessons from other country experiences. Second, managing volatility takes into account the following: intervention, expanding inflow channels, administrative actions, and balance between short-term compulsions and long-term risks.

(iii) Policy Responses and Outcomes

In India, the prudent policy responses to volatility in capital flows and exchange rate volatility can be broadly classified into three categories: administrative measures, market-based measures, and direct intervention in exchange markets.

A. *Administrative Measures*

1. WITHDRAWAL OF THE FACILITY OF CANCELLATION AND REBOOKING OF CONTRACTS AVAILABLE UNDER CONTRACTED EXPOSURES
The turnover of transactions increased during volatile periods and most of the increase was on account of corporates undertaking a hedge and reversing the same intra-day.[12] A position undertaken to take advantage of the one way movement intensifies the move adding to the demand/supply pressures in the market. While the move reflects the hedging intention of the corporate, it may not be conducive for the market volatility if the same is undertaken to speculate on the market movements. The action led to reduced liquidity in the forex markets and took away certain leeway provided in managing the forex risk by corporates. In order to provide a small flexibility to exporters and bring in an extra bit of liquidity in to the markets, exporters were allowed to cancel and rebook 25 per cent of the total contracts booked for hedging their export exposure.

2. REDUCTION IN THE LIMIT AVAILABLE TO IMPORTERS UNDER THE PROBABLE EXPOSURES (PAST PERFORMANCE FACILITY)
It is well known that given the historical performance of the rupee, Indian importers generally stay unhedged (corporate generally hedge

---

[12] While undertaking a hedge in a volatile market stands to reason, reversing it on the same day does not in any way reflect the medium to long term view of the corporate.

around 40 per cent of their ECBs loans) or have a very small hedge ratio. Even corporates who have both import and export exposures prefer to have their import exposures unhedged while almost fully utilizing their export exposures. The same approach is followed in case of probable exposures also. In the current depreciating trend of rupee, these excess unutilized limits were a cause of concern when used for speculation. Hence, the limits for importers were reduced to 25 per cent.

3. PAST PERFORMANCE FACILITY MADE AVAILABLE TO EXPORTERS AND IMPORTERS ONLY ON DELIVERY BASIS

The past performance facility was made available to corporates in addition to the facility based on actual exposures so as to allow them to plan ahead for managing their foreign currency exposures. Both facilities together amounted to almost double the exposures of the corporates and without any delivery mandate on either could be/were used for speculative purpose. Hence, to avoid speculation in past performance facility, where the contracts are booked without any current exposure, the facility was made available on delivery basis.

4. NET OVERNIGHT OPEN POSITION LIMIT

Net Overnight Open Position Limit (NOOPL) of banks was reduced for positions involving rupee as one of the currencies. Later, positions undertaken in the currency futures/options segment in the exchanges, open positions of the overseas branches of Indian banks, and net option positions of banks were excluded from the above limit.

5. INTRA-DAY LIMIT OF BANKS

Intra-day limit of banks, for positions involving rupee as one of the currencies, was fixed by RBI linking the amount to their NOOPL. Later, the limit was fixed at five times their NOOPL, for positions involving rupee as one of the currencies.

6. POSITIONS UNDERTAKEN IN THE CURRENCY FUTURES/OPTIONS SEGMENT IN THE EXCHANGES

While presence of an underlying exposure is an essential requirement in the OTC segment, no such requirement is in place for the exchange-traded derivatives segment. On account of having a subset of participants, common to both the markets, the volatility of one market gets imposed on the other. To deal with this, even if partially, position limits of banks were revised on exposures to exchange traded products and positions undertaken in the currency futures/options segment in the exchanges so as to reduce the arbitrage between the two markets.

Apart from the above administrative measures, some quantitative measures were also undertaken to minimize volatility.

1. Policy relating to FII investment in government securities and long-term infrastructure bonds was revised on 30 November 2011 and 25 June 2012, respectively, and the nonresident investor base was broadened.
2. Qualified Foreign Investors (QFIs), that is, nonresident investors other than SEBI, registered FIIs and foreign venture capital investors (FVCIs) were allowed to invest in equity shares of Indian companies and Indian corporate debt securities.
3. Revision in guidelines related to EEFC accounts to enhance short term foreign exchange inflows. However, keeping in view the operational convenience, the erstwhile stipulation of allowing credit of 100 per cent foreign exchange earnings to the EEFC account was restored on 31 July 2012, subject to conversion of monthly foreign exchange accruals to rupees within the next month.

B. Market-based Measures

The market-based measures undertaken to minimize volatility included (a) deregulation of interest rate ceiling on the NRE deposits and NRO accounts, (b) upward revision of the interest rate ceilings on FCNR (B) deposits, and (c) upward revision of the all-in-cost ceiling for ECBs and making it compulsory to bring back immediately the ECBs proceeds meant for rupee expenditure. In the wake of recent phases of volatility witnessed in the rupee's exchange rate, the hedging issue has also come to the forefront from the accounting perspective, which needs further discussion and examination, in order to understand the economic reasons for corporates not willing to adopt hedging as part of their risk-management strategy.

C. Intervention Strategy

The policy approach has been that the exchange rate of the Indian rupee should be market-determined and the Reserve Bank should be intervening only to manage excessive volatility for ensuring orderly conditions without targeting any particular level or band for the Indian rupee (Figure 5.9). While the policy does not target any particular level of exchange rate, the Reserve Bank is well aware that any sharp movement of a unidirectional nature (in the current scenario, the bias is of depreciation) has a tendency to fuel further expectations of depreciation. Therefore, the intervention policy not only aims at quelling the excessive volatility, but also attempts to moderate speculative expectations of one-way downward movement of Indian rupee. Like any other asset price, the exchange rate is shaped to a large extent by the expectations component apart from the normal forces of actual demand and supply. The choice of market segment for intervention can vary from spot to outright forward depending on the prevailing market conditions.

Whether the Reserve Bank intervenes in the spot or in the outright forward market, the impact on the inter-bank spot rates is the almost the same and it gets reflected immediately.[13] Since the spot market is the most liquid segment, any large-scale operations may not always be possible through outright forward route. Therefore, the strategy has an appropriate mix of spot as well as forward interventions. Another issue which comes up for discussion is whether the intervention strategy will remain the same when central bank is buying dollars or selling dollars. The strategy depends on a host of factors, including the prevailing rupee liquidity conditions. This brings us to the issue of adequacy of reserves which has emerged as an important parameter in gauging a country's ability to absorb external shocks.

There are both long-term and short-term issues in relation to the central bank's role in external management. Should the exchange rate be a policy instrument for long-term growth? Are the choices and trade-offs different between large and small economies? These are important questions in the current global debate. Particularly, the EMEs are worried that volatile capital flows—alternate surges and

---

[13] At the same time, having a choice of operating in either spot or forward depending on the prevailing market conditions gives greater manoeuvrability in intervention operations.

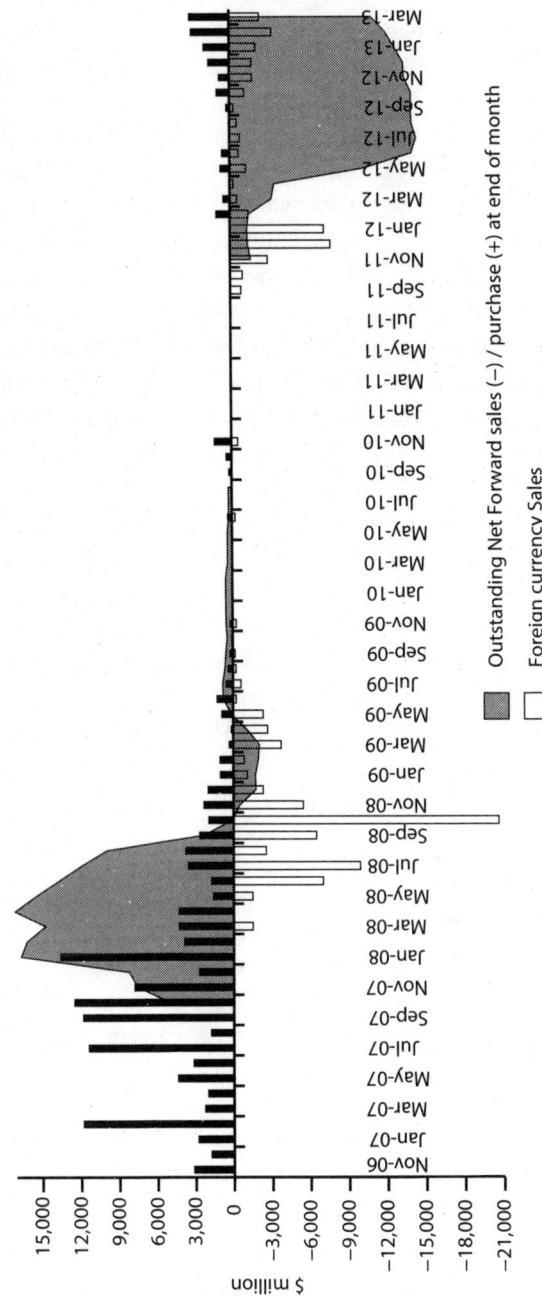

FIGURE 5.9   Market Interventions of the Reserve Bank of India

Source: Database on Indian Economy, Reserve Bank of India.

ebbs—would destabilize their domestic economies through exchange rate appreciation/sharp depreciation. What should central banks be doing to deal with this situation? While the justification for capital controls is subject to several conditions, clearly, many countries that do not meet all those conditions would be equally tempted to use controls as a way of protecting themselves against the threats to stability from volatile capital flows and exchange rates and domestic liquidity conditions. Is this an argument for capital controls? One may agree with this to a limited extent, reflecting the conditions during the crisis and how different groups of countries have emerged from it. However, the specific conditions, both domestic and global, that would determine the desirability of capital controls for specific countries need to be thought through (Gokarn 2010). Intervention to manage the exchange rate is another way in which a central bank may contribute to external stability. From a short-term perspective, the decision to intervene in order to avoid destabilizing both exporting and import-competing domestic producers needs to be viewed in the overall context of domestic conditions. Shirakawa (2010) argues that in a situation in which policy rates are already at the zero boundary, exchange rate appreciation, which helps dampen inflationary pressures, would allow the low interest rate scenario to persist, thereby raising the risks of an asset price bubble. The Reserve Bank's policy on exchange rates has been articulated as broadly noninterventionist, except when confronted with excessively volatile, lumpy, or disruptive flows. This is an approach consistent with the notions of 'flexibility' or 'constrained discretion' used in the context of boundary conditions for traditional approaches to monetary policy. Essentially, these are conditions that would presumably trigger some deviation from normal policy if abnormal circumstances were to arise. What would constitute abnormal conditions, of course, cannot be explicitly indicated but will presumably be defined by specific circumstances in which actions are taken. From the standpoint of financial stability, shocks to domestic asset prices led by uneven capital flows become a concern for central banks. Such pressures on asset prices can cause capital losses for entities which have large exposure to such assets and can be a source of instability. These adverse spillovers of volatile capital flows are minimized through prudential sectoral exposure limits on banks' lending, risk weights and provisioning norms.

V. Conclusion

Some key lessons from the experience with alternating phases of ebbs and surges in capital flows in the post-GFC period suggest: (a) global factors, particularly those which add to uncertainties, tend to aggravate currency volatility, (b) the drivers of currency volatility become more dominant if CAD is high, (c) addressing domestic drivers of currency dynamics holds key to stabilization, (d) direct measures are most effective when fundamental factors are dealt with, and (e) concerted domestic policy action can help offset global pressures.

The important message that comes out of the analysis of various episodes of volatility and the policy response is that flexibility and pragmatism are needed in exchange rate policy in developing countries, rather than adherence to strict theoretical rules. In the face of large capital flows, considerations of maintaining a competitive exchange rate, on the one hand, and controlling inflation, on the other, create conflicting objectives for a central bank. In such situations, central banks need to take a very cautious path while handling large capital inflows. The promptness of the central bank could be judged by effectiveness with which it resolves such conflicting policy objectives without any loss of inflows while keeping inflation within manageable limits. India's exchange rate policy with focus on managing volatility with no fixed rate target while allowing the underlying demand and supply conditions to determine the exchange rate movements over a period in an orderly way has stood the test of time.

With specific externalities associated with cross-border flows of foreign saving, welfare considerations require that policy measures should be used to counter these externalities, which are essentially differences between social and private marginal costs. The approach to capital flows thus involves a judgment as to how important externalities are and what combinations of policies to use to minimize their impact and consequently has to be country and case specific. Hence, it is important that policymakers have the flexibility and discretion to adopt policies that they consider appropriate to mitigate risks through macroeconomic, prudential, and capital account management policies. As regards multilateral strategies to managing capital flows, it is, thus, difficult to follow an approach that seeks to establish, standardize, prioritize, or restrict the range of policy responses of the member countries that are facing large surges in volatile capital inflows. The objective of public policy in managing capital flows should be to close this gap by ensuring that the true costs of these negative externalities are transferred to the agent(s) imposing these costs and are not borne by the country/society at large. To the extent that lumpy and volatile flows are a spillover from policy choices of advanced economies, managing capital flows should not be treated as an exclusive problem of EMEs. How this burden is to be shared raises both intellectual and practical challenges.

The ongoing debate on the desirability and merits of capital controls will become more constructive if the distinction between strategic and tactical controls is recognized. Countries must first decide their pecking order of capital flows and what they will do to enforce it. For any country, this will emerge from a combination of factors related to external vulnerability and tolerance for risk. Research clearly has a role in distinguishing between superior and inferior options for strategic controls, depending on country characteristics and objectives. Tactical controls, on the other hand, are essentially emergency responses to intense pressure and will largely depend on the country circumstances—what the pressures are, what instruments are immediately available, and which of them is likely to have the quickest impact. India's approach to hierarchy (pecking order) in capital flows suggests that policy has been successful in reinforcing stability objectives—reflected in significantly lower volatility of long-term capital flows.

VI. Epilogue: Exchange Rate Management in India, May–October 2013

After several months of relative stability, May 2013 saw the beginning of a period of high turbulence for the rupee. The proximate cause of this was the announcement by the US Federal Reserve Board Chairman that the institution was now thinking of rolling back on its third asset purchase programme (QE3). However, this 'shock' came at a time when the economy's vulnerability had increased quite significantly. The main manifestation of this was the widening of the CAD, which, for the full fiscal year 2012–13, recorded 4.7 per cent of GDP. The previous year saw it touching 4.2 per cent; these were the first occasions ever in which the gap exceeded 3 per cent, a threshold that was generally considered by policymakers to be 'safe', in the sense that it could be relatively easily financed by capital inflows in a wide range of global financial conditions.

As described earlier in this chapter, the rupee had been through two relatively turbulent periods in 2011 and 2012, during which a combination of policy responses had been used. Intervention in the form of selling dollars from the foreign exchange reserves had been combined with two other categories of measures. One, the upper limits on foreign investment into rupee-denominated debt, both government and corporate, were successively increased. Two, several administrative measures, which essentially limited the flexibility of market participants, including banks, to take undue advantage of the currency movements, were imposed. The first, though clearly involving higher external vulnerability, was consistent with the broader objective of capital account management of gradually reducing restrictions on debt inflows. The second set of measures were seen as deviation from the path of capital account liberalization, but were recognized as necessary in the short term to contain a potential runaway spiral in the exchange rate, which would be extremely destabilizing for the economy.

Both episodes ended when global financial conditions changed, as a result of central bank actions in the advanced economies. This time, however, the precipitating factor was itself a central bank action, so the nature of the shock was intrinsically different. Given the likelihood of persistent pressure on the currency, particularly in the face of the very large CAD, the policy response was also quite different from the two earlier episodes.

Figure 5.10 depicts the movement of the rupee-dollar exchange rate during the period 1 May–31 October, to provide a backdrop to the discussion of policy responses. As indicated, the rupee depreciated steadily from early May, with the movement accelerating in mid-July and the pressure becoming particularly intense during August. There was some recovery towards the end of August, with relative stability being achieved towards the middle of September, after which there was a period of relative calm. Over the period displayed, the rupee depreciated by 14.3 per cent. However, the lowest point during the period was reached on 28 August, when the rupee was 27.2 per cent below its value on 2 May.

In the initial phase of this period, the main policy response was in the form of intervention. However, as the trend continued and no obvious

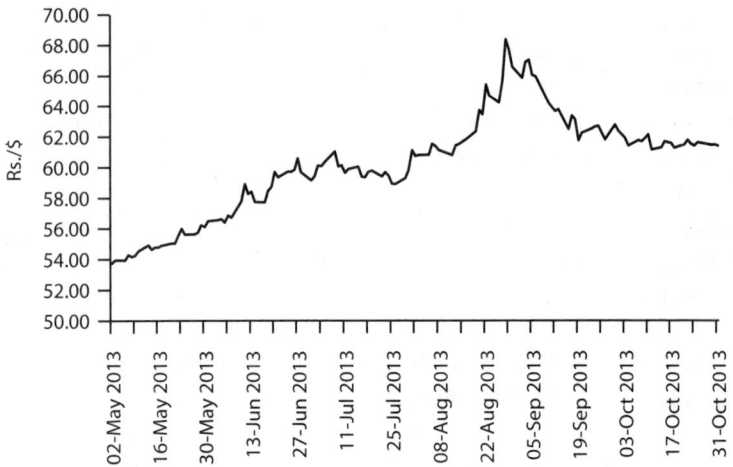

FIGURE **5.10**   The Rupee-Dollar Exchange Rate Movement, May–October 2013
Source: Database of Indian Economy, Reserve Bank of India.

reversal was in sight, in mid-July, the nature of the response changed significantly. Monetary policy instruments were used to deal with exchange rate movements. This was done by sharply raising the upper bound of the policy rate corridor. The Marginal Standing Facility (MSF) rate, which was what banks paid to access liquidity when all other channels were unavailable, was increased by 200 basis points. In addition, banks were now required to maintain their cash reserve as a proportion of their liabilities on a daily basis, as opposed to on a fortnightly basis in normal circumstances. Both these combined to put an enormous squeeze on market liquidity, as a consequence of which the yield curve moved sharply upwards. Following these measures, limits were imposed on individual banks' access to the repo window, which further reduced the amount of liquidity in the system; banks with a larger capacity to borrow and on-lend were now discouraged from exploiting this arbitrage.

The impact of these measures on market interest rates clearly marked it out as a monetary action. In effect, the focus of monetary policy shifted from managing the growth-inflation trade off to resisting rupee depreciation. It must be pointed out, however, that given the heightened inflationary pressures that rupee depreciation would inevitably exert, these measures were entirely consistent with inflation management, both in terms of their potential impact on the exchange rate itself and through a more conventional monetary policy channel.

The main rationale of these measures, which were positioned by the policy authorities as being temporary in duration, was that speculative activity was significantly reinforcing the downward pressure on the rupee. Tightening domestic liquidity was a way to restrict speculative trading, simply by making it more expensive to borrow in rupees in order to take dollar positions. The measures were not projected as monetary tightening, even though the impacts were exactly the same.

As it happened, the rupee movement did not appreciably change in the wake of these measures. In August, the next set of capital account measures were announced. The annual allowance for individuals and companies to remit money out of the country for asset acquisition purposes were brought down sharply. It is debatable whether these were binding in any case and, consequently, whether the actions would have had any material impact on actual outflows. But the market seems to have had perceived it as willingness of authorities to deviate from broad thrust towards increasing rupee convertibility. While this may have had some positive impact in terms of indicating the government's resolve, it might have raised concerns among investors and thus reinforced pressures on the currency.

One important measure was to incentivize banks to mobilize deposits in their foreign branches and subsidiaries by offering them a discounted swap facility for the dollars raised. In effect, they could reduce their costs of rupee funds by bringing in more dollars. This appeared to have worked well, even though it raised the level of dollar liabilities, with implications for long-term vulnerability.

One external factor that exerted enormous pressure during the second half of August was the developments on the Syrian front. The prospect of armed intervention in Syria caused crude oil prices to spike for a few days, besides impacting global capital flows adversely. This is when the rupee reached its trough. As those risks abated, the process of recovery began. When the US Federal Reserve announced that it was postponing the taper indefinitely, global markets almost instantaneously returned to normal and, since then, the rupee has seen relative stability. Even the tensions surrounding the budget reconciliation and the raising of the debt ceiling in the US did not cause much instability.

It is difficult to separate out the impact of various policy measures, external developments, either positive or negative, and other factors on the dynamics of the rupee during this short, but extremely turbulent period. But, some tentative inferences can be attempted. One, higher vulnerability in the form of a widening CAD clearly magnifies the impact of any external shock on the exchange rate. This indicates the need for a structural response to the deficit, in order to contain currency risks. Two, there are risks in taking actions that are perceived to be ineffective, which have to be weighed against not taking any action at all; the former course commits the authorities to an escalating series of actions, which may exacerbate the overall macroeconomic impact. Three, if the shock is global, the resolution also needs to have a global element; it is difficult for individual countries to fully deal with such shocks entirely by themselves.

At the time of writing, many of the liquidity tightening measures taken during this period had been reversed and the monetary policy process was on its way to returning to its conventional position. However, the capital control measures had not been done away with.

References

Ariyoshi, A., K.F. Habermeier, B. Laurens, I. Ötker, K.J.I. Canales, and A. Kirilenko. 2000. 'Capital controls: Country experiences with their use and liberalization', *IMF Occasional Paper 190*.

Bakker, Age F.P. 1996. *The Liberalization of Capital Movements in Europe*. Kluwer Academic Publishers.

Calvo, G.A., and F.S. Mishkin. 2003. 'Mirage of exchange rate regimes for emerging market countries', *Journal of Economic Perspectives* 17(4): 99–108.

Calvo, G.A., L. Leiderman, and C. Reinhart. 1993. 'Capital inflows and real exchange rate appreciation in Latin America: The role of external factors', IMF Staff Papers 40: 108–51.

De Gregorio, J., S. Edwards, and R. Valdés. 2000. 'Controls on capital inflows: Do they work?' *Journal of Development Economics* 63(1): 59–83.

Edison, H., and C. Reinhart. 2001. 'Stopping hot money', *Journal of Development Economics* 66(2): 533–53.

Edwards, S. 1999. 'How effective are capital controls?' *Journal of Economic Perspectives* 13(4): 65–84.

Frankel, J. 1999. 'No single currency regime is right for all countries', Essays in International Finance No. 215, August, Princeton University, New Jersey.

Ferruci, G., V. Herzberg, F. Soussa, and A. Taylor. 2004. 'Understanding capital flows to emerging market economies', *Financial Stability Review*, Bank of England, June.

Gokarn, Subir. 2010. 'Monetary policy considerations after the crisis: Practitioners' perspectives', *Plenary Lecture at the Conference on Economic Policies for Inclusive Development*, organized by Ministry of Finance, Government of India and National Institute of Public Finance and Policy, New Delhi, 1 December.

Hoe, Ee. 2001. 'Challenges for exchange rate policy in the emerging markets in Asia', *Remarks, South-East Asia Conference organized by South-East Asian Bank Representatives in London and Bank of England's Centre for Central Banking Studies*, London.

IMF. 2005. *IEO evaluation report on the IMF's approach to capital account liberalization 2005*, Independent Evaluation Office, International Monetary Fund, August.

Jalan, Bimal. 2003. 'Exchange rate management: An emerging consensus?' *RBI Bulletin*, September.

Johnston, R.B., Salim M. Darbar, and Claudia Echeverria. 1997. 'Sequencing capital account liberalization—Lessons from the experiences in Chile, Indonesia, Korea, and Thailand', *IMF Working Paper No. 97/157*, November.

Kaminsky, G., and C. Reinhart. 1999. 'The twin crises: The causes of banking and balance of payments problems', *American Economic Review* 89: 473–500.

Magud, N., and C.M. Reinhart. 2004. 'Capital controls: An evaluation', presented at NBER's International Capital Flows Conference, Santa Barbara, California, 16–18 December.

Mohan, Rakesh. 2003. 'Challenges to monetary policy in a globalising context', lecture delivered at the Central Bank of Sri Lanka, Colombo, November.

Mundell, R.A. 1963. 'Capital mobility and stabilization policy under flexible exchange rates', *Canadian Journal of Economics and Political Science* 29(4): 475–85.

Neely, C.J. 1999. 'An introduction to capital control', *Federal Reserve Bank of St. Louis Review* November/December.

Prasad, Eswar S., and Raghuram G. Rajan. 2005. 'Controlled capital account liberalisation—A proposal', *IMF Policy Discussion Paper No. 05/7*.

Reddy, Y.V. 2000. 'Issues in managing capital account liberalisation', *RBI Bulletin*, August.

Shirakawa, Masaaki. 2010. 'Advanced and emerging economies: Two-speed recovery', *Bauhinia Distinguished Talk*, Bauhinia Foundation Research Centre, Hong Kong SAR.

6

ABHIJIT SEN GUPTA

RAJESWARI SENGUPTA

Negotiating the Trilemma and Reserve Management in an Era of Volatile Capital Flows in India

Net capital flows to emerging markets have exhibited a sharp increase in volatility in the recent years, driven by widely shifting risk perceptions, uncertainty about advanced countries' recovery prospects, and quantitative easing in advanced economies (Forbes 2012). Net private capital flows to emerging markets rebounded strongly in late 2009 after experiencing a massive drop during the Global Financial Crisis (GFC). The trend slowed down in the second half of 2010, then surged again during the first half of 2011. However, the worsening debt crisis in Europe and a downgrade of US sovereign rating in the second half of 2011 caused investor sentiment to deteriorate, as a result of which net capital flows plunged across most emerging economies.

The rise in volatility of capital flows has significantly enhanced the intricacies involved in balancing diverse objectives of healthy growth rate, sustainable current account deficit, competitive exchange rate, adequate external capital to finance investment, moderate inflation, targeted monetary and credit growth rate, minimizing financial fragilities, and maintaining adequate reserves. This has rekindled the debate on appropriate macroeconomic and capital flow management measures.

Several emerging markets have also grappled with this conundrum. Countries such as Brazil, Peru, the Republic of Korea, and Indonesia have used both prudential macroeconomic measures such as allowing the exchange rate to appreciate, sterilized foreign exchange intervention, and low interest rates as well as capital flow management measures such as tax on inflows, additional capital requirements for foreign exchange credit exposure, minimum holding period, and withholding tax to manage capital flow volatility.

India, like other emerging markets, too has been subject to these capricious capital flows in the recent years. Sustained differential in growth potential of the advanced economies and India, ageing population in the developed countries, easy liquidity, and declining home bias in the advanced economies resulted in capital flows surging to India in the pre-GFC period well in excess of the current account deficit. Net capital flows increased from $17.3 billion in 2003–04 to over $107.9 billion in 2007–08. This resulted in the rupee appreciating steeply, which dented competitiveness of the Indian exports. The rapid inflow of capital soon turned into an outflow with the outbreak of the sub-prime crisis in 2007. Unnerved by the extreme uncertainty, global investors exited India and other emerging economies to return to safe havens in advanced economies. The direction of capital flows changed once again with the signs of ebbing of the GFC. The two speed recovery and quantitative easing by advanced economies drove global excess liquidity into emerging economies, including India, during 2010 and early 2011. However, this trend was short-lived. The deepening of the eurozone sovereign debt crisis in the second half of 2011 as well as deteriorating domestic fundamentals resulted in global capital reversing direction yet again.

A number of challenges have emanated from India's greater integration with the global capital market during the last two decades and the rise in capital flow volatility. These include managing the policy tradeoffs under the well-known macroeconomic trilemma—maintaining a stable exchange rate, keeping an open capital account open, and retaining monetary autonomy. To this end, we empirically quantify the various policy objectives under the trilemma. We find that instead of adopting corner solutions, India has opted for the middle ground or an intermediate regime juggling the three policy objectives as per the demands of the macroeconomic situation. We find that in the recent years, there has been a discernible shift towards greater monetary policy autonomy to tackle growing domestic inflationary pressure. This has been balanced with greater flexibility of the exchange rate, which has acted as a shock absorber in a period of volatile capital flows. Our results are consistent with recent evidence on India's trilemma management.[1]

In the context of the financial trilemma, it may be reasonable to conjecture that the RBI imposed capital controls to manage exchange rate stability (ERS) and not exclusively to moderate certain types of capital inflows. To this end, we calculate the exchange market pressure index (EMPI) in India, track its evolution over the last couple of decades, and also analyse the impact of trade and capital inflows on the EMP indices. We find that a deteriorating trade balance and decline in portfolio equity inflows are associated with a higher EMP while positive changes in stock market returns lower the EMP.

A possible way for authorities to manage the trade-offs under the trilemma is by accumulating or dissipating reserves. We find that the RBI has intervened heavily in the foreign exchange market in the face of growing capital flows. Moreover, using empirical methods, we find that much of this intervention has been asymmetric, with the RBI mostly intervening in the foreign exchange market to prevent an appreciation of the currency but adopting a hands-off approach during periods of depreciation. However, this trend seems to have dampened in the recent times with the RBI allowing the exchange rate to move in either direction with greater freedom.

Asymmetric intervention, unless sterilized, often leads to a sharp increase in reserve money and fuels inflationary pressure. We evaluate the magnitude of sterilization using empirical tools. We find that between 1998 and 2004, most of the concomitant rise in international reserves was offset by corresponding declines in the net domestic assets (NDA) through sterilization efforts by the RBI. Thus, the RBI indeed succeeded in insulating the money supply from the effects of its intervention in the foreign exchange market. However, owing to rising fiscal costs of sterilization, less than 30 per cent of the rise in international reserves was offset by a corresponding fall in NDA after 2004, implying

---

[1] See Hutchison et al. (2011), Aizenman and Sengupta (2013), and Sen Gupta and Manjhi (2012) among others.

only a partial sterilization. This resulted in monetary autonomy being partially sacrificed.

Finally, we evaluate the impact of the volatile capital flows on India's external vulnerability. Historically, reserve accretion has been a result of net capital inflows being greater than the current account deficit, and the RBI intervening in an asymmetric manner. The build-up of reserves meant that India was comfortably placed on the various traditional reserve adequacy indicators, such as, import cover, ratio of reserves to short-term debt, and ratio of reserves to monetary aggregates at the time of the sub-prime crisis in 2007–08. However, since then, India's reserve cover has declined sharply following a surge in capital outflows and widening current account deficit. In fact, a cross-country comparison shows that between 2007 and 2011, India witnessed one of the highest erosions of reserve cover across a spectrum of emerging economies.

The rest of the chapter is structured as follows. In Section II, we outline India's approach towards capital account liberalization and its impact on composition of liabilities as well as efficacy of some of the recent measures in stemming exchange rate appreciation and rise in asset prices. Section III analyses how India has negotiated the macroeconomic trilemma, outlining the changes in preference accorded to the various policy objectives. It also evaluates the extent to which the trilemma is binding in India. In Section IV, we calculate the EMPI to test the conjecture that capital account management in India focused on ensuring ERS and not exclusively on moderating certain types of capital inflows. We also investigate the major determinants of EMPI in India. Section V analyses the nature of RBI's intervention in the foreign exchange market, and the extent to which the RBI has been able to sterilize the impact of these interventions. Finally, Section VI evaluates the impact of rising current account deficit, volatile capital flows on India's external vulnerability.

I. Capital Account Liberalization in India

Capital account liberalization in India has taken place in a gradual manner, and has been viewed as a continuous process rather than a one-off event. Throughout most of the post-Independence period until the early 1980s, India had a relatively closed capital account. Most of the external financing was primarily confined to external assistance through multilateral and bilateral sources on concessional terms to or through the government. This approach was associated with an import-substitution strategy due to export pessimism, and relied on a host of tariffs and quotas to limit the need for foreign exchange.

It was in the 1980s that the scenario started changing as a widening current account deficit on account of higher oil prices, rise in demand for imports as a result of selective liberalization, and a sharp depreciation of the rupee in the second half of the 1980s necessitated the demand for additional finance. Consequently, the traditional sources of financing had to be supplemented with additional foreign capital and India resorted to short-term borrowings, external commercial borrowings (ECBs), and deposits by non-resident Indians (NRIs).

The subsequent phase of liberalization was under the overall reform process that was initiated after the balance of payment (BOP) crisis in 1991. On the external front, the reforms included dismantling of trade restrictions, move towards current account convertibility, a market-oriented exchange rate regime, and a gradual opening up of the capital account. However, with the Latin American debt crisis of the early 1980s and the Asian financial crisis of 1997 fresh in mind, India prioritized certain kinds of flows and agents in the liberalization process (Mohan and Kapur 2009; Reddy 2008). In particular, India favoured nondebt flows such as foreign direct investment (FDI) and portfolio investment flows over debt flows. Currently, barring a few sectors, FDI is universally allowed. Some of the sensitive sectors such as banking, aviation, multi-brand retail, and insurance are subject to caps.

Portfolio flows have also witnessed significant liberalization, though there still exist separate investment caps on sub-accounts of foreign institutional investors (FIIs), individual FII, and aggregate FII in a company. In contrast, debt flows are subject to numerous restrictions including borrowers and lenders having to satisfy eligibility conditions, minimum maturity period, ceilings on interest rate spread, and end-use restrictions. With India registering higher growth and inflation than the advanced economies, nominal interest rates tend to be higher and this interest rate differential is likely to persist in the foreseeable future. In this set-up, a liberalized regime for debt flows would attract hot money to take advantage of not only the interest rate differential but also the exchange rate expectations, which become self-fulfilling for a period, before an ultimate costly reversal. IMF (2012) and Sen Gupta and Sengupta (2013) provide a detailed list of the regulations governing inflow and outflow of various forms of foreign capital.

Thus, there has been a clear hierarchy in the liberalization of capital flows in India where equity flows have been given preference over debt flows. Within equity flows, FDI has been the preferred choice compared to portfolio investments, while within debt flows longer term flows have been preferred over short-term flows. This hierarchy has resulted in significantly modifying India's composition of external liabilities in the 'desired' manner.[2] From comprising 95 per cent of India's total external liabilities in 1990, the share of debt liabilities have dropped to 33.2 per cent in 2007. Over the same period, the share of portfolio liabilities have increased from less than 1 per cent to nearly 50 per cent, while that of FDI has increased from 4 per cent to 17.2 per cent. As is evident from Figure 6.1, the change in composition of liabilities in India towards nondebt creating flows has been in line with international experience. However, India along with some of the other emerging markets like Brazil and the Republic of Korea witnessed a greater preponderance of portfolio flows, while in other countries like the People's Republic of China (PRC) and Chile, FDI played a greater role.

Another key objective of management of capital flows in India is to stem rapid appreciation of the real exchange rate. Rajan and Subramanian (2005), Johnson et al. (2007), and Prasad et al. (2007) show that excessive capital inflows could result in rapid exchange rate appreciation, which can hurt exports of emerging markets. Even a short-term appreciation can have lingering implications in the form of permanent loss of export market share and reductions in manufacturing capacity. Moreover, bulk of the exports of developing countries like India tends to be concentrated in labour-intensive, low and intermediate technology products with very thin profit margins. As a result, sharp exchange rate volatility caused by capricious capital flows can have severe employment, output, and distributional consequences.

The need for capital flow management measures is also driven by the existing state of financial development. Prasad and Rajan (2008) con-

---

[2] Studies such as Kose et al. (2009) find that stocks of FDI and portfolio liabilities are associated with better risk sharing outcomes while stocks of debt liabilities are not. The nondebt flows are also more stable than debt flows.

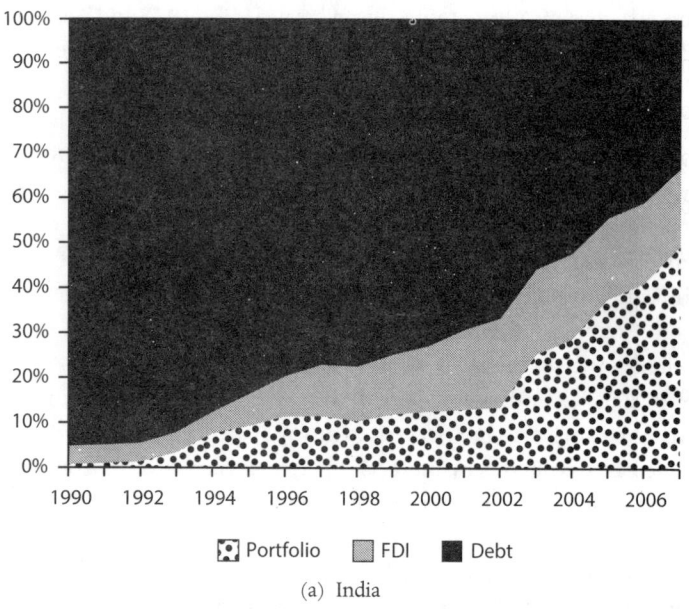

(a) India

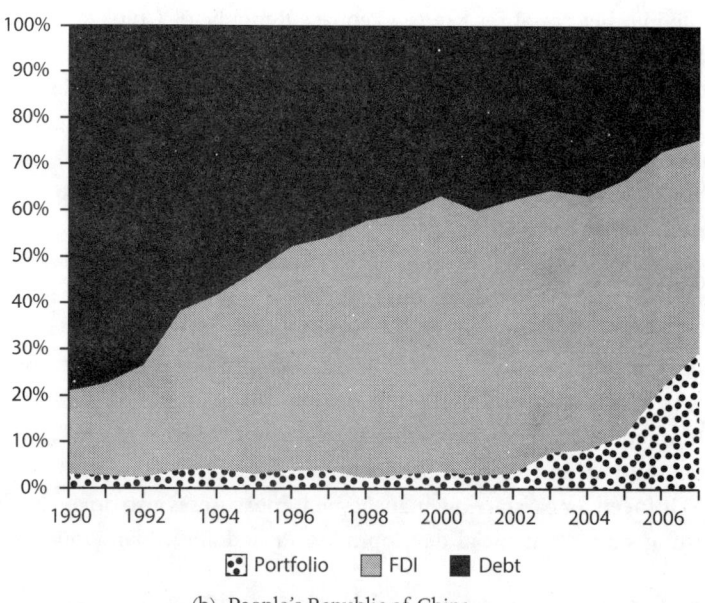

(b) People's Republic of China

(*Cont'd*)

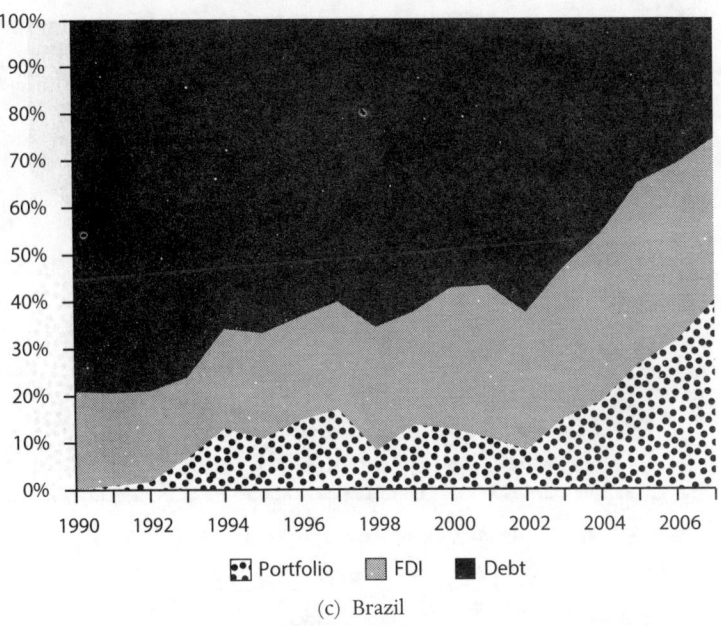

(c) Brazil

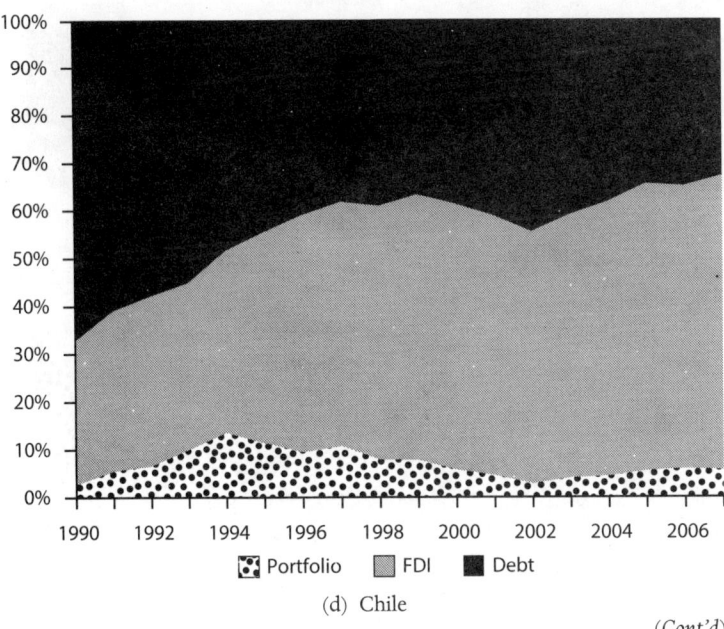

(d) Chile

(Cont'd)

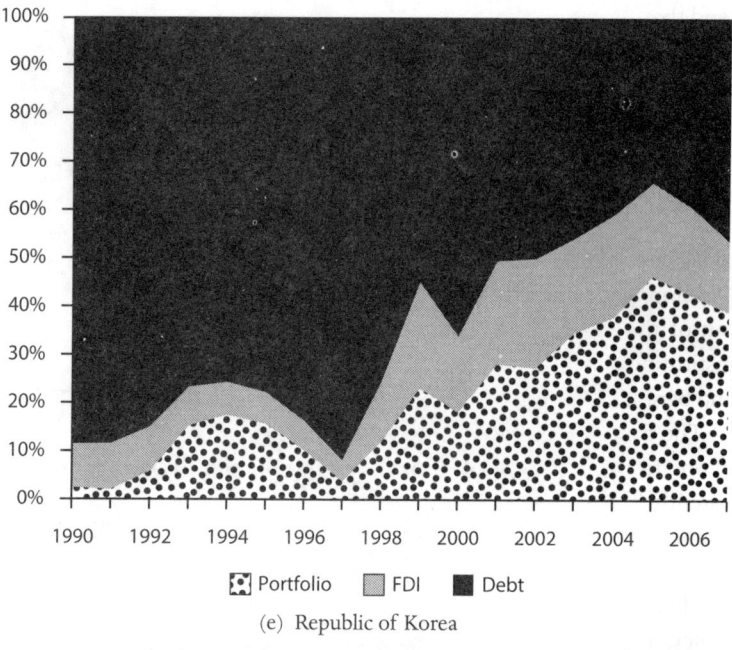

(e) Republic of Korea

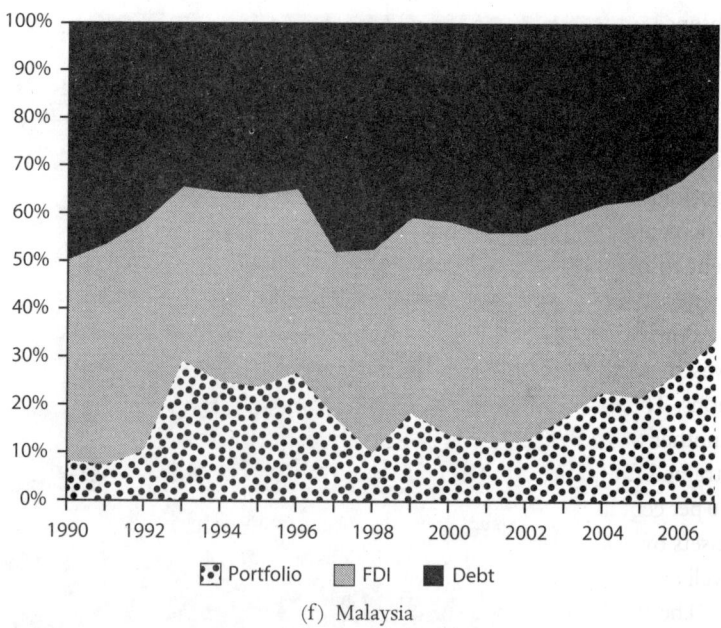

(f) Malaysia

FIGURE 6.1   Composition of Liabilities
Source: Lane and Milessi-Ferreti (2007).

tend that in an underdeveloped financial system, foreign capital is likely to be channelled towards easily collateralized, nontradable investments like real estate, leading to asset price booms, with subsequent busts severely disrupting the economy. Moreover, Aghion et al. (2009) argue that higher levels of exchange rate volatility can stunt growth, especially in countries with thin financial markets. Despite insignificant progress in the last two decades, India's level of financial development continues to lag considerably behind the advanced economies. The 2012 Financial Development Report of the World Economic Forum ranked India 40 out of the 62 countries covered. In particular, India ranked poorly on institutional and business environment, financial stability, and access and banking services.

The calibrated liberalization of the capital account was also driven by the fact that fiscal deficit and inflation rates in India have been consistently higher than international levels. Both RBI (2006) and Planning Commission (2009) have pointed out that the adverse effect of a rising fiscal deficit and high inflation rates would be transmitted much faster in a liberalized capital account regime. These include pro-cyclical fiscal policy, increased volatility of bond yields, increase in monetary base in absence of adequate sterilizing instruments, and difficulties in securing funds to finance the fiscal deficit.

India started experiencing steadily rising levels of foreign capital since the early 2000s, which turned into a surge after 2005 due to excess global liquidity and a strong domestic economy. Net capital flows increased fourfold, from $24.9 billion in 2005–06 to $107.9 billion in 2007–08. As a percentage of GDP net capital flows more than doubled from 4 per cent to over 9.5 per cent during this period. The surge was driven by increased foreign purchases of debt and securities and higher borrowings by domestic residents. The first response to the surge in capital flows was to accumulate reserves and sterilize the effect of these interventions. The RBI purchased $26.8 billion foreign exchange in 2006–07 and another $78.2 billion in 2007–08. Such a scale of interventions severely strained the monetary base. The reserve money growth accelerated to 30 per cent in 2007, almost completely driven by accumulation of foreign assets by the central bank. Broad money growth peaked at 25 per cent, well over the central bank's target of around 15 per cent.

The RBI attempted to sterilize the monetary impact of intervention and contain the growth in monetary base by reducing its holding of domestic assets and increasing the reserve requirements. The reduction of domestic assets took the form of selling Market Stabilization Scheme (MSS) bonds. The stock of these bonds increased steadily from Rs 373 billion in January 2006 to over Rs 1.7 trillion in October 2007. However, as mentioned previously, in spite of this sterilization, reserve money growth accelerated to over 30 per cent in 2007. The interest expenses on MSS bonds led to rising cost of sterilization. Kohli (2011) estimates the cost of sterilization increased from Rs 7.6 billion per month in 2006 to over Rs 31 billion in 2007. The sterilization cost, involving interest payments on MSS bonds and opportunity costs to the banking sector due to the rise in reserve ratio is estimated to have peaked at 0.42 per cent of GDP in March 2008.

The rising costs of sterilization forced RBI to incompletely sterilize the interventions in the foreign exchange market leading to a growth in money supply and intensification of inflationary pressures. To combat these pressures, outflows were liberalized and the pace of monetary tightening was accelerated with the repo and the reverse repo rate rates being raised by a cumulative 125 basis points in 2006 and 2007. An appreciating currency and a widening interest rate differential provided a very attractive option to the domestic borrowers to access foreign funds. Rising interest rates attracted further inflows, especially in the form of foreign borrowings by domestic firms, thereby further reinforcing currency appreciation and monetary tightening pressures. The simultaneous currency appreciation and inflationary pressure also reduced the competitiveness of Indian products in global markets in real terms.

With the surge in capital flow persisting and the inflationary and currency pressures not abating, the government introduced a series of measures to regulate the flow of foreign capital inflows. A majority of these measures were imposed on debt flows. In particular, access of corporations to foreign currency funds was capped and conversion of foreign currency loans into Indian rupees was restricted. The ceilings on interest rate for foreign borrowings were reduced. In the case of other flows, the use of Participatory Notes (PNs), an offshore derivative product, allowing overseas retail investors to participate in the Indian stock market, were banned while interest rates on nonresident deposits were also lowered.

To get a preliminary idea about the efficacy of some of the measures aimed at managing capital inflow, we look at the currency and stock price movement before and after the introduction of these measures.

Data on the bilateral rupee-dollar exchange rate is sourced from the RBI, while data on daily stock index is taken from National Stock Exchange (NSE). To be deemed effective these measures must reverse or at least slow down the rate of appreciation observed prior to their introduction. Figure 6.2 and Table 6.1 highlight the impact of some of the measures, enacted during 2007 and 2009 to manage the inflow of foreign capital, on stock prices and the exchange rate. We focus on the average daily change in the exchange rate and stock prices over a 30-day period before and after introduction of the measures.

We find that the evidence of the efficacy of capital controls in restricting exchange rate appreciation is mixed at best. While the reduction

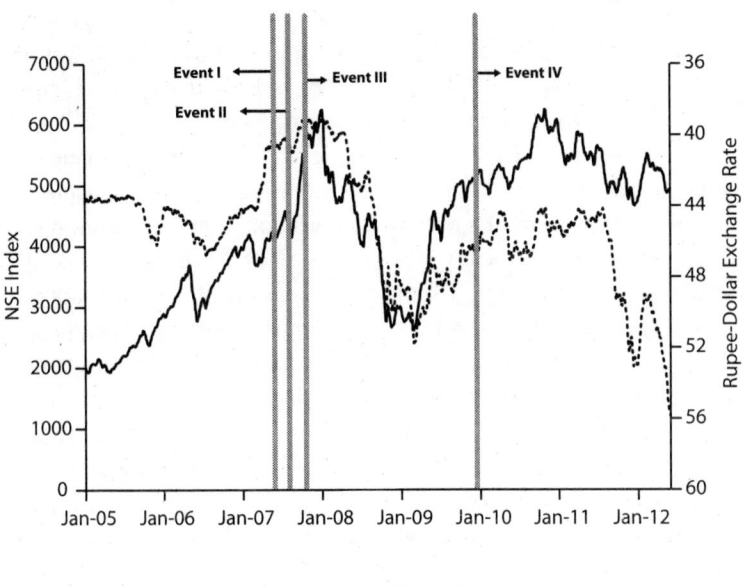

FIGURE 6.2 Impact of Capital Controls on the Currency and Stock Prices
Source: Authors' calculation.
Note: Event I refers to the reduction in all-in-cost ceilings for ECBs. Event II refers to measures introduced to restrict conversion of ECBs into rupee. Event III refers to Security and Exchange Board of India's tightening of rules for purchase of shares and bonds in Indian companies through the PN route. Event IV refers to re-imposition of all in cost ceilings for ECBs that were discontinued during the GFC and discontinuation of the buyback of Foreign Currency Convertible Bonds.

TABLE **6.1**   Impact of Capital Controls on Currency and Stock Prices (Tabulated)

	Date of Introduction	Average Daily Currency Appreciation (Percentage)		Average Daily Stock Price Increase (Percentage)	
		Before	After	Before	After
Event I	22 May 2007	0.198	−0.003	0.395	0.113
Event II	7 August 2007	0.029	0.027	0.092	0.271
Event III	17 October 2007	0.125	−0.026	0.670	0.181
Event IV	10 December 2009	0.023	0.026	0.196	−0.159

Source: Authors' calculation.

of all-in-cost ceilings in May 2007 and the restrictions on Participatory Notes (PNs) in October 2007 led to a reversal of rupee appreciation, the restrictions on conversion of ECBs into rupees in August 2007 and the re-imposition of the all-in-cost ceilings in December 2009 failed to reverse or slowdown the pace of appreciation significantly. In fact there was a slight increase in the pace of appreciation after the reimposition of all-in-cost ceilings. Even in the case of stock price movement, the impact of capital controls is found to be ambivalent. The stock prices also continued to increase after the introduction of the various capital controls in 2007, although there was a moderation of the pace of increase after the reduction in ECB ceiling in May 2007 and restrictions on PNs in October 2007. The latter restriction had a particularly strong impact as the PNs were an important source of FII investment in equities. In contrast, the restriction on conversion of ECBs into rupees introduced in August 2007 was associated with threefold acceleration in stock prices. Finally, the reimposition of the all-in-cost ceilings and discontinuation of the buyback of Foreign Currency Convertible Bonds had a negative impact on the stock prices.

Our simple analysis indicates that the introduction of capital control measures did not always lead to a reversal or even a slowdown in the rate of exchange rate appreciation or the stock prices. However, this is not to conclude that these measures were ineffective due to the absence of counterfactuals. Moreover, to rigorously estimate the efficacy of capital controls, one would have to also look at the impact of these measures on the volume and composition of flows (Patnaik and Shah

2011) and the extent to which they allowed the monetary policymaker to act in an independent manner (Kohli 2011).

The calibrated approach towards liberalization is reflected in the steady increase in India's extent of financial integration with the rest of the world. Gross capital flows have increased nearly 22 times from $42.7 billion in 1991–92 to over $932.3 billion in 2010–11. As a share of GDP, this amounted to an increase from 15.5 per cent in 1991–92 to 55.2 per cent in 2010–11. Much of the increase in financial integration occurred between 2003–04 and 2007–08. Given the impressive economic performance indicated by close to 9 per cent growth rate, higher domestic interest rates and a strong currency, India's risk perception was quite low during 2003 to 2007. Furthermore, this period was associated with favourable global conditions in the form of ample liquidity and low interest rates in the global markets—the so-called period of Great Moderation.

Despite the sharp increase in extent of financial integration during the last two decades, India has not kept pace with other emerging markets. The extent of capital account liberalization has been primarily determined using two kinds of measures. The first set looks at the de jure openness, focusing on laws governing the movement of capital in and out of the country. Most of such measures are based on the IMF's Annual Report on Exchange Arrangements and Exchange Restrictions, which gives a binary evaluation on various categories of transactions. Several studies including Chinn and Ito (2008) and Edwards (2007) have used these scores to create an index of capital account openness. Figure 6.3 looks at the degree of de jure capital account openness index across emerging markets. Over the last 40 years, there has been an increase in the extent of capital account openness, reflected in the upward shift of the median line. However, India has not liberalized at the same pace, as a result of which it has shifted from being in the middle of the distribution of countries, ranked according to their openness, during the 1970s and 1980s, towards the more restrictive end of the spectrum in the last two decades.

However, the existence of regulations often does not accurately capture the actual level of financial integration as they depend critically on the effectiveness of the enforcement and macroeconomic fundamentals. A country with strict controls but lax enforcement can experience large private capital flows. Alternately, a country with extremely liberal

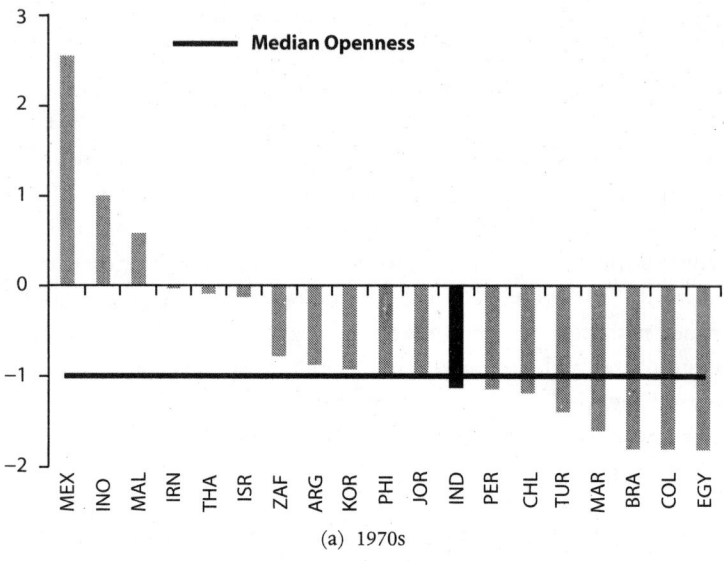

(a) 1970s

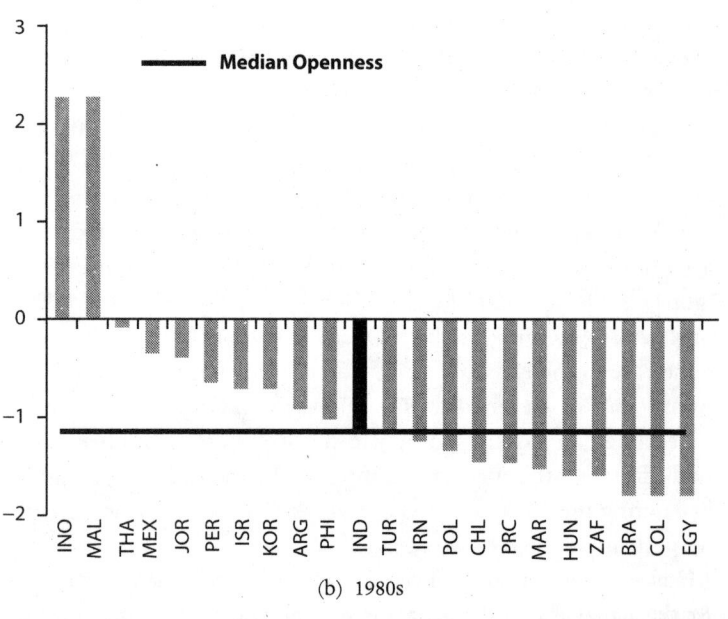

(b) 1980s

(*Cont'd*)

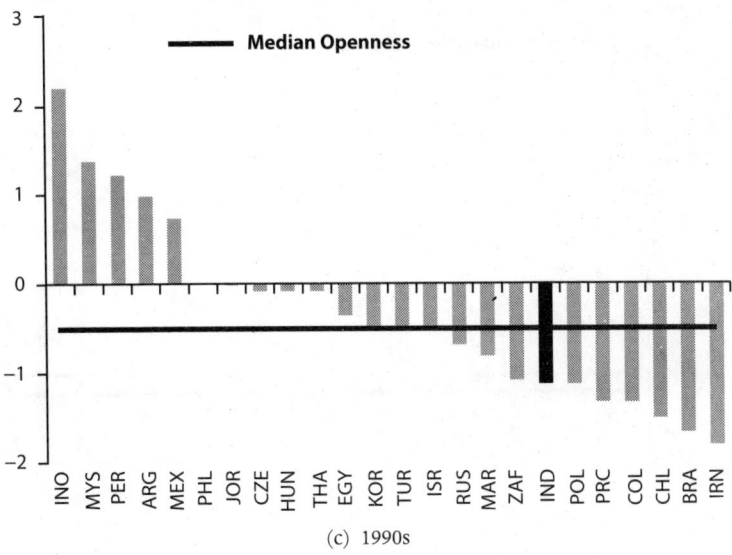

(c) 1990s

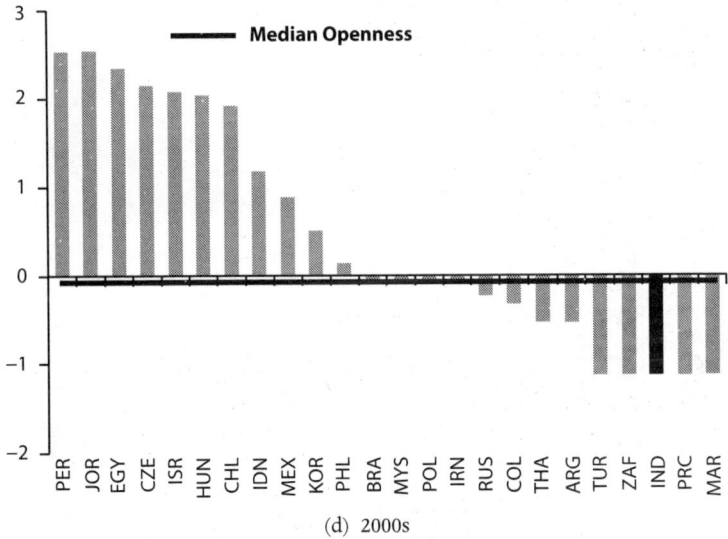

(d) 2000s

FIGURE **6.3** Cross-country Comparison of De Jure Openness
Source: Chinn and Ito (2008).
ARG=Argentina; BRA=Brazil; CHL=Chile; COL=Colombia; CZE=Czech
Republic; EGY=Egypt; HUN=Hungary; IND=India; INO=Indonesia;
IRN=Iran; ISR=Israel; JOR=Jordan; KOR=Republic of Korea; MAL=Malaysia;
MAR=Morocco; MEX=Mexico; PER=Peru; PHI=Philippines; POL=Poland;
PRC=People's Republic of China; RUS=Russian Federation; THA=Kingdom of
Thailand; TUR=Turkey; ZAF=South Africa

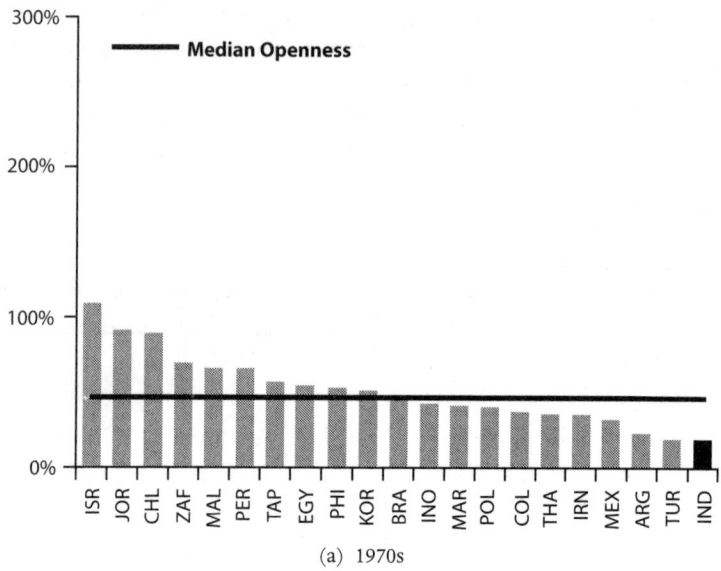

(a) 1970s

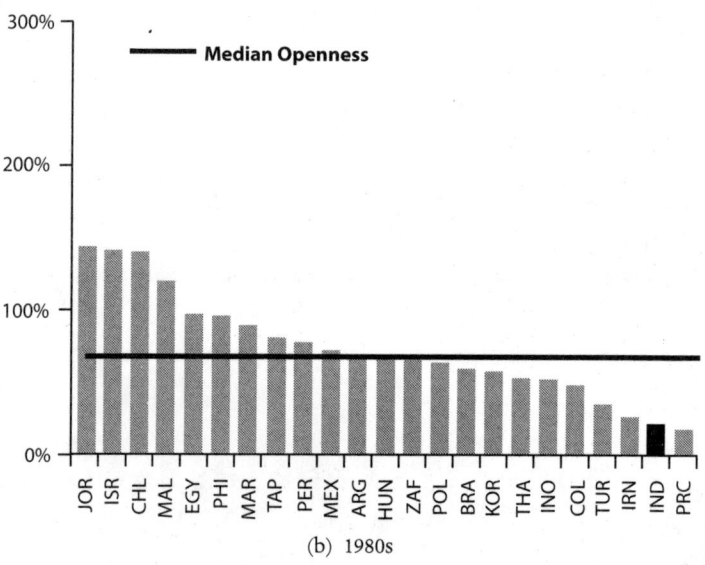

(b) 1980s

(Cont'd)

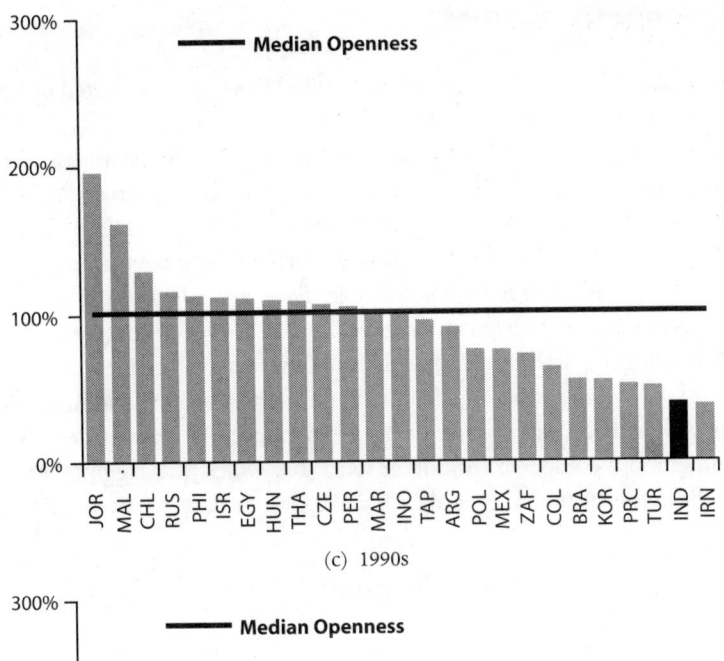

(c) 1990s

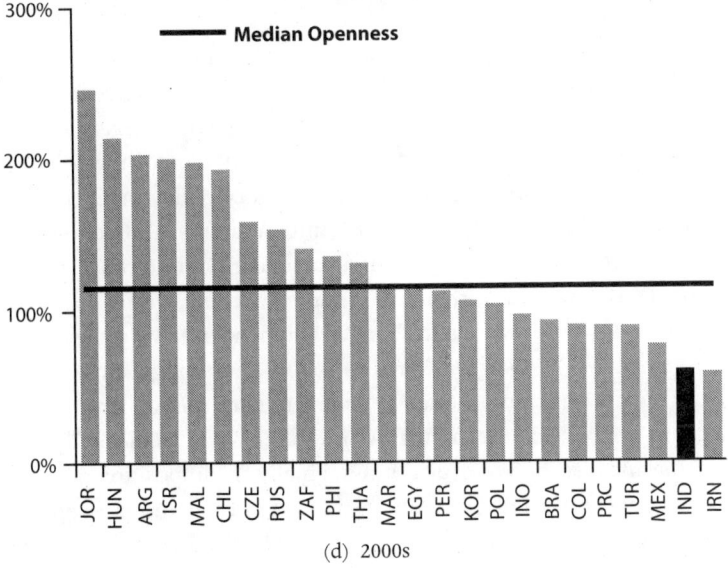

(d) 2000s

FIGURE 6.4   Cross-Country Comparison of De Facto Openness

Source: Lane and Milessi-Ferreti (2007).

ARG=Argentina; BRA=Brazil; CHL=Chile; COL=Colombia; CZE=Czech
Republic; EGY=Egypt; HUN=Hungary; IND=India; INO=Indonesia;
IRN=Iran; ISR=Israel; JOR=Jordan; KOR=Republic of Korea; MAL=Malaysia;
MAR=Morocco; MEX=Mexico; PER=Peru; PHI=Philippines; POL=Poland;
PRC=People's Republic of China; RUS=Russian Federation; TAP=Taipei,China;
THA=Kingdom of Thailand; TUR=Turkey; ZAF=South Africa

capital account regime can witness limited flows due to limited opportunities for economic returns.

The de facto measures focus on an outcome-based measure of financial integration. These measures involve sum of gross flows or gross stocks of foreign assets and liabilities as a ratio of GDP to indicate the extent of risk sharing. Several de facto measures including Lane and Milessi-Ferreti (2007) are available. Even according to the de facto measures, India has been at the lower end of the spectrum (Figure 6.4). According to the Lane and Milessi-Ferreti measure, which is based on the ratio of foreign assets and liabilities to GDP, most of the Latin American as well as East Asian countries have experienced far greater degree of integration, compared to India. Even PRC, which was lagging behind India in the 1980s, has overtaken India during the last two decades.

II. Negotiating the Trilemma

India's increased integration with the global capital markets during the last two decades has increased the complexity of macroeconomic management. In particular, India had to negotiate the well-known macroeconomic trilemma. The standard formulation of the trilemma argues that it is impossible to attain monetary policy independence, ERS, and capital market integration simultaneously. Only two of the three objectives can be obtained at a particular point in time. A stable exchange rate regime with an open capital account would imply that the monetary authority can no longer independently vary the domestic interest rate, which will have to follow the foreign interest rate. Alternatively, retaining monetary independence and an open capital account implies that exchange rate movements will be dictated by the volume and direction of capital flows. Finally, the imposition of capital controls breaks the link between the interest rate and the exchange rate and allows a country to retain exchange rate stability with monetary independence.

India, like other emerging markets, seeks to achieve each of the three aforesaid objectives with varying degrees. While capital flows aid growth by providing external capital to sustain an excess of investment over domestic savings, a competitive exchange rate helps to maintain a sustainable current account balance. An independent monetary policy stabilizes the economy in the face of domestic and exogenous shocks. However, given the impossibility of attaining the three goals simultaneously, India had to juggle the conflicting objectives. Moreover, the sharp increase in the volatility of the capital flows in the recent years has created a tension between monetary management and exchange rate management. Rajan and Subramanian (2005), Johnson et al. (2007), and Prasad et al. (2007) show that excessive capital inflows could result in rapid real exchange rate appreciation, which can hurt exports of emerging markets. Even a short-term appreciation can have lingering implications in the form of permanent loss of export market share and reductions in manufacturing capacity. Alternatively, if the central bank intervenes to prevent the exchange rate from appreciating, it is likely to lead to an increase in money supply, fuelling inflationary pressures.

In this section, we seek to analyse India's management of the conundrum of macroeconomic trilemma, the extent to which India has been bound by the trilemma, and if the trilemma has remained underutilized. Following Aizenman et al. (2010a,b) we quantify the various policy objectives under the trilemma. We use quarterly data and cover the period 1996–97Q1 to 2011–12Q3. Our coverage is dictated by the availability of the data at a quarterly frequency, especially data on GDP.

Monetary Independence

Following Aizenman et al. (2010a,b), the extent of monetary independence is measured as the inverse of the quarterly correlation of the interest rates between India and the US. The US is taken as the base country following Aizenman et al. (2010a,b) and Obstfeld at al. (2010), who argue that Indian monetary policy through this period has been most closely linked to the US. The Monetary Independence Index (MI) is given by

$$\text{MI} = 1 - \frac{corr\left(i_i, i_j\right) - (-1)}{1 - (-1)} \tag{1}$$

where i_i and i_j are the three-month Treasury Bill rates for India and the US, respectively, and $corr(i_i, i_j)$, refers to the correlation of the interest rates over a quarter. The data is taken from Global Financial Database.

By definition, *corr* (i_i, i_j) can take a maximum value of 1 and a minimum value of −1. MI is thus a min-max normalization of this correlation. It is obtained by subtracting the minimum value from the observed correlation and then divided by the range of values. Thus, MI can theoretically take a value between 0 and 1 with a higher value indicating greater degree of monetary independence. However, we find that for India, the index ranges between 0.11 and 0.85. Hence, we rescale this index to lie between 0 and 1.

Exchange Rate Stability

We make use of the methodology introduced by Frankel and Wei (1994) to create an index of ERS. The degree of influence that major global currencies have on the Indian rupee can be estimated using the following estimation model

$$
\Delta \log \varepsilon_{INR,t}^{CHF} = \alpha_0 + \beta_{US} \Delta \log \varepsilon_{USD,t}^{CHF} + \beta_{EUR} \Delta \log \varepsilon_{EUR,t}^{CHF}
$$
$$
+ \beta_{JAP} \Delta \log \varepsilon_{JPY,t}^{CHF} + \mu \tag{2}
$$

where $\varepsilon_{i,t}^{CHF}$ is the exchange rate of currency i against the numéraire currency, which in this case is the Swiss franc, where currency i can be the US dollar, Japanese yen, and the euro. For the period prior to the introduction of the euro, we consider the German deutsche mark. Under this estimation, $\hat{\beta}_i$ which is the estimated coefficient on the rate at which currency i depreciates against the numéraire currency indicates the weight of currency i in the basket. In the case where the currency under observation is pegged to a particular currency or a basket of currency, we will have $\hat{\beta}_i = 1$ or $\sum_{i=1}^{I} \hat{\beta}_i = 1$ for the i currencies that are a part of the basket. Moreover, pegging to an individual or a basket of currencies implies a higher goodness of fit. In our estimation we use daily data, with the data being sourced from the Database on the Indian Economy, Reserve Bank of India, and Global Financial Database. We apply the estimation over a quarter and take the goodness of fit, or the adjusted R^2 as the measure of ERS. A higher R^2 indicates greater pegging to an individual or a basket of currencies. Again, we normalize the index so that it lies between 0 and 1.

Capital Account Openness

The index of capital account openness (KO) is based on a de facto measure of openness instead of a *de* jure one as it is the actual volume of flows that creates a conflict between monetary independence and ERS as opposed to controls governing the movement of capital. A country with high de jure openness can have low capital flows and hence be able to simultaneously stabilize exchange rate and retain monetary autonomy. Alternatively, a country with low de jure openness can experience large flows due to low enforcement of capital controls, and face a trade-off between ensuring monetary independence and ERS. Hence, KO is based on net capital flows. The index is constructed as the ratio of absolute value of net capital flows to GDP.

$$KO = \left| \frac{\text{Net Flows}}{\text{GDP}} \right| \qquad (3)$$

The focus on net capital flows is based on the fact that it is the capital account balance that is crucial for the trilemma. If capital inflows in a country were to be matched by an equal amount of outflows, the central bank will still have the option of retaining monetary independence with a stable exchange rate. The construction of the capital account openness index does not impose an upper bound of 1. Hence, to make this index comparable with ERS and MI indices, we normalize this index to lie between 0 and 1.

In Figure 6.5, we highlight the evolution of the three indices over the period 1996–97Q1 to 2011–12Q3. While ERS exhibited a downward trend since the early 2000s, KO witnessed an upswing till the onset of the GFC. The GFC led to a sharp drop in KO, as flows to emerging markets, including India dried up globally. Since 2010–11, KO has shown signs of revival, although the various components of the capital account have displayed considerable volatility. Finally, MI witnessed significant volatility, although there is a perceptible upward trend since early 2000s.

The entire period from 1996–97Q1 to 2011–12Q3 was one of significant changes in domestic and external conditions and required the balancing of the three trilemma objectives as per the macroeconomic demands. To effectively evaluate the shift in the policy stance over the period of time, we divide the entire sample into four equal

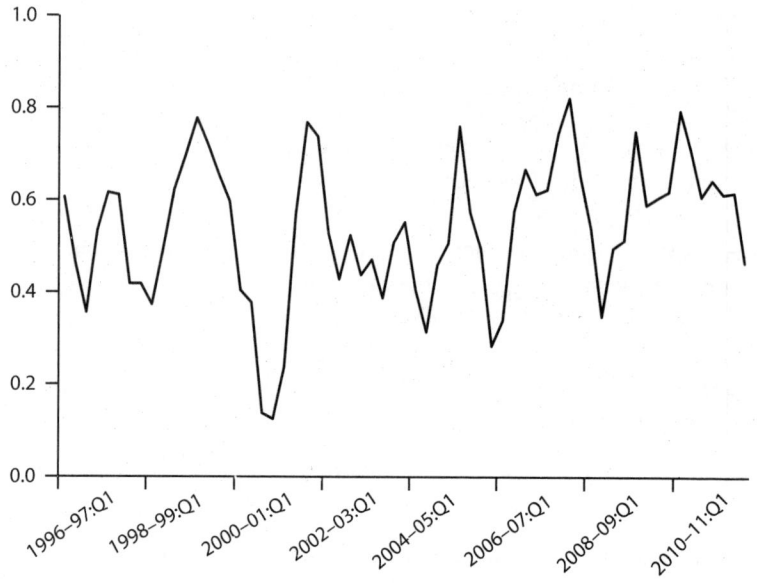

(a) Monetary Independence Index

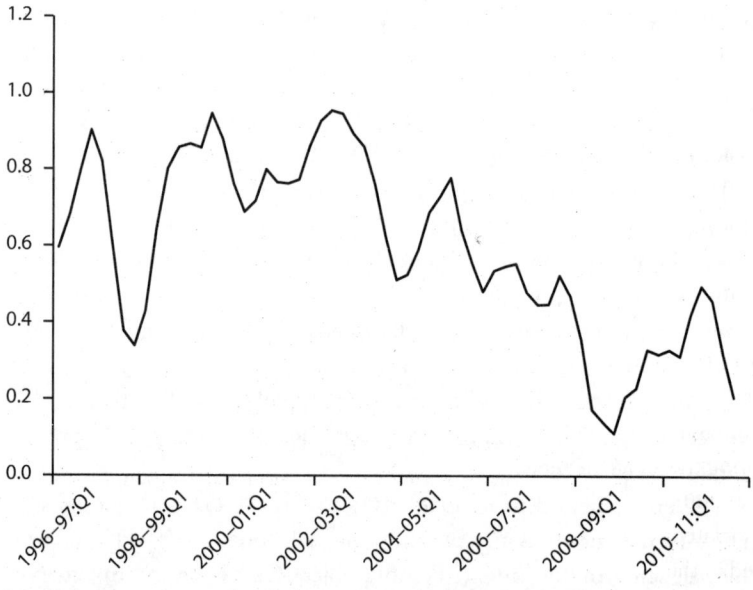

(b) Exchange Rate Stability Index

(Cont'd)

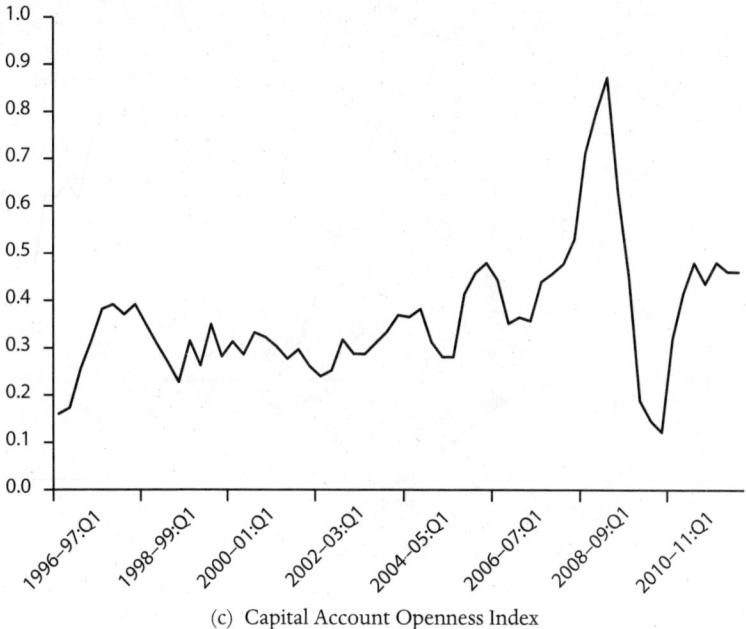

(c) Capital Account Openness Index

FIGURE **6.5** Evolution of the Trilemma Indices
Source: Authors' calculations.

sub-periods—Phase-I: 1996–97Q1 to 1999–2000Q4, Phase-II: 2000–01Q1 to 2003–04Q4, Phase-III: 2004–05Q1 to 2007–08Q4, and Phase-IV: 2008–09Q1 to 2011–12Q3. While the first three phases include 16 quarters, the last phase includes 15 quarters.

As pointed out in Aizenman et al. (2010a,b), policymakers can garner greater flexibility vis-à-vis monetary and exchange rate management in the short run by accumulating or dissipating reserves. Consequently, we also focus on, the absolute change in reserves (as a percentage of GDP).[3] Like the other indices we also normalize this index to lie between 0 and 1. In Figure 6.6, we illustrate the average of the various policy dimensions during these four phases using the diamond chart developed in Aizenman et al. (2010a,b). The rising extent of capital account openness has been associated with a drop in ERS. MI witnessed a drop in Phase-II but recovered in the following phases.

---

[3] We use data on actual intervention by the RBI to exclude valuation changes. The data is from *Handbook of Statistics on the Indian Economy*.

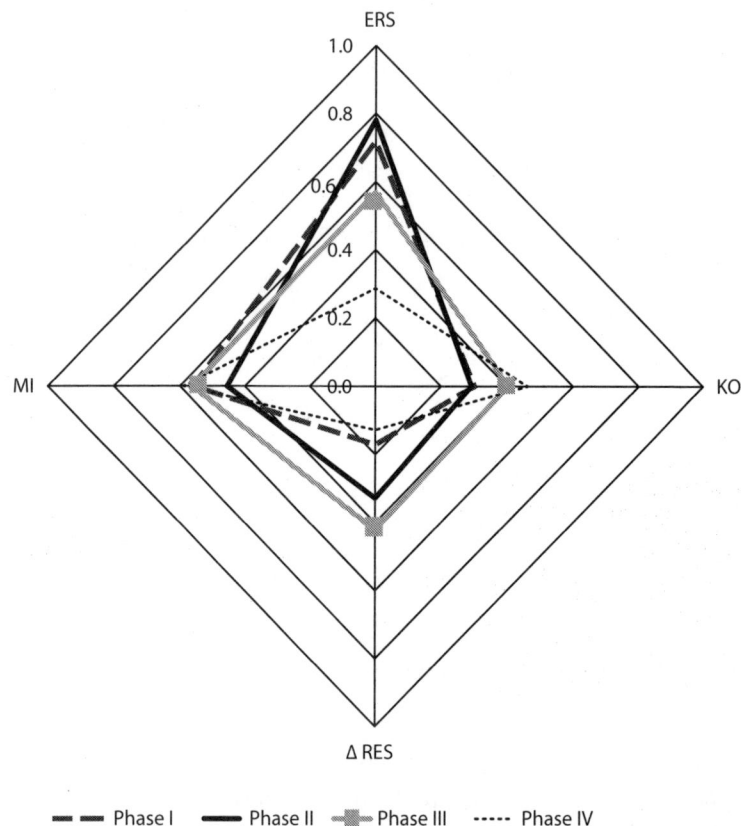

FIGURE **6.6** Configuration of the Trilemma Objectives and International Reserves

Source: Authors' calculations.

Next, we examine the validity of the trilemma framework by testing whether the weighted sum of the three trilemma policy variables adds up to a constant—here set to be 2. We estimate the relationship for the entire period as well as the four phases outlined in the previous lines. The results are given in Table 6.2. We find that the overall fit is extremely high with R^2 being above 0.93 across all the specifications. While the estimates for ERS and capital account openness are significant across all the specifications, it is not the case with monetary independence.

TABLE 6.2 Testing the Validity of the Trilemma Framework

	Whole Sample	Phase-I	Phase-II	Phase-III	Phase-IV
	1996–97Q1 to 2011–12Q3	1996–97Q1 to 1999–2000Q4	2000–01Q1 to 2003–04Q4	2004–05Q1 to 2007–08Q4	2008–09Q1 to 2011–12Q3
Monetary Independence	0.656***	0.684**	0.125	0.158	1.244**
	[3.448]	[1.986]	[0.516]	[0.861]	[2.711]
Exchange Rate Stability	1.388***	1.093**	1.511***	1.908***	1.774*
	[9.444]	[2.268]	[5.001]	[7.813]	[1.813]
Capital Account Liberalization	2.012***	2.419**	2.473***	1.997***	1.357**
	[8.392]	[2.918]	[3.078]	[5.861]	[2.696]
Observations	63	16	16	16	15
R^2	0.954	0.949	0.980	0.989	0.934

Source: Authors' calculations.

Notes: Robust standard errors in parentheses.

*, **, and *** indicate correlations significant at 10 per cent, 5 per cent, and 1 per cent, respectively.

To obtain the contribution of each trilemma policy orientation, we multiply the coefficients with the average for each phase. The results are outlined in Figure 6.7. The high goodness of fit implies that the contributions add up to being very close to 2 across all the phases.

The increase in ERS from Phase-I to Phase-II, and Phase-III was associated with a sharp drop in monetary independence. During Phase-II and Phase-III, the RBI intervened heavily in the foreign exchange market to prevent the rupee from appreciating in the face of strong capital inflows. It purchased $55.6 billion of foreign assets in Phase-II, and another $134 billion in Phase-III. The RBI tried to sterilize these interventions, initially through depletion of its stock of government bonds. However, as it started to run out of government bonds towards the end of 2003, a new instrument for sterilization—MSS bonds—were introduced. Nevertheless, owing to rising fiscal cost of sterilization, the RBI could only partially sterilize the flows, which resulted in loss of monetary independence during Phase-II and Phase-III. Phase-IV witnessed a resurgence of monetary independence with a decline in both

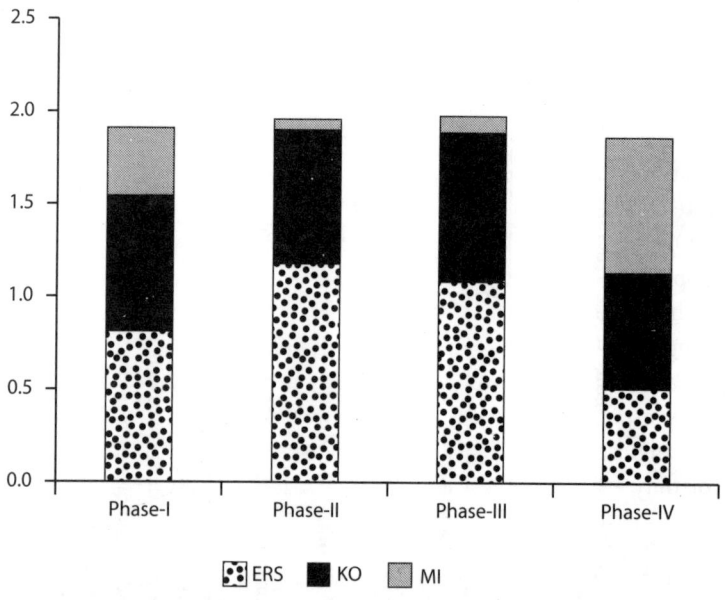

FIGURE 6.7   Contribution to the Trilemma
Source: Authors' calculations.

ERS and capital account openness. The outbreak of the subprime crisis in the US led to a flight to safety of foreign capital from India, which intensified after the collapse of the Lehman Brothers. The outflow was managed by allowing the rupee to depreciate and limit intervention in the foreign exchange market. Several measures such as increasing the cap on foreign investment in corporate bonds and raising the interest rate on NRI deposits were undertaken to attract greater capital inflow. At the same time a more independent monetary policy was pursued to bolster the Indian economy.[4]

Capital flows have remained volatile during most of Phase-IV having been influenced by investor uncertainty over the advanced economies' recovery prospects, large swings in risk aversion, loose monetary policy in the advanced economies, and changing domestic fundamentals. During this period, RBI intervened in a limited manner in the foreign exchange market and allowed the exchange rate to move with greater freedom. The rupee appreciated by nearly 17 per cent between March 2009 and April 2010. Similarly, between August 2011 and December 2011, the rupee depreciated by 19 per cent on the back of a widening current account deficit and weak capital inflows. The drop in capital inflows and greater exchange rate flexibility allowed the RBI to pursue a more independent monetary policy. After the initial softening of monetary policy to stimulate growth, the RBI started tightening the monetary policy from March 2010 in response to high and persistent inflation. This was in contrast with the advanced economies, which were continuing to follow a soft monetary policy to stimulate growth.

Overall, we find that instead of opting for corner solutions, India has adopted an intermediate regime while negotiating the trilemma. This has been buttressed by selective capital flow management measures. In doing so, India has resorted to a multiple instrument approach. The overall policy architecture encompasses active management of capital flows, especially volatile and debt flows, moderately flexible exchange rate regime with the RBI intervening at times to prevent excessive volatility, sterilization through various instruments like MSS bonds and

---

[4] The RBI took a series of measures to counter the drop in liquidity in the aftermath of collapse of Lehman Brothers. These included lowering of key policy rates, Cash Reserve Ratio (CRR), and Statutory Liquidity Ratio (SLR), unwinding of MSS bonds, opening up of new refinance windows, lowering of prudential norms related to provisioning and risk weights.

changes in CRR, and building up of a stockpile of reserves. In recent years, in response to the increase in volatility of capital flows, India has opted for greater flexibility of the exchange rate, with the objective of retaining higher monetary independence.

III. Impact on the Exchange Market Pressure Index

A. Measurements and Evolution of EMP Indices

The RBI's management of capital account could be driven by a desire to moderate certain types of capital inflows or to manage ERS. It may be reasonable to conjecture that the goal was the latter in the context of financial trilemma. Accordingly in this section we measure the exchange market pressure (EMP) in India, discuss its evolution over time and also analyse a few crucial macroeconomic factors that may have affected the EMP over the last couple of decades. EMP is a combination of exchange rate depreciation and international reserves loss-a concept pioneered by Girton and Roper (1977), and applied frequently in the analysis of EMEs (Frankel 2009). A positive (negative) EMP indicates a net excess demand (supply) for foreign currency, accompanied by a combination of reserve loss (gain) and currency depreciation (appreciation).

In order to measure EMP in India, we follow the methodology of Aizenman et al. (2012), who investigate the factors explaining EMP in emerging markets during the 2000s. The first measure of EMP is the un-weighted sum of percentage nominal depreciation and percentage loss of reserves:

$$EMP_{i,t} = \frac{\Delta e_{i,t}}{e_{i,t-1}} - \frac{\Delta IR_{i,t}}{IR_{i,t-1}} \tag{4}$$

where $e_{i,t}$ stands for nominal rupee exchange rate per US dollar and $IR_{i,t}$ denotes international reserve holdings (excluding gold) by India during quarter t.[5] $\Delta e_{i,t}$ and $\Delta IR_{i,t}$ denote changes in nominal exchange

---

[5] Since EMP is defined using a combination of percentage changes in exchange rate and reserves, there could be several variants of these ratios; we chose the ones mentioned in equations (4)–(6) based on ease of interpretation and also relevant studies in the EMP literature such as Aizenman and Hutchison (2010), Frankel (2009), Aizenman, Lee, and Sushko (2010) among others.

rate and international reserve holdings, respectively between quarters t and $t-1$.

Our second measure, EMP (IR/M-Base), is defined as the un-weighted sum of percentage exchange rate depreciation and international reserve loss, with reserve loss deflated by the monetary base or M2:

$$EMP_{i,t}^{IR/M-Base} = \frac{\Delta e_{i,t}}{e_{i,t-1}} - \frac{\Delta IR_{i,t}}{M_{i,t-1}\Big/e_{i,t-1}} \tag{5}$$

where $M_{i,t-1}$ stands for M2 in local currency units of India in quarter $t-1$, and the monetary base is converted to US dollars. According to the monetary model-based EMP measure popularized by Girton and Roper (1977), specification (5) provides a real measure of international reserve loss, normalized by the monetary base.

The third and final measure, EMP (Standardized), is the weighted sum of demeaned percentage nominal exchange rate depreciation and percentage loss of international reserves where the weights are inverses of the historical standard deviation of each series:

$$EMP_{i,t}^{Standardized} = \frac{1}{\sigma_{i,\Delta e}}\left(\frac{\Delta e_{i,t}}{e_{i,t-1}} - \mu_{i,\Delta e}\right) - \frac{1}{\sigma_{i,\Delta RES}}\left(\frac{\Delta IR_{i,t}}{IR_{i,t-1}} - \mu_{i,\Delta RES}\right) \tag{6}$$

where $\mu_{i,\Delta e}$ and $\mu_{i,\Delta RES}$ denote the historical means of percentage nominal exchange rate depreciation and percentage changes in international reserve holdings. Similarly, $\sigma_{i,\Delta e}$ and $\sigma_{i,\Delta RES}$ represent historical standard deviations of both these series for India.

Figure 6.8 shows the time-series evolution of the three EMP indices as measured above, with the un-weighted EMP on the left axis and EMP (IR/M-Base) and EMP (Standardized), on the right axis.

As can be seen from the figure, all three EMP indices display a fair amount of fluctuations during the early 1990s, representing the period of heightened macroeconomic volatility during and in the aftermath of the 1991 BOP crisis in India. The un-weighted measure of EMP (left axis) indicate that between 1990Q1 and 1990Q4, India went from an average 5 per cent combined nominal appreciation and gains in international reserve holdings to a 50 per cent combined nominal depreciation and international reserve loss. The fluctuations in all three EMP series continue throughout the 1990s, shooting up during the 1997–1998 Southeast Asian currency crisis.

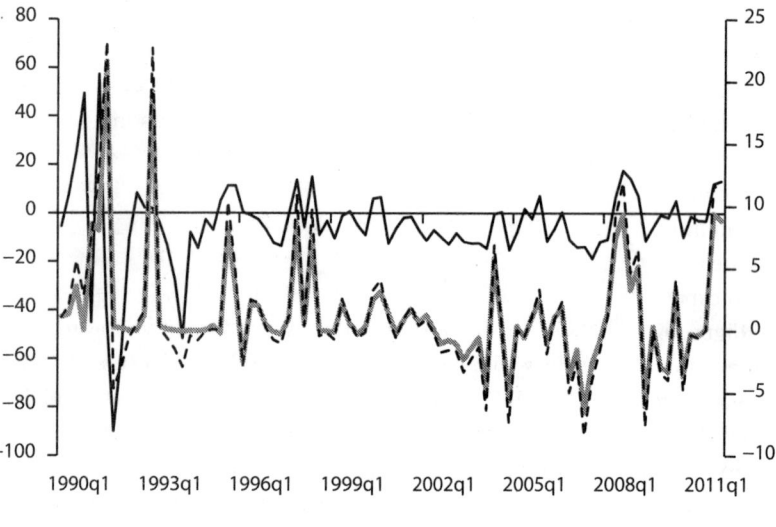

FIGURE **6.8**   Evolution of the EMP Indices, 1990Q1–2011Q4
Source: Authors' calculations.

From 1999Q1 to 2008Q1, all three EMP indices are on average negative, implying net excess supply of foreign currency, alleviated by a combination of reserve gain and appreciation. According to the un-weighted EMP, during this period Indian economy experienced, on average, a 7 per cent combined nominal currency appreciation and gains in international reserve holdings. This also coincides with the period of Great Moderation in the global economy during which all EMEs, in general, experienced nominal currency appreciation and massive accumulation of international reserves.

The downward/negative trend in the EMPs through the early and mid-2000s gets interrupted by a sharp upward movement between 2008Q2 and 2009Q1—the period of global economic and financial turbulence centering around the collapse of Lehman Brothers in the US. Between 2008Q1 and 2008Q4, India went from an average 10 per cent combined nominal appreciation and gains in international reserve holdings to a 14 per cent combined nominal depreciation and international reserve loss. This is quite comparable to the EMP of other EMEs who during the same period went from an average 10 per cent combined nominal appreciation and gains in international reserves holdings to a 20 per cent combined nominal depreciation and international reserve loss (Aizenman et al. 2012).

Like other EMEs, the EMP in India (by all three measures) came down by 2009Q2 and switched back to net nominal currency appreciation combined with hoarding international reserves. This trend continued in India till the end of 2010. Since then, however, the EMP has been on the rise again, given the massive currency depreciation that India has been experiencing in the wake of the eurozone sovereign debt crisis.

Figure 6.9 to Figure 6.11 depict the EMP indices in India for three sub-periods 1990Q1 to 1998Q3; 1998Q4 to 2004Q1; 2004Q2 to 2010Q3, based on the exchange rate regimes identified in Patnaik et al. (2011).

Clearly, positive movements in the EMP (indicating currency depreciation and reserve loss) were relatively more frequent in the first sub-period than in the second reflecting the fact that India had begun to actively accumulate reserves from late 1990s onwards. In Figure 6.10, the sharp upward movement in the EMP indices coincides with the onset of the GFC in 2008Q3.

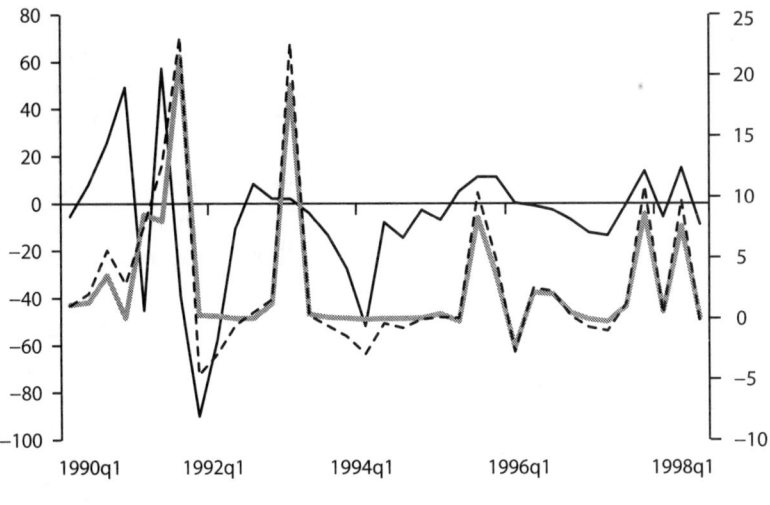

FIGURE **6.9** EMP Indices, 1990Q1–1998Q3
Source: Authors' calculations.

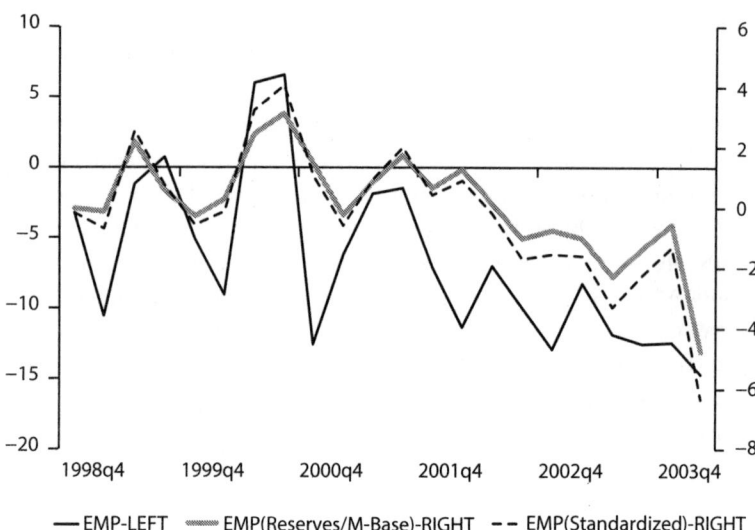

FIGURE **6.10**   EMP Indices, 1998Q4–2004Q1
Source: Authors' calculations.

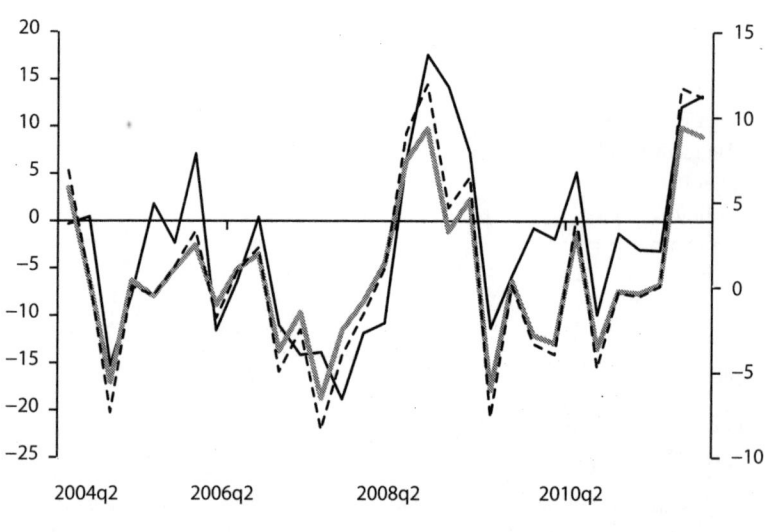

FIGURE **6.11**   EMP Indices, 2004Q2–2011Q4
Source: Authors' calculations.

B Estimation of EMP determinants

In this sub-section we use a multivariate time-series regression framework in order to estimate the link between EMP and selected explanatory variables. The objective is to quantify the statistical as well as economic significance of these factors in accounting for EMP patterns over the sample period. Following Aizenman et al. (2012), in our first specification we include trade balance to GDP ratio, share of net FDI inflows, and net portfolio equity inflows in GDP separately and we also control for year on year WPI inflation.[6] Estimation results are reported in Table 6.4. The three columns pertain to the three different EMP measures as detailed in the previous section. The last two measures are used as dependent variables in the time-series regressions as robustness check for our baseline results on column 1.

As can be seen from column 1 of Table 6.3, a deteriorating trade balance is associated with a higher EMP, a result that makes intuitive sense.

TABLE 6.3   Factors Affecting EMP in India (1990Q1–2011Q4)

Variables	EMP	EMP(Reserves/ M-Base)	EMP (Standardized)
Trade Balance	−1.420***	−0.096	−0.095
(Percentage of GDP)	[0.578]	[0.263]	[0.074]
Net FDI Inflows	−1.073	−0.137	−0.083
(Percentage of GDP)	[0.944]	[0.448]	[0.124]
Net Portfolio Equity	−1.667**	−0.661*	−0.206**
Inflows (Percentage	[0.758]	[0.366]	[0.098]
of GDP)			
WPI Inflation	−1.667	0.198	0.071
	[0.429]	[0.218]	[0.058]
Observations	60	60	60
R^2	0.1892	0.0858	0.1306

Source: Authors' calculation.

Notes: Robust standard errors in parentheses.

*, **, and *** indicate correlations significant at 10 per cent, 5 per cent, and 1 per cent, respectively

[6] We are constrained by the number of observations and hence have not added too many controls in the EMP estimations for lack of sufficient degrees of freedom.

When EMP is standardized or deflated by monetary base, the estimated coefficient of trade balance continues to have the predicted sign, but it is no longer statistically significant. An increase in net portfolio equity inflows lowers the EMP. This effect is both statistically and economically significant. For instance, a 10 percentage point rise (decline) in portfolio equity inflows (outflows) is associated with a 16.7 percentage point lower EMP when measured using the un-weighted index. The association between EMP and equity flows is also robust to the normalization of reserves by monetary base as well as standardization of the EMP index. Neither WPI inflation nor the share of net FDI inflows in GDP seems to have any significant impact on the EMP over the sample period.[7]

We had also incorporated percentage change in stock market returns (BSE Index) as well as the ratio of short-term external debt to GDP in the EMP estimations. Stock market returns happened to be highly correlated with WPI inflation and trade balance. When added without these two explanatory variables in the regression, stock market returns were found to be significantly associated with EMP measured using all three indices. In other words, positive changes in stock returns lower the EMP and vice versa. Quarterly data on short-term external debt is available only from 2006Q1 onwards from the Quarterly External Debt Statistics (QEDS) database maintained jointly by the BIS–IMF–World Bank. When added to the estimation, external debt was found to be negatively associated with EMP—a lower short-term external debt ratio increases the EMP, but the effect was found to be statistically significant only for the un-weighted EMP index. These results are not reported here for brevity but are available upon request. Our results, thus, primarily highlight the importance of portfolio equity flows and also stock market returns to some extent, in accounting for EMP in India from 1990Q1 to 2011Q4.

IV. Intervention and Sterilization by the RBI

A RBI's Intervention in the Foreign Exchange Market

As discussed in sections III and IV, India has had an active foreign exchange management policy, with active intervention by the RBI in the foreign exchange market and very large growth in foreign exchange reserves,

---

[7] We also conducted the estimation using Newey-West standard errors and results came out to be the same.

even though India formally moved to market-determined exchange rate system in 1993. According to RBI's stated objective, these foreign exchange interventions are aimed at ironing out the excessive volatility of exchange rate, and not necessarily to defend any particular value of the rupee. However, the sustained buildup of reserves since the early 2000s contradicts this argument. Foreign exchange reserves climbed from around $150 billion in mid-2005 to over $300 billion in mid-2010, a doubling in just five years, making India one of the largest reserve-holding countries in the world. Management of exchange rate volatility would imply that reserve holdings do not change much over a period of time.

Both the dramatic rise in reserves as well as the monthly intervention data (Figure 6.12) indicate substantial and sustained US dollar purchases by the RBI, and sales of the Indian currency in the foreign exchange market. In other words, the RBI has purchased significantly more US dollars than it has sold since April 1997, thereby intervening in the foreign exchange market in an asymmetric manner to prevent the rupee from appreciating sharply. India also had a current account deficit in the BOP from late 1990s onwards, implying that the official purchases of foreign exchange were offsetting the substantial private capital inflows into the economy. These capital inflows are in turn related to partial relaxation of capital account restrictions, one part of the macroeconomic trilemma. Hence, maintaining a relatively open capital account required the RBI to intervene actively in the foreign exchange market to prevent the resultant rupee appreciation.

Next, we test the validity of the hypothesis that the central bank in India has intervened in an asymmetric manner in the foreign exchange market. Following Pontines and Rajan (2011) and Srinivasan et al. (2008), we assume that the central bank controls a proxy measure of intervention defined as the percentage change in foreign exchange reserves (R_t). The central bank intervenes in the foreign exchange market to minimize the following loss function.

$$L_t = \frac{1}{2}\left(R_t - R^*\right)^2 + \frac{\phi}{2}\left(\left(\tilde{\varepsilon}_t - \varepsilon^*\right)^2 + \frac{\theta}{3}\left(\tilde{\varepsilon}_t - \varepsilon^*\right)^3\right) \qquad (7)$$

which can be rewritten as

$$L_t = \frac{1}{2}\left(R_t - R^*\right)^2 + \frac{\phi}{2}\left(\tilde{\varepsilon}_t - \varepsilon^*\right)^2 + \frac{\phi\theta}{6}\left(\tilde{\varepsilon}_t - \varepsilon^*\right)^3$$

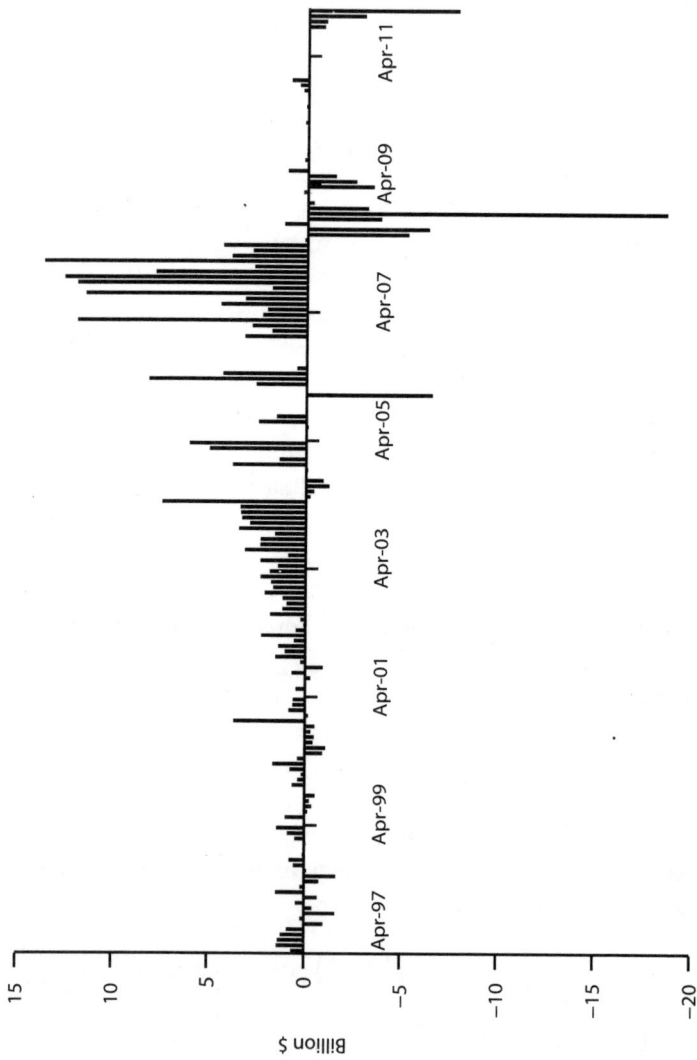

FIGURE 6.12 Net Sale or Purchase of US Dollar by RBI.
Source: Database of the Indian Economy, Reserve Bank of India.

Here $\tilde{\varepsilon}$ is the percentage change in exchange rate with the exchange rate being defined as the foreign currency price of the domestic currency. The central bank is concerned with deviation of reserves as well as the exchange rate from their respective target values R^* and ε^* with $\phi > 0$ being the relative weight the central bank puts on stabilizing exchange rate. With India not following a preannounced band or target for the exchange rate, is assumed to equal zero. The first quadratic term on the right hand side implies that the central bank's loss increases with deviation of any size and direction. While drawing down of reserves raises a country's vulnerability to external shocks, accumulation of reserves has associated costs such as cost of sterilization. Similarly, the second term indicates that the central bank is cognizant about the dangers of sharp appreciation as well as depreciation. Exchange rate depreciations trigger fears of financial distress, especially in countries where financial markets are vulnerable. In contrast, exchange rate appreciation can result in misallocation of resources between tradeables and nontradeables and fear of excessive credit booms.

Now, if $\theta = 0$ the right most term drops out and the central bank is equally concerned about an appreciation $(\tilde{\varepsilon} > 0)$ or depreciation $(\tilde{\varepsilon} < 0)$ as either would raise the value of the loss function. However, $\theta \neq 0$ introduces an asymmetry in the loss function as appreciation and depreciation have a differential impact on the value of the loss function. A positive θ implies that the value of the central bank's loss function is higher in case of an appreciation and lower in case of depreciation compared to the case where if $\theta = 0$. Such a central bank would resist appreciation and adopt a 'hands-off' approach in case of depreciation. Conversely, a negative θ results in central bank resisting depreciation and adopt a hands-off approach in case of appreciation.

The central bank faces a trade-off between stabilizing reserves and exchange rate simultaneously, as interventions can reduce the extent of exchange rate deviation.

$$\tilde{\varepsilon}_t - \varepsilon^* = \alpha_0 + \alpha_1 R_t + \eta_t \tag{8}$$

where $\alpha_1 > 0$ and η_t is independent and identically distributed with zero mean and variance σ_s^2. Minimizing equation (7) by choosing R subject to the constraint given in equation (8) yields the following optimality condition.

$$R_t = R^* - (\phi\alpha_1)\tilde{\varepsilon}_t - \frac{\phi\theta}{2}\alpha_1\tilde{\varepsilon}_t^2 \qquad (9)$$

Following Pontines and Rajan (2011), the optimality condition can be altered to an empirically testable reduced form

$$R_t = \beta_0 + \beta_1\tilde{\varepsilon}_t + \beta_2\tilde{\varepsilon}_t^2 + \upsilon_t \qquad (10)$$

where $\beta_1 = -\phi\alpha_1$ and $\beta_2 = -\frac{\phi\theta}{2}\alpha_1$ are the reduced form parameters.

The reduced form parameters provide information on the degree of asymmetry in exchange rate stabilization with $\theta = \frac{2\beta_2}{\beta_1}$.

To empirically estimate equation (10) we use monthly data from April 1994 to December 2011. The data is sourced from RBI's Database on the Indian Economy. The dependent variable R_t is defined as $(\Delta \log R_t)*100$ while $\tilde{\varepsilon}_t$ refers to $(\Delta \log \varepsilon_t)*100$. While the data from April 1997 points to actual RBI intervention, the data prior to April 1997 refers to changes in reserves, and hence are inclusive of valuation changes.

Zeileis et al. (2010) argue that the exchange rate regime in India has evolved considerably during the last two decades. Despite India announcing a move to a market-determined exchange rate system in 1993, the rupee continued to be tightly pegged to the US dollar through most of the subsequent period. It was only 2004 onwards that India moved to a basket peg. Based on Zeileis et al. (2010), we identify four sub-periods: Phase-I: April 1993 to August 1998; Phase-II: September 1998 to March 2004; Phase-III: April 2004 to May 2008; and Phase-IV: June 2008 to December 2011.[8]

We use the Generalized Method of Moments (GMM) to estimate Equation 10. The orthogonality conditions implied by the inter-temporal optimization and rational expectations paradigm make the GMM

---

[8] Zeileis et al. (2010) further subdivides Phase-I into two periods, April 1993 to March 1995 and March 1995 to August 1998, with the rupee being tightly pegged to the US dollar in the first sub-period while witnessing greater flexibility in the second sub-period. However, in our analysis due to absence of higher frequency data on reserves, we are forced to combine these two periods to ensure adequate degrees of freedom.

approach appealing. Moreover, the GMM approach does not require strong assumptions about the distribution of shocks. We follow Hansen (1982) and use an optimal weighting estimate of the covariance matrix, which accounts for auto-correlation and heteroskedasticity in the error term. We employ a variable lag Newey-West estimate of the covariance matrix.

In the GMM estimation, a larger set of instruments improves the estimation performance by including more moment restrictions. However, in relatively small samples, this comes at the cost of the precision of the weighting matrix. Hence, in our analysis the optimal set of instruments is decided by the Hansen (1982) over-identifying restriction test (*J*-statistics) with a rejection of these restrictions indicating that some of the variables fail to satisfy the orthogonality conditions. We use 12 lags of R_t and $\tilde{\varepsilon}_t$, the current value of federal funds rate and its eight lags as instruments.

The estimates of the intervention reaction function and the asymmetric preference parameter are reported in Table 6.4. The *J*-statistic

TABLE 6.4 Estimates of Policy Preference (Dependent variable: Percentage change in reserves)

	Apr 1993 to Aug 1998	Sep 1998 to Mar 2004	Apr 2004 to May 2008	Jun 2008 to Dec 2011
	Phase-I	Phase-II	Phase-III	Phase-IV
β_0	−0.023	0.864***	1.138**	0.707***
	[0.035]	[0.026]	[0.05]	[0.033]
β_1	−0.509***	−3.366***	−0.630***	−1.410***
	[0.069]	[0.221]	[0.120]	[0.03]
β_2	0.053	−2.164***	−0.243***	−0.377***
	[0.034]	[0.654]	[0.055]	[0.087]
θ	0.208	1.286***	0.771***	0.535***
	[0.152]	[0.040]	[0.013]	[0.004]
Observations	49	67	50	43
J-statistics	9.38	10.19	9.93	11.55

Source: Authors' calculations.

Notes: Standard errors in parentheses.

*, **, and *** indicate correlations significant at 10 per cent, 5 per cent, and 1 per cent, respectively.

indicates that the null hypothesis of valid over-identifying restrictions cannot be rejected at the conventional significance level. Of primary interest to us is the parameter, θ, which indicates the extent of asymmetric intervention. As can be seen from Table 6.1, barring Phase-I, θ is positive and economically and statistically significant across all specifications, implying that the RBI has been intervening in an asymmetric manner during appreciation and depreciation pressures since 1998.[9]

Moreover, θ varies across the various phases, indicating shifting weight on the extent of asymmetric intervention. The parameter, θ, takes the highest value during Phase-II indicating the central bank's strong concern for appreciation of the rupee. Interestingly, despite India's reserves increasing by nearly \$196 billion during Phase-III, compared to an increase of \$87 billion in Phase-II, the parameter, θ, takes a higher value in Phase-II. This could be driven by the fact that the dependent variable in our estimation is the growth rate of reserves, rather than the absolute increase in reserves. While reserves grew by 165 per cent over Phase-III, Phase-II witnessed a growth of around 287 per cent due to a low base at the beginning of the phase. Finally, as discussed in Section IV, in Phase-III the rupee experienced greater volatility compared to Phase-II.

The positive and significant value of θ in Phase IV indicates that the asymmetric intervention continued even during this period, although the extent was lower than previous phases. The lower coefficient was driven by the fact that India witnessed limited pressures of appreciation during this phase as rising risk averseness of international investors and slowing down of domestic growth rate mitigated the capital flows. During the third and fourth quarter of 2008 and again since the third quarter of 2011, the rupee witnessed strong depreciation pressures. The central bank allowed the rupee to depreciate during these periods by intervening in a very limited manner in the foreign exchange market. This limited intervention by the central bank at the time of depreciation pressure also contributed to a positive and significant value of θ.

Sterilization of RBI's Intervention in the Foreign Exchange Market

In the pursuit of managing the macroeconomic trilemma, the RBI intervened actively in the foreign exchange market to ensure currency

---

[9] The standard errors of θ are obtained using the delta method.

stability, rapidly accumulated reserves, and also sterilized its intervention in order to ensure monetary independence.[10] As mentioned in Section III, from 2000Q1 to 2008Q4, the RBI actively purchased foreign currency assets in order to prevent the rupee from appreciating in the face of strong capital inflows. Between 2000 and 2003 RBI sterilized the interventions [increase in net foreign assets (NFAs)] so as not to allow any inflationary impact on monetary policy, by selling off government bonds (decline in NDA) and absorbing the excess liquidity from the system. However, 2003–04 onwards, the rising fiscal costs of sterilization forced the RBI to only partially sterilize its foreign exchange interventions. In this context, we try to find out to what extent the RBI has succeeded in limiting the impact of international reserve accumulation on the money supply and maintaining monetary autonomy in the face of large inflows of capital into India against the backdrop of financial liberalization.

To this effect we estimate a basic sterilization equation wherein the change in NDA is regressed on the change in NFA. In this regression, the magnitude of the estimated coefficient of NFA is an indicator of the extent to which the RBI has managed to insulate the money supply from international reserve accumulation. We also include the lagged dependent variable and lagged industrial production (12 month lag of log IIP) to control for other factors influencing the growth of money supply in the economy. We use monthly data from the RBI database and divide the sample into sub-periods primarily based on the exchange rate regimes identified in Patnaik et al. (2011). The sub-periods are: Jan 1990 to Sep 1998 (rupee pegged to the dollar); Oct 1998 to Mar 2004 (rupee moving to a basket peg with relatively more flexibility); Apr 2004 to Aug 2010 (higher flexibility in rupee).

---

[10] Intervention is usually defined as the official purchase and sale of foreign currencies that a country's monetary authorities undertake in order to influence future currency movements. In the case of unsterilized intervention, monetary authority buys (sells) foreign exchange or foreign assets due to which its monetary base increases (decreases) by the amount of the purchase (sale). On the other hand, through sterilized intervention the central bank can insulate the domestic monetary base from the effect of purchase (sale) of foreign assets by undertaking a corresponding amount of sale (purchase) of domestic or local currency bonds.

TABLE **6.5**   Effect of Net Foreign Assets (NFA) Accumulation on Net
Domestic Assets (NDA) (Dependent variable: Change in NDA)

Variables	Jan 1990 to Sep 1998	Oct 1998 to Mar 2004	Apr 2004 to Aug 2010
Change in NFA	−0.208	−0.609***	−0.269*
	[0.231]	[0.128]	[0.152]
Lagged change in NDA	0.226***	−0.052	0.158*
	[0.094]	[0.187]	[0.094]
Lagged change in log of IIP	−11829.18	−9133.15	115470.10***
	[9543.64]	[10163.47]	[31567.53]
Constant	878.367	1523.943	4227.436**
	[607.92]	[1005.134]	[1929.542]
Observations	41	66	76
R-Squared	0.0994	0.2122	0.2487

Source: Authors' calculations.

Notes: Newey-West Standard errors in parentheses.

*, **, and *** indicate correlations significant at 10 per cent, 5 per cent, and 1 per cent, respectively.

As can be seen from Table 6.5, the estimated coefficient of change in NFA or the sterilization coefficient is statistically significant only in the last two sub-periods and has the highest magnitude (0.61) in the second sub-period which continues from the end of 1998 to the middle of 2004. This implies that almost 60 per cent of the rise in NFA was offset by corresponding fall in NDA through RBI's sale of government bonds. However, the magnitude of NFA goes down significantly in the third sub-period, during which, less than 30 per cent of the rise in NFA seems to have been sterilized by a concomitant decline in NDA. Thus, post-2004, the RBI has, on average, let the money supply grow in the face of rising NFA holdings and relaxation of capital controls.

Thus, monetary autonomy seems to have been compromised in the later part of 2000s, during which capital account restrictions were relaxed significantly and India joined the ranks of several other EMEs who began accumulating massive international reserves—the so-called period of Great Moderation. This is also consistent with our previous finding in Section III (see Table 6.3 and Figure 6.6) that the period 2004–2009 witnessed a loss of monetary independence in the face of rising ERS, capital account openness, and only partial sterilization by the RBI.

A partial resurgence of monetary independence happened only after 2010, when exchange rate became more flexible and capital inflows into the economy slowed down owing to renewed global economic turmoil against the backdrop of the eurozone crisis.

V. India's Reserve Management

As has been described in Section 5.1, India's reserve accumulation has been driven by the central bank's policy of leaning against the wind. Reserve accretion was a result of net capital inflows being greater than the current account deficit, with the central bank accumulating the excess flows. The build-up of reserves meant that India was comfortably placed on the various traditional reserve adequacy indicators—import cover, ratio of reserves to short-term debt, and ratio of reserves to monetary aggregates—at the time of the sub-prime crisis in 2007.[11]

However, since the outbreak of the sub-prime crisis in 2007, India has been witnessing a rising current account deficit and slowing capital inflows. The widening of the current account deficit has been driven by sluggish demand for Indian exports by advanced countries as well as high crude oil prices. Increase in risk aversion and deterioration of macroeconomic fundamentals have resulted in a slackening of capital inflows. In fact, a cumulative current account deficit between 2008–09Q1 and 2011–12Q3 of $164.3 billion and net capital inflows of $168 billion over the same period meant that the latter was just barely able to finance the deficit. This, in turn, kept foreign exchange reserves largely stagnant over this period, resulting in significant deterioration of reserve cover. In fact, as can be seen from figures 6.13a and 6.13b,

---

[11] The import cover or the number of months of imports that can be financed if all foreign inflows cease, is an important indicator for countries subject to shocks to the current account, and the balance of payment is dominated by the current account. The short-term debt cover served as a good indicator of crisis risk for most crisis episodes except the recent GFC. Similar to the import cover, the short-term debt cover is based on the formulation that countries should be able to fulfill their immediate debt obligations even if they are cut off from the market for an entire year. The monetary aggregate metric captures short-term foreign currency debt amortization and other forms of net foreign currency exposure of the domestic financial system as well as the threat of a domestic bank run under a convertible currency.

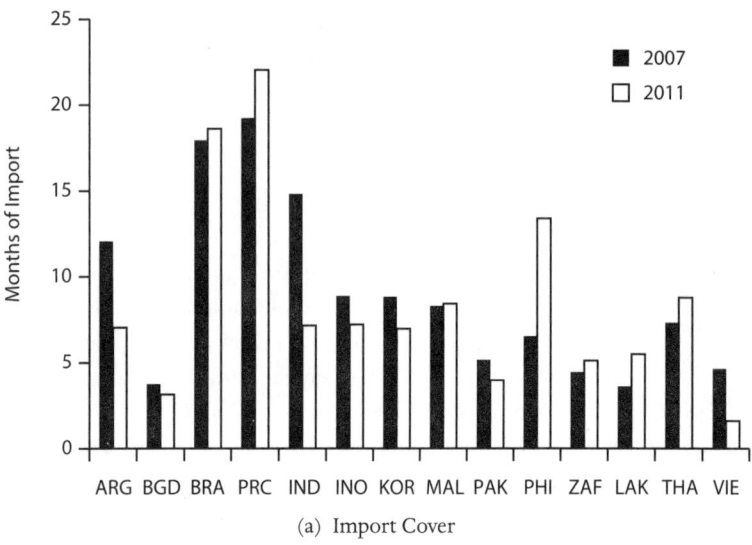

(a) Import Cover

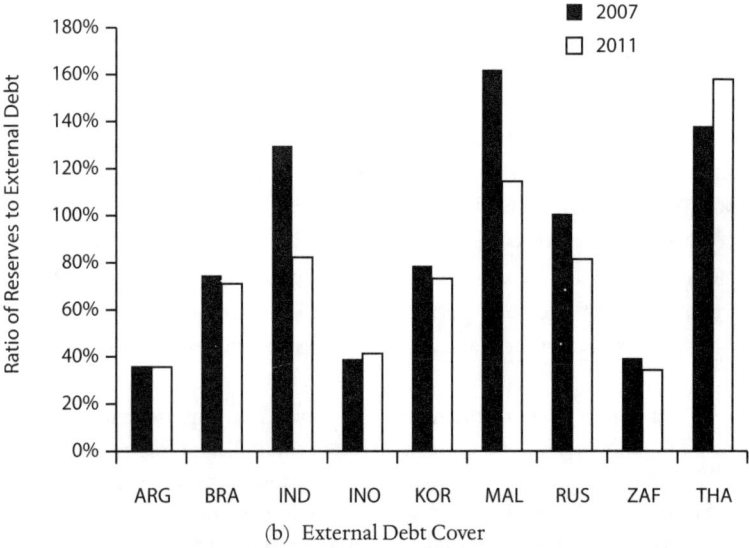

(b) External Debt Cover

FIGURE 6.13 Reserve Adequacy Measures in Selected Emerging Economies
Source: Authors' calculations and *World Development Indicators*, World Bank.
ARG=Argentina; BGD= Bangladesh; BRA=Brazil; PRC=People's Republic of
China; IND=India; INO=Indonesia; KOR=Republic of Korea; LAK= Sri Lanka;
MAL=Malaysia; PAK= Pakistan; PHI=Philippines; RUS=Russian Federation;
THA=Kingdom of Thailand; VIE= Viet Nam; ZAF=South Africa.

between 2007 and 2011, India witnessed one of the highest erosion of reserve cover across a spectrum of emerging economies.

Figures 6.14a and 6.14b trace out the evolution of the various reserve adequacy indicators. India's reserve cover reached a peak around 2008–09Q2, and has been declining steadily since. While at the end of June 2008, India's reserves could fund 136 per cent of India's total external debt, by December 2011, the reserve cover had dropped to only 87 per cent. More importantly, while in June 2011, India's reserves were almost eight times its holding of short-term debt (original maturity), this had halved to less than four times in December 2011. Rising import bill and stagnant reserves also meant that the import cover of reserves nearly halved from 15.1 months to 7.8 months over the same period.

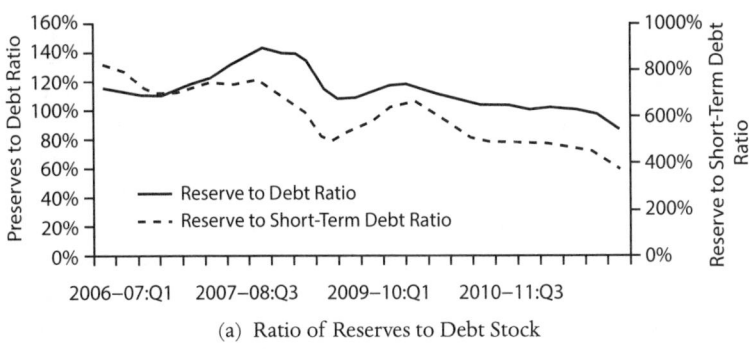

(a) Ratio of Reserves to Debt Stock

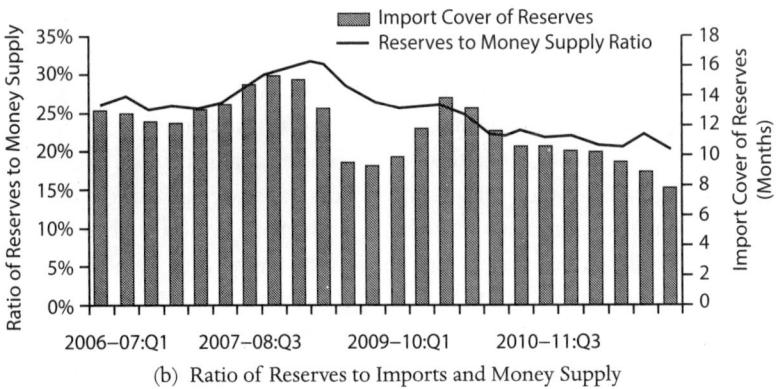

(b) Ratio of Reserves to Imports and Money Supply

FIGURE 6.14 Tracing the Reserve Adequacy Measures in India
Source: Authors' calculations and Database on the Indian Economy, Reserve Bank of India.

The monetary aggregate metric, measured as the ratio of reserves to broad money also deteriorated from around 31.5 per cent in June 2008 to around 20 per cent in December 2011.

VI. Conclusion

There is now an emerging consensus that countries need to actively manage their capital account to avoid vulnerabilities associated with financial crisis. While it is widely agreed that capital flows aid growth by providing external capital to sustain an excess of investment over domestic savings, in the recent years, many emerging markets, including India, have experienced significant volatility in the quantum of capital flows. Such volatility complicates macroeconomic management challenges by feeding into real exchange rate misalignment, excesses in credit market, asset price booms and busts, and exacerbating overall financial fragility. Furthermore, the diverse objectives of robust growth rate, sustainable current account deficit, competitive exchange rate, adequate external capital to finance investment, moderate inflation, minimizing financial fragilities, and maintaining adequate reserves also need to be balanced in an era of volatile capital flows. All these trade-offs further reiterate the need to actively manage capital flows. While capital controls can be effective, they are generally not foolproof, and are vulnerable to leakages through financial engineering. In such circumstances, a gamut of policy measures has to be used to ensure financial stability of the economy.

In this chapter we analyse India's experience in negotiating the trade-offs involved in capital account management. We find that to minimize risks associated with financial fragilities, India has adopted a calibrated and gradual approach towards opening of the capital account, prioritizing the liberalization of certain flows. India has also resorted to a multiple instrument approach while dealing with capital inflows. The overall policy architecture encompasses active management of capital flows, increasingly flexible exchange rate regime with the RBI intervening from time to time, sterilization of these interventions through multiple instruments like MSS bonds and CRR, and building up of a stockpile of reserves.

Using empirical methods, we find that instead of adopting corner solutions, India has embraced an intermediate approach in managing the conflicting objectives of the well-known financial trilemma, balancing the three policy objectives as per the demands of the macroeconomic situation. We find that in recent years there has been a discernible shift towards greater monetary policy autonomy to tackle growing domestic inflationary pressure. This has been balanced with greater flexibility of the exchange rate, which has acted as a shock absorber in a period of volatile capital flows.

Our results also indicate that the intermediate approach has been associated with an asymmetric intervention in the foreign exchange market by the RBI, with the objective of resisting pressures of currency appreciation, resulting in large-scale reserve accumulation. However, sterilization of this asymmetric intervention has been partial at times, leading to rapid increase in monetary aggregates and fuelling inflation. Finally, we conclude that while the greater flexibility in exchange rate since 2007, has allowed the pursuit of a more independent monetary policy and has permitted the exchange rate to act as a shock absorber, the hands-off approach has resulted in reserves remaining virtually stagnant since 2007, leading to a significant deterioration in the reserve adequacy measures.

REFERENCES

Aghion, P., P. Bacchetta, R. Rancière, and K. Rogoff. 2009. 'Exchange rate volatility and productivity growth: The role of financial development', *Journal of Monetary Economics* 56 (4): 494–513.

Aizenman, J., M. Chinn, and H. Ito. 2010a. 'The financial crisis, rethinking of the global financial architecture, and the trilemma', *Asian Development Bank Institute Working Paper No. 213*, April.

———. 2010b. 'The emerging global financial architecture: Tracing and evaluating the new patterns of the trilemma's configurations', *Journal of International Money and Finance* 29 (4): 615–41.

Aizenman, J., and M. Hutchison. 2010. 'Exchange market pressure and absorption by international reserves: Emerging markets and fear of reserve loss during the 2008-09 crisis', *NBER Working Paper 16260*.

Aizenman, J., J. Lee, and V. Sushko. 2012, 'From the great moderation to the global crisis: Exchange market pressure in the 2000s', *Open Economies Review* 2 (4): 597–621.

Aizenman, J., and R. Sengupta. 2013. 'The financial trilemma in China and a comparative analysis with India', *Pacific Economic Review* 18 (2): 123–46.

Chinn, M., and H. Ito. 2008. 'A new measure of financial openness', *Journal of Comparative Policy Analysis* 10 (3): 307–20.

Edwards, S. 2007. 'Capital controls, sudden stops, and current account reversals', in S. Edwards (ed), *Capital Controls and Capital Flows in Emerging Economies: Policies, Practices and Consequences*, pp. 73–120. University of Chicago Press.

Forbes, K. 2012. 'The 'Big C': Identifying and mitigating contagion', *MIT Sloan School Working Paper 4970-12*.

Frankel, J. 2009. 'New estimation of China's exchange rate regime', *Pacific Economic Review* 14 (3): 346–60.

Frankel, J.A., and S.J. Wei. 1994. 'Yen bloc or dollar bloc? Exchange rate policies of the East Asian Economies', in T. Ito and A.O. Krueger (eds), *Macroeconomic Linkages: Savings, Exchange Rates, and Capital Flows*, pp. 295–333. University of Chicago Press.

Frankel, J. 2009. 'New estimation of China's exchange rate regime', *Pacific Economic Review* 14 (3): 346–60.

Girton, L., and D. Roper. 1977. 'A monetary model of exchange market pressure applied to the postwar Canadian experience', *American Economic Review* 67 (4): 537–48.

Hansen, Lars Peter. 1982. 'Large sample properties of generalized method of moments estimators', *Econometrica* 50 (4): 1029–54.

Hutchison, M., R. Sengupta, and N. Singh. 2011. 'India's trilemma: Financial liberalization, exchange rates and monetary policy', *World Economy* 35 (1): 3–18.

IMF. 2012. 'Liberalizing capital flows and managing outflows', International Monetary Fund, Washington D.C. Available at http://www.imf.org/external/np/pp/eng/2012/031312.pdf. Accesed in January 2014.

Johnson, S., J.D. Ostry, and A. Subramanian. 2007. 'The prospects for sustained growth in Africa: Benchmarking the constraints', *IMF Working Paper 07/52*.

Kohli, R. 2011. 'India's experience in navigating the trilemma: Do capital controls help?' *ICRIER Working Paper 257*, June.

Kose, M.A., E. Prasad, K. Rogoff, and S.J. Wei. 2009. 'Financial globalization: A reappraisal', *IMF Staff Papers* 56 (1): 8–62.

Lane, P., and G.M. Milessi-Ferreti. 2007. 'The external wealth of nations mark II: Revised and extended estimates of foreign assets and liabilities: 1970-2004', *Journal of International Economics* 73 (2): 223–50.

Mohan, R., and M. Kapur. 2009. 'Managing the impossible trinity: Volatile capital flows and Indian monetary policy', *Stanford Center for International Development Working Paper No. 401*.

Obstfeld, M., J.C. Shambaugh, and A.M. Taylor. 2010. 'Financial stability, the trilemma, and international reserves', *American Economic Journal: Macroeconomics* 2 (2): 57–94.

Patnaik, I., A. Shah, A. Sethy, and V. Balasubramaniam. 2011. 'The exchange rate regime in Asia: From crisis to crisis', *International Review of Economics and Finance* 20 (3): 32–43.

Patnaik, I., and A. Shah. 2011. 'Did the Indian capital controls work as a tool of macroeconomic policy?' *NIPFP Working Paper No. 87*.

Planning Commission. 2009. *A Hundred Small Steps: Committee on Financial Sector Reforms.* New Delhi: Sage Publications India.

Pontines, V., and R. Rajan. 2011. 'Foreign exchange intervention and reserve accumulation in emerging Asia: Is there evidence of fear of appreciation?' *Economic Letters* 111 (2): 252–5.

Prasad, E.S., and R.G. Rajan. 2008. 'A pragmatic approach to capital account liberalization', *IZA Discussion Paper No. 3475*.

Prasad, E.S., R. Rajan, and A. Subramanian. 2007. 'Foreign capital and economic growth', *Brookings Papers on Economic Activity* 1: 153–230.

Rajan, R.G., and A. Subramanian. 2005. 'What undermines aids impact on growth?' *IMF Working Paper 05/126*.

RBI. 2006. 'Report of the committee on fuller capital account convertibility', Reserve Bank of India.

Reddy, Y.V. 2008. 'Management of the capital account in India: Some perspectives', *Reserve Bank of India Bulletin*, February.

Sen Gupta, A., and G. Manjhi. 2012. 'Negotiating the trilemma: The Indian experience', *Global Economy Journal* 12 (1): 1–20.

Sen Gupta, A., and R. Sengupta. 2013. 'Management of capital flows in India', *South Asia Working Paper Series No. 17*, Asian Development Bank, Manila.

Srinivasan, N., V. Mahambare, and M. Ramachandran. 2008. 'Preference asymmetry and international reserve accretion in India', *Applied Economics Letters* 16 (15): 1543–6.

Zeileis, A., A. Shah, and I. Patnaik. 2010. 'Testing, monitoring, and dating structural changes in exchange rate regimes', *Computational Statistics and Data Analysis* 54 (6): 1696–706.

7

LUIZ AWAZU PEREIRA DA SILVA
RICARDO EYER HARRIS*

Sailing through the Global Financial Storm

Brazil's Recent Experience with Monetary and Macro Prudential Policies to Lean Against the Financial Cycle and Deal with Systemic Risks

Introduction

The global financial crisis of 2008–12 prompted a renewal of both analytical thinking and policy practices regarding the interaction and mutual complementarity between monetary and prudential regula-

* The views expressed are those of the authors and do not necessarily reflect those of the Central Bank of Brazil. We thank participants at the International Monetary Fund-World Bank Conference in Bali, Indonesia, November 2011 and the International Monetary Fund Article IV Mission in May 2012 for useful interactions and comments. This chapter is an updated version that originally appeared in a World Bank Study, 'Dealing with the Challenges of Macro Financial Linkages in Emerging Markets', in Otaviano Canuto and Swati Ghosh (2013).

tory policies, given the simultaneous objectives of macroeconomic and financial stability (Box 7.1).

Many of these issues were present before the global financial crisis, but have been thoroughly revisited since, essentially because (a) overwhelming evidence showed that macro financial linkages allowed for the buildup of significant financial risk in an environment of macroeconomic stability without adequate regulation; (b) analysts realized that the cost of mopping up after crises such as that of 2008 is extraordinarily high, suggesting that prevention is preferred to remedies; and (c) destabilizing side effects resulted from the unprecedented injections of global liquidity by monetary authorities of advanced economies, exacerbating sudden floods of capital into emerging economies.

Box 7.1   The Global Financial Crisis: Origin and Policy Responses in
Emerging and Advanced Economies

Long before the crisis—since the mid-1990s—Brazil had adopted standard macroeconomic policies, including an inflation-targeting framework, to control inflation and anchor expectations. Fiscal policies were strengthened to ensure that markets perceived debt dynamics as sustainable. Together with many (though not all) emerging markets, Brazil opted for a flexible exchange rate regime as a first buffer against capital market mood swings and volatility. Last but not least, Brazil did not embark on the fashionable financial deregulation movement of the 1990s, keeping a conservative prudential regulatory framework for its financial sectors, which remained tightly supervised and well capitalized.

Advanced economies did not follow the same path, perhaps because of the absence of emergencies, less pressure—at that time—from markets or rating agencies, and a self-reassuring belief in their own singularity. In those countries, private and public debt increased, sometimes beyond existing institutional fiscal pacts such as the Maastricht treaty in the Eurozone. Financial deregulation was conducted with great confidence on the capacity to dissipate risk using sophisticated derivative products that priced financial instruments very well, except under tail events. Last but not the least, the monetary policy response to shocks in the United States (for example, the burst of the Internet bubble or the 9/11 attack) managed to produce quick recoveries. However, they relied on prolonged periods of low-interest rates that did not translate into higher inflation because of the concomitant disinflationary pressure of the People's Republic of China's (PRC's) exports of durable goods. Nevertheless, financial conditions were eased by enough to conceivably trigger excessive risk-taking behavior by both lenders and borrowers. In that context, in addition to agency problems, classic Minsky problems of financial market behavior were exacerbated, including procyclicality, very high leverage, deterioration of lending standards, and excessive credit financing increasingly riskier borrowers.

In many advanced economies, excessive credit (including in the housing market) allowed for a pattern of arguably unsustainable consumption financed by debt. Current account deterioration was large enough to trigger the debate about global imbalances. The benign view* was that these current account deficits and surpluses were a win-win situation for both developing and developed countries. Surplus developing economies would benefit from deep developed consumer markets to export their goods and services, and deficits could always be financed by a host of new financial instruments. The opposite view# was that this was an unstable equilibrium. In addition, lax macro prudential regulation of financial sectors reacted with lags and/or too timidly to the accumulation of risks. And, since many financial institutions were global by definition, risks would cross borders and spread potential financial instability worldwide. The 'benign view' prevailed and the crisis eventually struck, beginning in mid-2007 (the subprime debacle in the United States) and continuing until the Lehman Brothers spike in mid-September 2008.

The crisis caught emerging and advanced economies in different positions along the spectrum of macro and financial fragility: the former were ending a cycle of macro policy consolidation and had stronger financial sectors that had been tested through crises; the latter were at the peak of a cycle of credit-fueled growth and had allowed their financial sectors to become highly vulnerable to shifts in confidence and changes in asset price valuation in their balance sheets. Since policymakers in advanced economies had thoroughly studied the Great Depression, liquidity provision to troubled banks was swift and massive. Together with a first round of fiscal stimulus, that response avoided an even greater collapse of interconnected global markets. Happily, for the first time, many emerging markets—Brazil was a case in point—could also implement countercyclical policies to support activity. But, after a rebound, advanced economies faced a dwindling recovery by the end of 2010. Additional fiscal policy action then met local political economy constraints in the United States and the Eurozone, as well as bond market suspicion of how advanced economies' debt stocks would remain marketable (at sustainable prices) in an environment of prolonged

(Cont'd)

Box 7.1. (*Cont'd*)

mediocre growth. With all advanced economies at the zero bound of their monetary policy rates, unconventional monetary easing emerged as the option of last resort, first with the US quantitative easing and (much) later with the European Central Bank's long-term refinancing operations (LTROs). In that context, global liquidity increased and resulted in significantly higher-than-usual capital inflows into emerging markets. As economic recovery continued to lag in advanced countries, monetary policy remained loose. Global excessive liquidity became a major driving force behind recent capital flows into emerging markets in general and Brazil in particular.

Notes: * For example, Cooper (2007), Dooley et al. (2009), and Caballero et al. (2008).

For example, as early as 2005; Roubini and Setser (2005), then Obstfeld and Rogoff (2009), and Borio and Disyatat (2011).

Going back to where it began, by the end of the 1990s and early 2000s the world economy was enjoying the so-called Great Moderation, partly due to the progressive—and successful—adoption by central banks of flexible inflation-targeting monetary policy framework. The perceived attraction of inflation targeting was to deliver low and stable inflation while minimizing growth fluctuations, relying on a simple policy instrument—namely, a short-term interest rate. At the same time, the framework took advantage of flexible exchange rates to smooth external pressures, thus avoiding the recognized pitfalls of pegged or fixed regimes and turning reserve accumulation into a healthy precaution rather than an absolute necessity. Provided that one's 'house was in order', this combination brought credibility and stability to macroeconomic policies and policy makers. The fact that the adoption of inflation targeting with flexible exchange rates was so widespread (despite notable holdouts) seemed to support, on a global as opposed to a merely local scale, a virtuous cycle of aggregate demand growth with low inflation and fewer threats to balance-of-payment positions. Meanwhile, regarding financial stability, a neat separation principle seemed to hold: regulators recommended the use of a set of well-tested and traditional microprudential instruments to ensure that financial intermediaries performed their function without engaging in practices that could undermine the robustness of the system. Things seemed to be going so well that central banking was becoming a boring business to the point that some countries even chose to convert to the model of split institutional responsibilities (that is, to separate the two objectives of price stability and financial stability)—and, in so doing, also split into separate entities the regulatory-supervisory and lender-of-last-resort functions.

The only nagging doubt was about how central banks should deal with asset price bubbles. The discussion was motivated by the late-1990s episodes of stock market booms and busts, after Japan's property market problems in the late 1980s. Should central banks react to rapidly rising asset prices, and, if so, how? As usual, the economics profession provided a divided answer, each side with a well-grounded rationale. One side of the divide[1] argued that higher asset prices had the propensity to enhance wealth effects transmitting into consumption and eventually consumer prices; thus it was warranted to 'lean against the wind' of asset price surges, acting in a preventive way. They also noted that financial imbalances may very well build up in an environment of stable prices; low and stable rates of inflation may even foster asset price bubbles due to excessively optimistic expectations about future economic prospects or to increased propensity to take on more risk. At a minimum, price stability should not be taken as a sufficient condition for financial stability. The opposite camp[2] claimed that pricking asset price bubbles with monetary policy instruments was bound to impact the base interest to such a degree as to do great damage to macroeconomic stability. They also argued that it is exceedingly hard to determine whether an ongoing rise in asset prices is justified by fundamentals or is a bubble. Therefore, the central banks could compromise their reputation by getting into the muddy business of attempting to identify bubbles ex ante.

In practical terms, the generally adopted protocol was to forsake any attempt to lean with the base policy rate against asset price inflation; but, if it turned out to have been a bubble, as it would prove to be by

---

[1] Mostly from the Bank for International Settlements (BIS) and, not surprisingly, from the Bank of Japan, but also Blanchard (2000), Borio and Lowe (2002), Cecchetti, Genberg et al. (2000), and Goodhart (2000).

[2] Mostly from the Anglo-Saxon academic community, for example, Bean (2003), Bernanke and Gertler (1999, 2001), Greenspan (2002), Kohn (2005), and Mishkin (2008).

eventually bursting, the solution was to clean up afterwards. The collateral damage caused by the bursting of the bubble on macroeconomic performance could presumably be remedied with a more accommodative monetary policy stance.

One could arguably detect that a partial departure from this general attitude was present when the Federal Reserve (FED), confronted with more evidence of herd behavior in stock and housing markets, tried to talk markets down[3] by suggesting that they were displaying 'irrational exuberance'. While that attempt involved a quasi-official verdict about the departure of asset prices from fundamentals, the fact that intervention remained purely verbal ultimately helped to enshrine the notion that conventional monetary policy instruments should not go out chasing asset price inflation.

But other types of nuance were later introduced into the debate, bringing the 'clean up after' camp (Mishkin 2010). closer to those advocating prevention. One key step in this direction was the realization that bubbles based on credit—as was notably the case of housing bubbles, as opposed to garden-variety stock market bubbles—might more clearly call for preventive intervention, considering the much more deleterious effects of the eventual market downturn on banks' balance sheet as compared to those of households'. The argument was that instead of getting into the tricky issue of whether increases in asset prices faithfully reflect the corresponding fundamentals, central banks should focus on the mutual interaction between asset price and credit dynamics, with one eye on the potential for unstable feedback loops and the other on their joint effect on aggregate demand.

Thus, credit connections rather than asset prices per se moved to center stage as the critical variable to observe in the rethinking of monetary and prudential-regulatory policies. After the full manifestation of the global 2008 crisis, a number of voices (CIEPR 2011) started calling

---

[3] The warning was made by Alan Greenspan during the dot com bubble on 5 December 1996:

Clearly, sustained low inflation implies less uncertainty about the future, and lower risk premiums imply higher prices of stocks and other earning assets. We can see that in the inverse relationship exhibited by price/earnings ratios and the rate of inflation in the past. But how do we know when irrational exuberance has unduly escalated asset values, which then become subject to unexpected and prolonged contractions as they have in Japan over the past decade? (Greenspan 1996)

on central banks to incorporate explicitly and systematically a financial stability objective into their reaction function, arguing that they should consider the interplay between the objectives of macroeconomic stability and financial stability. This new literature reflected a growing concern that, under lax regulation, the achievement of price stability may have been associated with an increased risk of financial instability.

In parallel, policy makers were also realizing that traditional microprudential tools had been insufficient to dampen financial risk. A number of proposals started to revisit prudential guidelines and to extend them to a larger macroeconomic dimension, with a view on the buildup of systemic risk. That was the idea behind 'macro prudential' regulation, aimed at strengthening the financial system and at encouraging more prudent lending behavior in economic upturns (for example, by raising capital requirements in a countercyclical way, to help choke off credit-related asset price bubbles in their early stages).[4] Macro prudential regulation became, naturally, the favorite candidate to fill this new role of guarding the crossroads between asset price and credit dynamics.[5]

In 2010, a paper by the Committee on the Global Financial System (CGFS) of the BIS mapped the available set of macro prudential instruments and frameworks and summarized the experiences in using them. The variety of existing tools is illustrated in Table 7.1, which organizes the various instruments according to the vulnerability they address and the financial system component they target.

The underlying idea was to use existing microprudential instruments in a more comprehensive way (that is, extend them to a macro prudential dimension) to 'lean against the financial cycle'. That implied a countercyclical calibration of these tools across all financial sector institutions. For example, during upturns in the financial cycle, regulation would increase buffers that could be used in downturns: higher capital and liquidity requirements, more stringent and forward-looking provisioning rules, limits to concentration, loan size, maximum debt-to-income levels, foreign exchange exposure, and so on. The expected result of

---

[4] The Turner Review [see Financial Services Authority (2009)], Brunnermeier et al. (2009), and BCBS (2010).

[5] See the financial regulatory agenda of the G-20 and Financial Stability Board (FSB), Committee on the Global Financial System (2010) , Galati and Moessner (2011), and IMF (2011b, 2011c).

TABLE 7.1 Macro Prudential Instruments by Vulnerability and Financial System Component

	Financial system component			
	Bank or deposit-taker		Nonbank investor	Securities market	Financial infrastructure
Vulnerability	Balance sheet*	Lending contract			
Leverage	capital ratio risk weights provisioning profit distribution restrictions credit growth cap	Loan-to-value (LTV) cap debt service/income cap maturity cap		margin/haircut limit	
Liquidity or market risk	liquidity/reserve requirements FX lending restriction currency mismatch limit open FX position limit	valuation rules (eg, MMMFs)	local currency or FX reserve requirements	central bank balance sheet operations	exchange trading
Interconnectedness	concentration limits systemic capital surcharge subsidiarisation				central counterparties (CCP)

* Capital and other balance sheet requirements also apply to insurers and pension funds, but we restrict our attention here to the types of institutions most relevant for credit intermediation.

Source: BIS (2010).

applying such brakes was that financial institutions would refrain—considering the higher costs of expanding certain components of their assets and the forward guidance provided by these messages—from engaging in excessive expansion of their lending, especially to riskier segments of the market. But the paper only alluded in passing to the possible interaction between monetary policy and macro prudential tools, listing strands of the literature that touched on how changes in the funding cost of banks would affect banks' lending behavior, or how bank capital would affect the transmission of monetary policy.

At the same time, empirical studies were carried out by the BIS and the International Monetary Fund (IMF), drawing lessons from country experiences in using macro prudential instruments. In particular, the IMF produced a comprehensive account of existing cases[6] showing that these tools were mostly introduced to reduce systemic risk, either in its time dimension and/or its cross-sectional dimension, and that they were quite effective. The study used cross-country comparisons to show that macro prudential tools have helped to dampen procyclicality of financial systems and that they do not seem to depend on the particular policy regime adopted by each country.

The global financial crisis would provide a stressful opportunity for Brazil to put to test these policy and analytical proposals.

The Effects of the Global Financial Crisis on Brazil

Brazil sailed quite well through the first acute phase of the global financial crisis. Nonetheless, the effects of the crisis were severe. After the Lehman Brothers episode, in the last quarter of 2008, trade flows contracted 6.9 per cent year-on-year (YOY); industrial production fell by 27 per cent quarter-on-quarter (QOQ); capital outflows rose by 36 per cent QOQ causing an exchange-rate depreciation spike of 32 per cent YOY; and credit growth fell by 35 per cent YOY. In one month (October 2008), trade financing fell by 30 per cent and the debt roll-over ratio went down from 167 per cent to 22 per cent. From July to October, liquidity ratios in Brazilian banks fell from 1.73 to 1.43. The Brazilian authorities took immediate action in face of the shock (Mesquita and Torós 2010). First, they addressed liquidity problems

[6] See Lim et al. (2011).

both in domestic and foreign currencies: bank reserve requirements were lowered, injecting about R$116 billion worth of liquidity (or 4 per cent of gross domestic product [GDP]) into the economy; lines of credit in foreign exchange were provided to the private sector; the central bank offered $14.5 billion (7 per cent of total international reserves at the end of 2008) in spot market auctions. Foreign exchange swap contracts to the tune of $33 billion were also offered by the central bank, helping an orderly wind-down of large foreign exchange derivatives exposures by domestic corporations (amounting to an estimated $37 billion at the end of September 2008). The second line of action was to calibrate policy instruments to provide stimulus to economic activity: the monetary policy base rate was lowered by a total of 500 basis points (bps), from 13.75 per cent per annum (p.a.) to 8.75 per cent p.a.; a number of tax breaks were put in place and the fiscal surplus target was reduced from 3.8 per cent in 2008 to 2.5 per cent of GDP in 2009; credit extension by public financial institutions rose by R$105 billion (3.3 per cent of GDP).

The response of the Brazilian economy was swift, and produced the expected V-shaped recovery pattern. Despite the strong policy-driven rebound throughout 2009, GDP growth was still zero for that calendar year, but in 2010, GDP grew 7.5 per cent YOY, domestic demand by 10.3 per cent, with private consumption expanding 7.2 per cent YOY and investment by 11.1 per cent YOY.

Meanwhile, advanced economies were struggling with their own recoveries and that initiated a second phase of the crisis. The crisis had revealed severe problems in the global banking system, which continued despite the unprecedented initial response of governments and central banks, combining fiscal stimulus, monetary expansion (with significant purchases and holding of bank debt, mortgage-backed securities (MBS), and Treasury instruments by central banks) and institutional bailouts. After an initial recovery in the second half of 2009 and early in 2010, the FED resumed its balance sheet expansion in August 2010 as it observed that the economy was not growing fast enough. In November 2010, the FED announced a second round of quantitative easing. Other central banks, all with policy rates already pressed against the zero lower bound, followed suit.

As a result, in 2010, policy rates were negative in real terms in advanced economies and expansionary monetary policy (including unconventional measures) resulted in provision of ample liquidity that affected international financial markets, contributing to high global liquidity. Although these policies of advanced economies may have been justified from the point of view of their domestic situation, it is now accepted that they created spillovers to emerging markets. Sluggish recovery in advanced economies and weak financial accelerators caused liquidity injections to remain largely on the balance sheets of financial institutions. Yield, risk, and growth differentials (low interest rates in advanced economies, narrowing relative risk premia, two-speed growth prospects) led to stronger demand for emerging market assets and put pressure on emerging currencies to appreciate.

Moreover, global liquidity was also affecting emerging markets (EMs) through its effects on commodity prices, further contributing to the appreciation of commodity currencies. Expanding global liquidity appears to be correlated with higher commodity prices, although fundamentals (excess long-term demand) may have given crucial support to these price rises. On the real demand side, strong economic growth in EMs, social structure changes in the PRC and India, and more resource-intensive development strategies have put pressure on commodity prices. But, most likely, global excess liquidity also played a role, in addition to fundamentals, in compounding rising trends in commodities and energy prices. Of course, it is far from trivial to attest and quantify causal relationships, as there is limited robust empirical evidence that excess global liquidity favored commodity financialization, and it is even harder to determine to what extent it was the causal factor behind price rises.

Nevertheless, higher commodity prices do improve fundamentals of commodity exporters; and that, in turn, triggers additional capital flows into these economies. Despite policy action in recipient countries, excess inflows contributed to the appreciation of several commodity-based currencies, as for instance in Australia, Canada, Brazil, and Chile, among others. The volume and intensity of capital flows in 2010 posed a challenge to policy makers in these countries because the impact of the overly liquid international environment was inflationary, in spite of the currency appreciation that inevitably took place, at a time when the strong post-crisis V-shaped recovery already gave rise to inflation pressures in EMs.

In a way, strong capital inflows were actually compounding the inflationary pressures already suffered by EMs as a consequence of their expanding domestic demand and globally rising commodity prices. Capital flows added fuel to local inflationary pressures as they exacerbated the procyclicality of local financial sectors in recipient economies: they contributed to an excessive expansion of domestic credit by lowering funding costs and relaxing local credit standards. Not only did the ample foreign funding to local credit markets intensify the impulse to aggregate demand, especially on the consumption side, but it also weakened the transmission of domestic monetary tightening, as conventional monetary policy instruments operate essentially through the funding costs of banks. Finally, excessive capital flows increased the risks of financial instability, since banks increased their foreign currency exposure at the same time as they lowered credit standards in response to higher liquidity. Therefore, 'sudden floods', that is, surges in capital inflows, can lead to credit and asset price bubbles, and can impact the exchange rates of commodity exporters[7].

In the second half of 2010 and early 2011, Brazil was facing exactly those challenges. The economy was showing signs of overheating (see Table 7.2), with domestic demand growing 5.7 per cent YOY in the first quarter of 2011, and inflationary pressures resulting from the resulting domestic supply-demand imbalances combined with global pressures on commodity prices. Local supply shocks and idiosyncratic regulated price adjustments also played a role: adjustments in urban transportation fares, which have a relevant weight in the consumer price index (CPI); atypical price hikes on food items, caused by unfavorable weather conditions in some production areas; and a supply shock in ethanol, an important fuel for the passenger car fleet (either used separately or as part of the regular gasoline blend). In addition, Brazil faced inflationary pressures stemming not from cyclical or momentary factors, but rather from structural social transformation, with a growing middle class boosting the demand for nontradables, while their rising incomes also represented a cost shock on labor-intensive sectors. Inflation in services was particularly representative of these latter trends[8].

The diagnosis of overheating in the economy was conducted *pari passu* with the monitoring of the buildup of potential threats to

---

[7] See Bank for International Settlements (2009), IMF (2011a), and Terrier et al. (2011).

[8] See Central Bank of Brazil (2011a) for a complete description of the macroeconomic scenario.

TABLE 7.2 Activity, Credit, Capital Flows, and Prices

	Unit	2009				2010				2011			
		Q1	Q2	Q3	Q4	Q1	Q2	Q3	Q4	Q1	Q2	Q3	Q4
Activity													
GDP	%YOY	2.9	0.7	-1.4	-0.3	2.5	5.4	7.6	7.5	6.3	4.9	3.7	2.7
Domestic demand	%YOY	-0.5	-0.2	1.0	7.6	10.8	9.8	8.4	7.1	5.7	5.3	2.3	2.0
Ind. Production	% YOY	-14.6	-12.3	-8.2	5.9	18.2	14.3	3.0	3.3	2.8	0.6	0.0	-2.0
Unemployment	%	8.6	8.6	7.9	7.2	7.4	7.2	6.6	5.7	6.3	6.3	6.0	5.2
Capital Flows (Gross)													
Reserves	$ b	190.4	201.5	221.6	238.5	243.8	253.1	275.2	288.6	317.1	335.8	349.7	352.0
Reserves	% YOY	-2.5	0.3	7.3	23.1	28.0	25.6	24.2	21.0	30.1	32.7	27.1	22.0
Portfolio	$ b	25.1	46.4	55.0	46.9	29.7	30.1	38.7	35.1	24.5	28.6	22.7	25.2
Portfolio % of GDP	%	8.6	13.4	11.9	8.9	5.8	5.6	7.1	6.4	4.1	4.6	3.6	4.0
Bank credit	$ b	2.3	5.2	4.0	8.1	10.3	7.6	12.3	13.2	25.7	15.3	14.4	4.8
Bank credit % of GDP	%	0.8	1.5	0.9	1.5	2.0	1.4	2.2	2.4	4.3	2.5	2.3	0.8
FDI	$ b	6.6	5.0	7.6	11.2	6.7	12.1	11.9	24.7	15.6	16.8	19.1	17.3
FDI % of GDP	%	2.3	1.4	1.6	2.1	1.3	2.3	2.2	4.5	2.6	2.7	3.0	2.7
Total	$ b	72.5	101.2	106.6	127.2	94.8	104.9	119.1	146.4	134.9	139.0	146.8	127.4
Total Percent of GDP	%	24.9	29.3	23.0	24.2	18.5	19.5	21.8	26.7	22.5	22.3	23.4	20.2
Credit (Oustanding)													
Consumer	% YOY	18.5	17.0	15.7	17.7	18.4	16.3	17.1	19.1	17.9	18.2	-16.9	13.9
Payroll-guaranteed	* YOY	22.6	30.3	33.9	36.1	37.2	29.7	27.8	28.4	21.8	19.5	17.8	12.5
Housing	* YOY	40.3	41.8	43.0	40.8	48.1	50.1	50.7	55.5	49.9	49.4	47.1	44.1

Ear-marked	% YOY	27.2	24.3	32.0	28.9	30.7	34.9	28.6	27.1	25.8	23.8	26.4	26.6
Nonearmaked	% YOY	23.6	17.0	10.4	9.1	10.9	13.2	15.7	17.7	18.0	17.8	15.7	14.7
Total	% YOY	24.7	19.1	16.6	15.0	16.9	19.8	19.9	20.9	20.6	19.9	19.4	18.8
Total Percent of GDP	%	40.7	41.5	43.6	43.7	43.1	43.6	44.3	45.2	45.2	46.0	47.4	49.0
Prices/Asset Prices													
CRB Metals ($)	%YOY	-48.1	-39.5	-10.3	48.6	85.2	43.5	17.6	27.8	30.0	35.1	25.9	-6.6
CRB Food ($)	% YOY	-21.9	-23.0	-25.4	7.6	20.2	14.0	27.4	26.8	38.2	40.4	27.8	6.9
CRB Total ($)	% YOY	-28.0	-24.7	-16.0	18.9	34.6	23.2	19.8	24.0	30.0	30.8	20.7	4.4
CPI (IPCA)	% YOY	5.6	4.8	4.3	4.3	5.2	4.8	4.7	5.9	6.3	6.7	7.3	6.5
CPE food	% YOY	9.3	5.0	4.1	3.2	5.6	5.1	5.4	10.4	8.8	8.9	9.9	7.2
CPE-services	% YOY	6.8	7.2	6.9	6.4	6.9	6.8	6.9	7.6	8.5	8.8	9.0	9.0
WPI (IGP-M)	% YOY	5.6	-0.6	-3.0	-4.4	0.5	5.0	9.3	13.9	13.5	9.7	7.6	4.3
Eft nominal	% YOY	30.4	19.0	1.1	-31.3	-25.9	-8.0	-5.7	-3.3	-7.4	-13.0	1.8	8.1
REER	%YOY	13.2	6.5	-6.2	-26.0	-20.0	-13.3	-9.0	-7.9	-6.3	-6.7	0.8	5.2
Real estate (SP)	%YOY	22.8	23.5	23.9	24.2	24.5	25.1	26.2	27.4	24.5	27.4	28.8	27.8
Real estate (RJ)	%YOY	13.9	15.0	17.6	20.6	23.5	29.0	34.7	38.6	41.7	44.0	42.3	37.3
BOVESPA	%YOY	39.9	-23.4	21.7	60.2	54.2	16.9	12.1	1.0	-2.6	2.4	-28.3	-20.0

Source: BCB and authors' calculations.

financial stability. Brazil had been going through an already long cycle of rapid credit expansion—about 22.2 per cent p.a. on average between 2005 and 2011—especially for consumer credit. To a large extent, such credit expansion corresponded to a process of natural deepening of financial markets in Brazil, with explanatory factors both structural and cyclical, including institutional improvements to loan contracts and collateral quality, strong fundamentals, in particular in the labor markets, and upward social mobility for about 40 million Brazilians, with new middle-class members now accessing credit. However, the fragility of the recovery in mature economies, combined with favorable perspectives for the Brazilian economy, intensified the inflow of foreign financing, part of which was directed to the local credit market (see Table 7.2). The central bank was concerned that excessive volume of inflows could exacerbate the already strong growth in local credit markets by increasing credit multipliers. Lower cost of external funding could also weaken the transmission mechanism of monetary policy through channels related to credit, diminishing its potency as an aggregate demand management instrument, as well as causing distortions in the price of domestic assets.

Credit Market Developments

Since the mid-2000s, the dynamism of the credit market in Brazil has been intense and has translated into a continuous growth in the credit-to-GDP ratio. Greater levels of credit penetration, among other factors, contributed to the amplification of the power of monetary policy in Brazil. In 2010, in particular, credit operations in the Brazilian financial system, having left behind the impact of the 2008–09 crisis, were again expanding briskly and in line with domestic demand growth, which was boosted by a buoyant job market, improvements of income levels, and strong confidence indicators.

Credit growth to households did not change the stability of debt-service-to-income ratios (see Table 7.3): higher volumes of debt as a proportion of income were compensated by lower costs and longer tenors. Interest rates and spreads for household loans declined, maturities lengthened, and delinquency rates [nonperforming loan (NPL) ratios] were following a downward trend. Social changes in Brazil explain the expansion of credit to households, especially car loans and

TABLE 7.3 Credit Market

	Unit	2009				2010				2011			
		Q1	Q2	Q3	Q4	Q1	Q2	Q3	Q4	Q1	Q2	Q3	Q4
Firms													
Total (growth rate)	%YOY	28.5	19.7	16.0	12.6	14.5	20.4	19.9	19.6	20.1	18.2	17.8	18.4
Average interest rate	%	30.2	28.2	26.4	26.0	26.2	26.8	28.8	28.4	30.4	31.0	30.8	29.3
Spread	p.p.	13.6	18.4	17.8	17.1	17.1	16.8	18.3	17.7	19.0	19.2	19.1	18.7
NPL(90days overdue)	%	1.94	2.55	2.75	2.43	2.20	1.97	1.80	1.68	1.73	1.84	1.90	1.91
Households-Total Credit													
Total (growth rate)	%YOY	20.1	18.4	17.3	18.3	20.0	19.0	19.9	22.5	21.2	22.0	21.5	19.3
Total Percent of GOP	%	17.7	18.5	19.3	19.3	19.3	19.3	19.6	20.1	20.3	20.7	21.4	22.0
Average rate	%	52.6	47.2	44.2	43.3	42.0	41.0	39.9	40.0	44.2	46.6	45.9	45.2
Spread over deposit	p.p.	41.6	37.3	34.3	32.5	30.9	29.2	28.5	28.3	31.7	34.1	34.2	35.0
Total Debt to Income	%	32.5	33.3	34.2	35.2	36.1	37.2	38.2	39.0	39.8	40.7	41.8	42.5
Total Debt Service to income	%	18.8	19.5	19.3	19.5	19.2	19.4	19.1	19.3	19.8	20.3	21.9	22.2
NPL (90days overdue)	%	7.1	7.0	7.1	6.5	6.1	5.7	5.4	5.0	4.9	5.2	5.3	5.5
Worst risk category/Total	%	9.4	9.2	9.1	8.8	8.3	7.9	7.6	7.1	6.9	7.2	7.4	7.6
Households-Consumer Credit													
Total (growth rate)	%YOY	18.5	17.0	15.7	17.7	18.4	16.3	17.1	19.1	17.9	18.2	16.9	13.9
Total Percent of GOP	%	13.0	13.7	14.2	14.2	14.0	14.0	14.1	14.5	14.4	14.5	14.8	15.0
Average rate	%	53.9	47.0	44.6	44.6	43.8	42.6	41.9	43.2	47.9	49.5	49.3	49.7

(Cont'd)

TABLE 7.3   (Cont'd)

	Unit	2009				2010				2011			
		Q1	Q2	Q3	Q4	Q1	Q2	Q3	Q4	Q1	Q2	Q3	Q4
Spread over deposit	p.p.	43.0	37.0	34.6	33.5	32.4	30.6	30.3	31.3	35.2	36.9	37.6	39.5
Average Maturity	months	13.0	14.8	15.1	15.2	15.5	15.7	16.1	16.2	16.2	16.3	16.5	17.6
NPL (90days overdue)	%	8.5	8.5	8.3	7.9	7.3	6.9	6.5	6.2	6.2	6.6	7.0	7.3
Worst risk category/Total	%	9.9	9.7	9.7	9.4	8.8	8.4	8.0	7.5	7.4	7.8	8.2	8.5
Households-Car loans													
Total (growth rate)	%YOY	-3.3	0.6	4.5	17.8	26.5	33.8	43.3	50.7	48.0	45.3	35.7	27.8
Total Percent of GOP	%	2.5	2.5	2.7	2.7	2.8	3.0	3.3	3.5	3.6	3.8	4.0	4.1
Average rate	%	32.0	28.6	26.0	25.4	24.3	24.0	23.6	23.8	28.1	30.4	29.1	27.3
Spread over deposit	p.p.	21.0	18.5	15.9	14.2	12.8	12.0	12.0	11.9	15.4	17.8	17.4	17.1
Average Maturity	months	N/A	16	17	17	18	19	19	20	20	19	19	19
NPL (90days overdue)	%	6.4	6.9	6.1	5.5	5.0	4.4	3.8	3.2	3.7	4.5	5.2	5.9
LTV (average)	%	71.2	72.0	74.7	74.9	77.4	77.9	786	77.8	70.6	74.9	73.6	71.9
Worst risk category/Total	%	6.3	6.6	6.0	5.5	4.8	4.2	3.6	2.8	3.1	3.6	4.2	4.8

Source: BCB and Authors' calculations.

loans guaranteed by automatic payroll deduction. However, that did not significantly affect the risk profile of the system's credit portfolio, even when taking into account the considerably larger group of new borrowers with little prior credit history and the impacts of the 2008–09 financial crisis on the domestic economic cycle. Indeed, payments overdue above 90 days for total credit to households were at a historical low of 4.98 per cent in December 2010.

Credit growth was more intense for loans with earmarked resources, boosted by Banco Nacional de Desenvolvimento Econômico e Social (BNDES) and mortgage lending (see Box 2). Total credit outstanding

---

Box 7.2 Housing Loans in Brazil

Early in 2011, some observers began warning about the risk of a 'housing bubble' in Brazil. Joe Leahy and Samantha Pearson of the *Financial Times*, for example, wrote on May 11, 'Across Latin America's largest economy, record prices for the country's commodities and surging foreign fund inflows—what the IMF calls "favorable tailwinds"—are driving a historic boom. Property prices are soaring, consumer credit is booming and bank profits swelling. But there are growing concerns over whether Brazil is becoming addicted to this windfall of easy money. Increasingly, there are fears that Brazil is heading for a bubble. "Experience tells us that whenever there is a lot of credit available for emerging markets economies, especially in South America, and if that's coupled with very high commodity prices, the tendency of our economies is to spend too much," said IMF western hemisphere director, Nicolás Eyzaguirre, a former Chilean finance minister...Anecdotes abound of beachfront apartments in Rio's fashionable Ipanema district selling for a third more than levels of late last year. In São Paulo, house prices have nearly doubled since 2008.'

However, these observations did not disentangle the structural and cyclical factors behind the upswing in housing markets in Brazil, nor did they take into account the small basis upon which this segment of the credit market was growing. True, mortgage lending, whose primary funding sources are saving account deposits and the Workers Severance Fund (FGTS), accounted for a major portion of the credit expansion. For decades, however, millions of Brazilians had stayed away from the housing market altogether, because of a nearly complete lack of financing. The rapid growth in mortgage lending helped many Brazilians start accessing the housing market. Mortgage lending in Brazil grew 56 per cent in 2010, and approximately 44 per cent in

2011. Nevertheless, mortgage debt is still quite low (4.6 per cent of Brazil's GDP), compared to international standards (Table B7.1.1). In Brazil, residential real estate loans still account for only 7.1 per cent of total bank loans. Given its incipient state, it is expected to continue driving housing-sector growth in the long term.

Mortgage lending gained momentum in Brazil not just because of the credit expansion and increases in income but also because of various legal and regulatory changes over the years. For instance, Law 10.931/2004 reduced a lender's mortgage origination risk by making it easier and faster to repossess a property in the event of default.[a] Earlier, in the case of delinquency, it took as long as six years for a bank to foreclose on a property.[b]

TABLE B7.1.1   Mortgage Loans: International Comparison

Selected countries	Mortgage loans/GDP (April 2011)	Residential real estate loans to total loans
Brazil	4.1	7.1
Eurozone	40.2	–
Germany	37.7	16.8
Spain	61.2	27.4
United States[a]	70.3	36.5
France	39.8	–
The Netherlands	66.1	23.6
Italy	22.9	18.1

Source: FED, Bureau of Economic Analysis, BCE, Eurostat and FSI.
Notes: [a]. December 2010.

a. It was made possible by the use of a mechanism called '*alienação fiduciária*'. In a mortgage issued with this feature, the title of the property used as loan collateral is placed with a trustee who, on behalf of the lender, has the right to sell such property in case of a borrower default—without court proceedings.

b. Another important legal change that helped boost mortgage lending in Brazil was the Law 10931/04 that amended the civil code to extend maximum mortgage tenors from 20 to 30 years.

in the financial system reached R$ 1,706 billion in December of 2010, corresponding to 46.4 per cent of GDP and resulting from YOY growth of 20.6 per cent. The nonearmarked credit portfolio reached R$ 1,116 billion in December 2010, after an increase of 16.9 per cent compared with the previous year. It represented 65.4 per cent of the total credit of the financial system. The household credit portfolio increased by 19.2 per cent, reaching R$ 560 billion. Loans for the acquisition of vehicles soared by 49.1 per cent and personal credit, mostly for consumption, increased by 24.7 per cent.[9]

On average and in aggregate terms, the general credit conditions were favorable because most of the credit expansion was taking place in lower-risk credit modalities. However, there were localized sources of risk coming from households' leverage increase and excessive lengthening of loan maturities in certain credit modalities. That risk was especially noticeable in consumer credit extended with loan maturities beyond prudent levels (for example, above 60 months for car loans) and with LTV ratios incompatible with the actual quality of the collateral.

Capital Flow Developments

In recent years, capital flows to Brazil have been related to a profound transformation of the Brazilian economy. For almost two decades, Brazil has been enjoying an environment of stability, thanks to having implemented a consistent macroeconomic policy framework. Combined with the adoption of other sound public policies, this framework enabled the country to resume a process of sustainable and inclusive growth after two decades of sluggish and irregular performance. Naturally, Brazil became an attractive destination for foreign capital, with attractive investment opportunities in numerous areas, resulting from the newly improved prospects combined with the backlog left by underinvestment during the preceding decades.

Alongside these structural factors, the long history of emerging market booms and busts shows that the buildup of financial risks is usually associated with periods of capital bonanzas that fuel credit booms, asset bubbles, and exchange rate misalignments. Those episodes frequently end in sudden stops and reversals of capital inflows that endanger the financial system and the real economy. Short-term inflows in particular contribute to the buildup of financial mismatches with potentially severe financial and macroeconomic consequences arising from the

[9] See Central Bank of Brazil (2011b).

combination of exchange-rate, pass-through, and mismanaged aggregate demand expansions.

The strong recovery of the Brazilian economy in the aftermath of the more acute phase of the global financial crisis reinforced these structural factors, such as recognition for the soundness of the policy framework and favorable long-term growth prospects. Together with temporary factors such as the difference between international and local interest rates, and excessive global liquidity, all this resulted in large short-term foreign inflows and domestic currency appreciation.

Table 7.2 describes recent developments regarding capital flows. During 2010, net capital inflows (defined as nonresidents' net flows into portfolio investments, depositary receipts, direct investment and external credits) amounted $125 billion,[10] compared with nearly $80 billion in 2009. Brazil had a historically high amount of equity issuance, totaling R$ 146 billion (mostly by Petrobras), of which 26 per cent were taken up by foreign investors. External debt issuance raised another $48 billion, approximately. Foreign direct investment net inflows amounted to $38 billion.

Therefore, managing the effects of large capital inflows has been one of the main policy issues in Brazil since the global crisis. Brazil managed those massive inflows primarily in standard textbook fashion, with aggregate demand contraction through fiscal and monetary policies, allowing significant currency appreciation while smoothing movements through sterilized reserve accumulation, which reduced the volatility of the exchange rate without, however, aiming at distorting its structural trend.

When Brazil's credit market was affected by capital inflows, a set of measures was consequently adopted, as discussed in the next section. There was evidence that multiple sources of foreign funding were transmitted into credit markets, in addition to the confidence factors associated with periods of abundant liquidity. External funding at low cost, despite tight domestic prudential rules, creates incentives to increase risk-taking and usually ends by distorting asset prices, including the exchange rate. In Brazil, excessive capital inflows contributed to the brisk pace of domestic credit growth, which fueled inflationary

---

[10] For the purpose of this chapter, the amounts of capital flows come from data on foreign exchange contracts, the same criteria used for IOF (Brazil's tax on financial operations) charges. Because of these methodological criteria, the figures may differ from BOP data.

pressures associated with domestic supply–demand mismatches and created fertile ground for the domestic transmission of pressures stemming from global commodity prices.

Brazil's Policy Responses to the Crisis

Brazilian policy makers relied on a comprehensive textbook toolkit of policy measures (see Table 7.4) to deal with the emerging risks of macroeconomic and financial instability at the end of 2010 and in early 2011. Standard aggregate demand management was conducted using fiscal and monetary policies to dampen supply–demand imbalances and to control inflation expectations. Macro prudential measures were adopted to reduce systemic financial risk stemming from rapid credit growth and large capital inflows.

Monetary Policy

On the monetary policy front, in the first half of 2011, the central bank took action and raised the policy rate by 175 bps in five consecutive monetary policy committee meetings. That followed the 200 bps increase of 2010 and totaled an overall rate hike of 375 bps.[11]

Fiscal Policy

On the fiscal front, in February 2011, the government reaffirmed its commitment to a strong fiscal stance with a steady reduction of the public-debt-to-GDP ratio and proposed a fiscal consolidation of R$ 50 billion of expenditure cuts. In August, it announced an additional R$ 10 billion savings. At the end of the year, the public sector successfully delivered on its commitment to a primary fiscal surplus of 3.1 per cent of GDP.

Macro Prudential Policy

On the macro prudential front, the central bank and the government were proactive in anticipating potential sources of risk to the Brazilian

---

[11] The reversal of the monetary policy tightening stance in August 2011 is discussed later in more detail.

TABLE 7.4 Macro Prudential, Monetary, and Fiscal Policy Measures

Policy Measures:	Unit	2009				2010				2011			
		Q1	Q2	Q3	Q4	Q1	Q2	Q3	Q4	Q1	Q2	Q3	Q4
On Activity													
Selic Base rate (average)	%	12.6	10.3	8.9	8.8	8.8	9.5	10.6	10.8	11.3	12.0	12.3	11.4
Selic Base rate increase	(+bps)	–250	–200	–50	0	0	150	50	0	100	50	–25	–100
Primary Fiscal Surplus													
Target	% GDP	–	–	–	2.50	–	–	–	3.10	–	–	–	3.09
Achievement	% GDP	–	–	–	2.00	–	–	–	2.70	–	–	–	3.11
Public Debt(Net)	% GDP	39.1	41.2	42.3	42.1	41.1	40.0	39.4	39.2	38.9	38.6	36.3	36.4
On Capital Flows													
Tax on Financial Transactions (IOF)													
Nonresident Fixed income	%	0	0	0	2	2	2	2	6	6	6	6	6
Derivative margin deposits	%	0.38	0.38	0.38	0.38	0.33	0.38	0.38	6	6	6	6	6
Equity	%	0	0	0	2	2	2	2	2	2	2	2	0
Reserve Requirement	%	N/A	N/A	N/A	N/A	N/A	N/A	N/A	N/A	Minimum between	Minimum between	Minimum between	Minimum between

		(1)	(2)	(3)	(4)	(5)	(6)	(7)	(8)	(9)	(10)	(11)	(12)
on Short FX Open Positions in Spot Market	%	5.38	5.38	5.38	5.38	5.38	5.38	5.38	5.38	60% of what exceeds $3 billion or Tier 1 capital 6	60% of what exceeds $1 billion or Tier 1 capital 6	60% of what exceeds $1 billion or Tier 1 capital 6	60% of what exceeds $1 billion or Tier 1 capital 6
External Credit inflows taxable maturity	days	90	90	90	90	90	90	90	90	360	720	720	720
FX Derivatives	%	N/A	N/A	N/A	N/A	N/A	N/A	N/A	N/A	N/A	N/A	1	1
On Credit													
Reserve Requirements (RR)													
Outstanding RR	R$ bi	174.9	179.4	186.0	193.6	233.2	279.5	301.3	395.2	400.9	413.6	434.7	448.5
Outstanding RR	% credit	14.0	13.9	13.7	13.6	15.9	18.1	18.5	23.0	22.7	22.7	22.4	22.0
Average ratio on Demand Deposits	%	42.0	42.0	42.0	41.0	42.0	42.0	42.9	43.0	43.0	43.0	43.0	43.0
Average ratio on Term Deposits	%	15.0	15.0	14.5	13.5	13.5	14.9	15.0	15.8	20.0	20.0	20.0	20.0
Tax on Financial Transactions (IOF) on domestic credit	%	0.0041	0.0041	0.0041	0.0041	0.0041	0.0041	00041	(10041	0.0041	0.0082	0.0032	0.0068

Source: BCB and Authors' Calculations.

economy and its financial system. Employing macro prudential measures they: (a) increased bank reserve requirements to dampen the transmission of excessive global liquidity to the domestic credit market; (b) increased capital requirements for specific segments of the credit market (essentially consumer loans) to correct a deterioration in the quality of loan origination; and (c) created reserve requirements on banks' short spot foreign exchange positions and taxed specific inflows to correct imbalances in the foreign exchange market and to deal with the intense and volatile inflows of capital.

The scope and direction of these policies is summarized in Table 7.5, using the same format as Table 7.1. In terms of macro prudential instruments, most of the balance-sheet vulnerabilities listed earlier were addressed either comprehensively or for specific segments of the credit market with higher financial risk; similarly, loan contracts and foreign currency liquidity were strengthened. Other features were not tightened but were already in place in Brazil, such as mark-to-market rules and the obligation for all financial institutions to register any derivatives contract in a clearing house or a data repository facility. The crisis revealed that this obligation had a loophole: nonfinancial firms with foreign exchange operations could use foreign counterparties to engage in derivatives trading outside Brazil's jurisdiction. This loophole was subsequently corrected by extending the registration requirement of overseas derivatives to nonfinancial firms and demanding the disclosure on the quarterly financial statements of publicly traded companies of sensitivity analysis of three scenarios based on their derivatives exposure.

Macro Prudential Measures in the Credit Market

This section looks at macro prudential measures used in the credit market and their results.

The Measures

Measures used in the credit market include reserve requirements, a tax on financial operations; and setting capital requirements for consumer loans.

TABLE 7.5 Macro Prudential Instruments by Vulnerability and Financial System Component

	Macroeconomic policies by area				
	2009	2010	2011Q1–Q2	2011Q3	2011Q4
Fiscal Policy	Loosening	Neutral	Tightening	Tightening	Tightening
Monetary Policy	Loosening	Tightening	Tightening	Loosening	Loosening

Macroprudential instruments by vulnerability and financial system component

		Financial system component			
		Bank or deposit-taker		Nonbank investor	Securities market	Financial infrastructure
		Balance sheet*	Lending contract			
Vulnerability	**Leverage**	Capital ratio	LTV cap		Margin/haircut limit	
		Risk weights				
		income cap	Debt service/			
		Provisioning	Maturity cap			
		Profit distribution restrictions	Margin/Haircut limit			
			Tax on household			
		Credit growth cap credit				

(Cont'd)

TABLE 7.5 (Cont'd)

Macroprudential instruments by vulnerability and financial system component

	Financial system component				
	Bank or deposit-taker		Nonbank investor	Securities market	Financial infrastructure
	Balance sheet*	Lending contract			
Liquidity or market risk	Liquidity / reserve requirements	Valuation rules (e.g. MMMFs)	Tax on FX deriv	Central bank balance sheet operations	Exchange trading
	FX lending restrictions				
	Currency mismatch limit				
	Open FX position limit		Tax on ext credit		
Interconnectedness	Concentration limits				Central counterparties (CCP)
	Systemic capital surcharge				
	Subsidiarisation				

* Capital and other balance sheet requirements also apply to insurers and pension funds, but we restrict our attention here to the types of institutions most relevant for credit intermediation.

☐ Used for some segments of the credit market

▨ Used for all financial system components

Source: Authors' calculations.

Reserve Requirements

As mentioned earlier, during the 2008–09 crisis, Brazil used reserve requirements (RRs) as an important mechanism to support financial stability and to facilitate liquidity reallocation among financial institutions[12]. In particular, to support the operations of small- and medium-sized banks, the central bank allowed larger banks to draw on portions of their required reserves if these funds were to be used to extend liquidity to small- and medium-sized banks.[13] These measures were progressively reversed and, in December 2010, the central bank moved further with the recomposition of reserve requirements by gradually eliminating these reductions (Figure 7.1). At the end of 2010 and in 2011, the central bank used reserve requirements again as a countercyclical buffer to smooth rapid credit growth, raising unremunerated reserve requirements on term deposits from 15 to 20 per cent[14] and the additional remunerated reserve requirements on demand and term deposit from 8 to 12 per cent.[15]

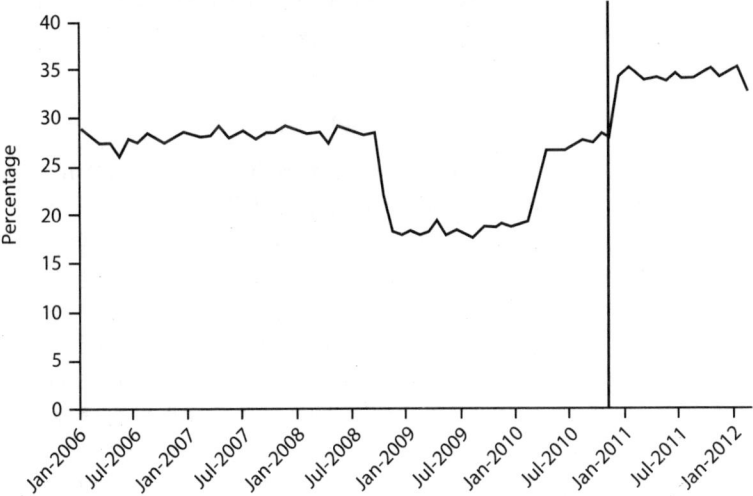

FIGURE 7.1   Total Reserve Requirements / Total Deposits (Percentage)
Source: BCB and authors' calculations.

[12] See Montoro and Moreno (2011), and Moreno (2011).
[13] Central Bank of Brazil, Circular 3,427/2008.
[14] Central Bank of Brazil, Circular 3513/2010.
[15] Central Bank of Brazil, Circular 3514/2010.

Nevertheless, the central bank protected sources of longer-term bank funding and exempted the Letras Financeiras (LF)—a bank-issued debenture with a minimum maturity of two years—from reserve requirements.[16] Previously, the Letras Financeiras were charged reserve requirements at the same rate as term deposits. Although maturity mismatch is inherent to the banking business, it is also a source of risk to be carefully monitored, so protecting LFs as a long-term source of funding for banks, in conjunction with shortening credit maturities for consumer credit as a result of the macro prudential measures adopted, is important to mitigate this risk.

Financial Operations Tax

With the same objectives in mind, in April 2011, the government raised the tax on financial operations (*Imposto sobre Operações Financeiras*; IOF) applying to credit operations for individuals[17] from 0.0041 to 0.0082 per cent per day, limited to a maximum charge over 365 days. Therefore, the maximum tax rate increased from 1.5 to 3 per cent.

Capital Requirements for Consumer Loans

As mentioned earlier, the diagnosis in the credit market was that the strong credit expansion to individuals, especially in car loans and payroll-guaranteed consumer loans, was increasingly done by lengthening maturities, increases in LTVs, and reductions in interest rates that were incompatible with the quality of risk (Table 7.6). These changes were translating into higher potential risk associated with higher household indebtedness and with maturity mismatches in the banking system. Since 2003, the tenors for consumption loans were extended and in some cases went beyond 72 months for car loans. As for payroll-guaranteed consumer loans, the tenors for public sector employees reached 60 months. This lengthening of loan tenors was not, however, accompanied by a similar extension in the maturity

[16] Central Bank of Brazil, Circular 3,513/2010.

[17] Government of Brazil, http://www.planalto.gov.br/ccivil_03/_Ato2011–2014/2011/Decreto/D7458.htm] Decree 7,458. Accessed in 2014.

TABLE 7.6   Maturity Limits and LTVs Used to Calibrate Risk-Weights for
Auto and Personal Consumer Loans, Brazil

Operation	Maturity and LTV	Risk Weight
Vehicles (financing and leasing)	between 24 and 36 months and LTV > 80%	150%
	between 36 and 48 months and LTV > 70%	
	between 48 and 60 months and LTV > 60%	
	more than 60 months and any LTV	
Payroll-deducted loan	more than 36 months	
Personal loan	more than 24 months	
	Other consumer loans	100%

Source: BCB and authors' calculations.

structure of banks' funding, which remained concentrated in demand deposits and term deposits with daily liquidity, thus constituting a source of financial vulnerability. The terms of some of these longer-tenor loans to households were not compatible with the quality of collateral and its associated risk. This characteristic was especially acute in vehicle financing, where the market value of pledged assets tends to decline rapidly. Given the growing size of these market segments, they represented a potential source of systemic risk if the prevailing market trends continued to go unchecked.

Macro prudential measures were thus adopted to curb the supply of excessively long-term consumer credit and car loans. In December 2010, the central bank raised capital requirements for household loans above 24 months by increasing the risk-weight factor (RWF), used for capital requirements calculation, from 75 to 150 per cent on most household credit modalities.[18] In practice, the total capital required from financial institutions for those loans increased from 8 to 16.5 per cent of risk-weighted assets (RWA). The rise on the RWF was not applicable to agricultural credit operations, mortgage loans, or credit for the acquisition of trucks and similar vehicles.

[18] Central Bank of Brazil, Circular 3,515, 3 December 2010.

The Results

The reserve requirements on demand and term deposits, the IOF tax rate on consumer credit, and increases on capital requirements for consumer loans were successful in reducing the growth of household credit to a more sustainable pace. These measures affected not only the volume of new loans, as shown in Figure 7.2, but also their interest rates and average maturities. The average interest rate rose to 30.4 per cent p.a. in May 2011, compared with 22.8 per cent p.a. in November of 2010 (see Figure 7.3). In the same period, the monthly origination of new loans fell from R$ 11.2 billion to R$ 8.8 billion and the average maturities declined from 45.7 to 43 months (see Figure 7.4).

Macro Prudential Measures on the Foreign Exchange Market

This section outlines the various instruments employed by Brazil to address systemic risk in the foreign exchange market, and provides an evaluation of their efficacy in the Brazilian context.

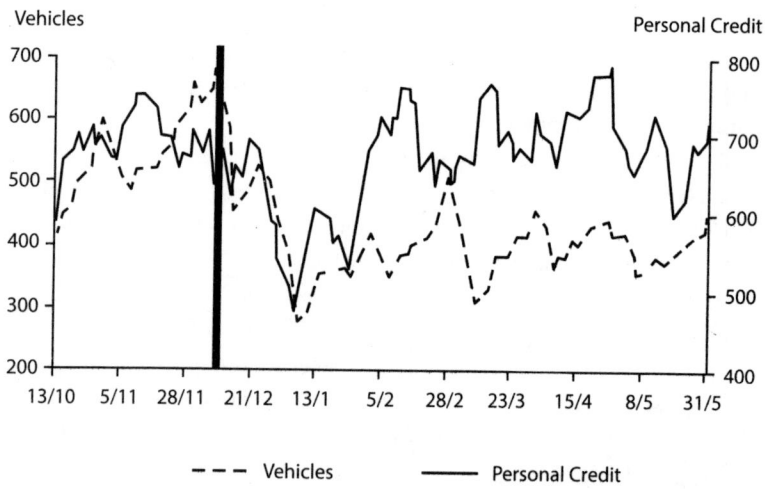

FIGURE 7.2   New Loans: Five-Day Moving Average for Vehicle Financing and Personal Credit (R$ millions)
Source: BCB and authors' calculations.

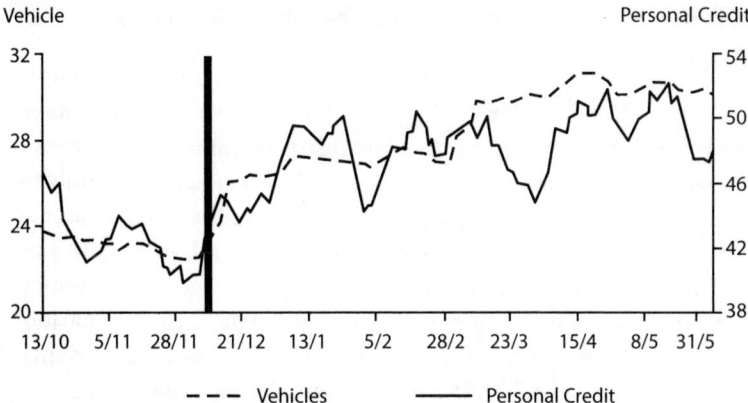

FIGURE 7.3   Interest Rates: Five- Day Moving Average for Vehicle Financing and Personal Credit (per cent p.a.)
Source: BCB and authors' calculations.

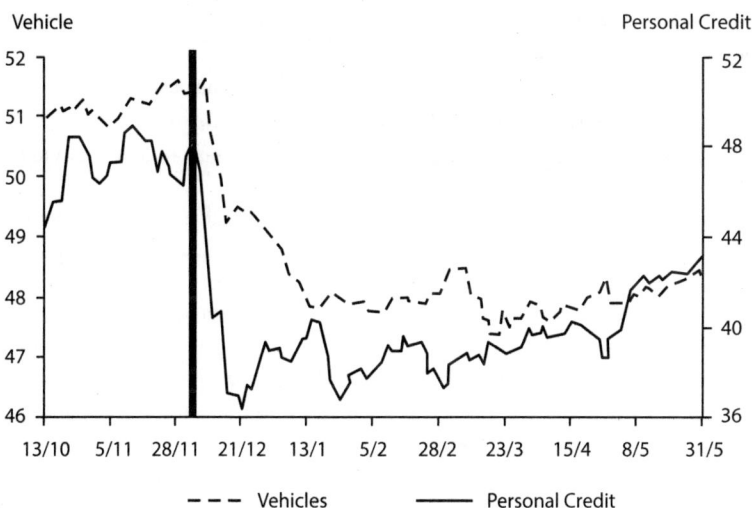

FIGURE 7.4   Average Maturity: Five-Day Moving Average for Vehicle Financing and Personal Credit (months)
Source: BCB and authors' calculations.

IOF Tax on Portfolio Investments by Nonresidents and on Margin Deposits on Derivatives

In October 2010, the IOF tax[19] for nonresidents' portfolio investment in fixed income instruments was raised,[20] first from 2 to 4 per cent, and later in the same month to 6 per cent. The IOF was also raised to 6 per cent (from 0.38 per cent) on incoming remittances destined to posting collateral on derivatives positions held at central counterparties for stocks, commodities, or futures trading.[21] Inflows for equity investments remained subject to a 2 per cent IOF tax rate. The IOF rate increases were meant to curb excessive short-term and speculative capital inflows and lengthen flow composition, in particular by discouraging short-term carry trades in both spot and futures markets, which were putting pressure on the domestic currency to appreciate.[22]

Additional technical measures were subsequently adopted to close possible loopholes that would have allowed foreign investors to bypass the higher IOF tax rate on fixed-income flows. For instance, to avoid arbitrage between the different IOF rates in force, any internal transfer of nonresident funds from equities to fixed income investments was required to be accompanied by a simultaneous foreign exchange transaction subject to IOF taxation.[23] Local banks were also forbidden to lend securities to foreign investors, which would allow them to avoid the tax

[19] The IOF is a tax of economic nature and is applicable to several operations, such as: credit, foreign exchange, securities, and insurance transactions. Each tax origin is based on a different trigger; in the case of a foreign exchange transaction, it is the settlement of the respective foreign exchange contract.

[20] The IOF on nonresident inflows for portfolio investments was used to limit excessive inflows before the crisis, from March to October 2008, with a 1.5 per cent tax rate, both for fixed income and equities. In October 2009, it was introduced again with a 2 per cent tax rate.

[21] In Brazil, about 90 per cent of the derivatives are standardized exchange-traded and cleared through a central counterparty. The BM&FBOVESPA is currently the only exchange in Brazil acting as central counterparty for every trade registered on its systems.

[22] A synthetic carry trade can be performed in the derivatives market by acquiring long positions on a high-yield currency [that is, the Brazilian real (BRL)] and short position on a funding currency (that is, dollars, yens, and so on).

[23] Otherwise, nonresidents would be able to enter the market with a first investment in equity, taxed at the 2 per cent IOF, and, later on, transfer funds to a fixed income investment, avoiding the payment of a higher 6 per cent IOF rate.

on derivative margin deposits. With this goal, the BM&F BOVESPA, Latin America's major securities, commodities, and futures exchange, was encouraged to exclude trust letters issued by domestic banks from the list of assets eligible as nonresident investors' collateral.

As shown in Figure 7.5, the foreign net inflows to fixed income plummeted since the IOF tax rate hike in October 2010, and have not yet recovered. This happened despite the fact that, according to one estimate, when considering the domestic interest rate, the Special Clearance and Escrow System (Sistema Especial de Liquidação e Custodia; SELIC) at the time of the measure compared with the Libor rate (as a proxy for funding costs), investment in a government bond by a foreign investor subject to the IOF would break even at a about nine months.[24,25]

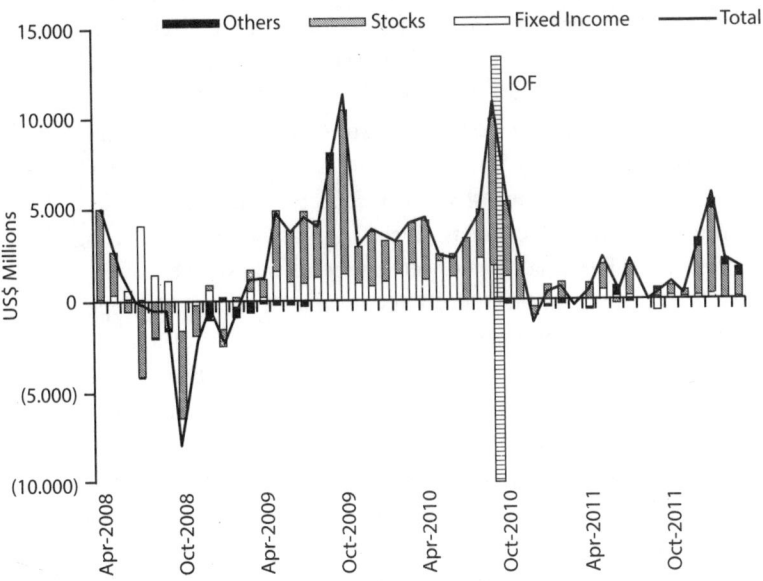

FIGURE 7.5   Portfolio's Net Inflows by Asset Class, Monthly Data
Source: BCB and authors' calculations.

[24] Although the flat one-time IOF hurdle is relatively less penalizing of returns on investments held for longer terms, the tax rate hike affected the liquidity of the primary market at the long end of the yield curve, where foreign investors are usually more active.

[25] Calculated as: $t = \log(1 - IOF)/\log[(1+e)/(1+i)]$, where e = external interest rate and i = domestic interest rate

Conversely, carry trades on derivatives markets were not significantly affected. Because the tax on derivatives transactions applied only to margin deposits posted as collateral at the clearinghouse, and not on the actual notional exposure, it had limited effectiveness. In fact, the foreign investor could use other assets that he already possessed in the country, such as government bonds or equities, to deposit as margin for his exposures and avoid the tax. Therefore, currency positions taken in the derivatives market enjoyed a favorable tax treatment compared with positions in the underlying cash market.

Bank Reserve Requirement on Open Short Positions In the FX Spot Market

In January 2011, the central bank imposed a 60 per cent unremunerated reserve requirement on banks' short positions in the foreign exchange spot market exceeding either $3 billion or Tier 1 capital, whichever is lower. In July, the limit was further tightened to $1 billion[26,27].

The diagnosis was that domestic banks could take advantage of the ample liquidity in global markets to significantly increase their funding abroad, and then invest those resources in Brazilian real (BRL)-denominated domestic assets, including loans, thus capturing the interest rate differential. There were concerns that such behavior could leave banks overexposed to currency mismatch and overly dependent on foreign liquidity, and hence vulnerable in the event of a large shock to the exchange rate or a rapid reversal of inflows. Technically, according to the regulations of the Brazilian foreign exchange market, banks open a short cash position when they sell foreign currency borrowed abroad resulting from drawings on external credit lines. Under those same regulations, although the operation is similar in accounting terms, when a bank contracts a direct loan or issues securities abroad (for example, commercial paper), it opens a long position. This aspect

---

[26] A five-day moving average methodology was also adopted for the calculation of the short position.

[27] In December 2012, BCB released Circular 3.619 withdrawing this limit back to $3 billion as the likehood of excessive short-term capital inflows was not high anymore and in order to inject further liquidity into the spot market.

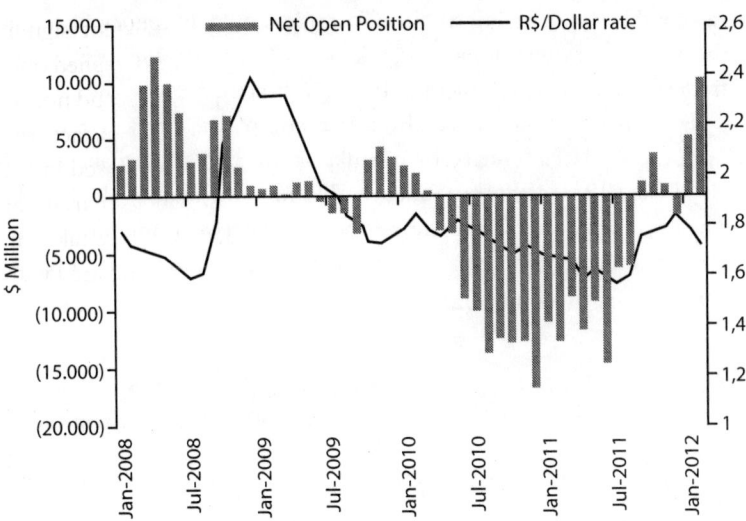

FIGURE 7.6   Net Open Positions of Banks, 2008–12
Source: BCB and authors' calculations.

is particularly important to understanding the rationale behind subsequent IOF measures.

Indeed, throughout 2010, as shown in Figure 7.6, banks increased exponentially their open foreign currency position. During that year, the financial system came out of a long position of $3.4 billion to a short position of $16.8 billion by year end. Therefore, not only was the system's position as a whole excessive but also some small- and medium-sized banks built positions in very large sizes compared to their respective Tier 1 capital.

The reserve requirement on short foreign currency positions was also intended to complement the rise in the IOF tax on nonresident's portfolio investments in reducing the attractiveness of carry-trade operations through long BRL derivatives positions. That was expected to be indirectly achieved by making it more expensive for banks—usually the counterparty of nonresidents' derivatives positions—to draw on their external credit lines. It was designed to impair an important channel for carry trades while reducing vulnerabilities in the banking sector. By limiting banks' ability to operate in spot and derivatives markets, or by raising the cost of doing so, the authorities could, in theory, also make the market less liquid and potentially less attractive for foreign carry traders, even without targeting the latter directly.[28]

Foreign investors are on the other side of the derivative transaction, usually large international banks acting as market makers in the US dollar/BRL offshore nondeliverable forward market (Figure 7.7). They take the role of bridge intermediaries between the onshore and offshore markets by relying on the domestic market to take the opposite net exposure of its offshore clients.

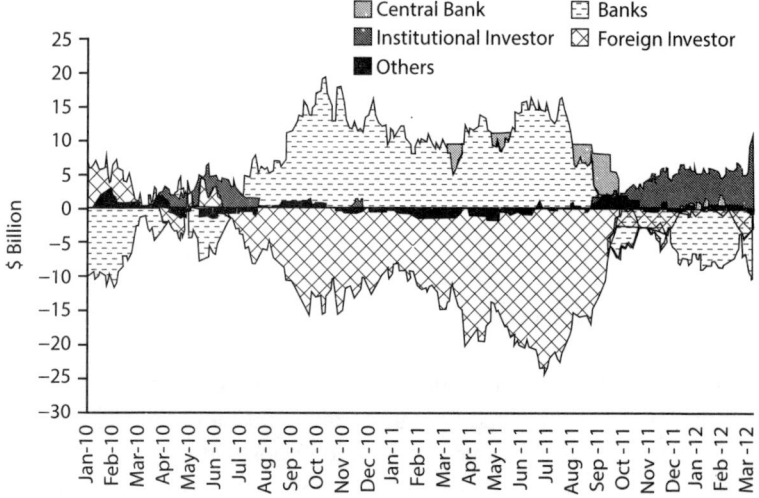

FIGURE 7.7   FX Derivatives Exposure by Type of Investor
Source: BCB and authors' calculations.

[28] This happens because local banks usually perform an arbitrage transaction in which they take a long foreign exchange position in the derivatives markets and hedge their exposures in the underlying cash market by drawing on an external credit line and selling the proceeds to the central bank, to another bank, or in the primary market (that is, to an importer) and invest it in BRL-denominated assets. They earn a currency risk-free arbitrage profit resulting from the difference between the onshore foreign currency interest rate – called '*cupom cambial*'—and the offshore external borrowing cost (Libor rate plus a spread). This transaction, in theory, does not influence the exchange rate trending path.

IOF Tax on External Credit Inflows

In March 2011, to curtail short-term speculative inflows while avoiding hampering longer-term flows, the authorities raised to 6 per cent the IOF tax rate on inflows related to direct external borrowing or debt securities issued by residents[29] with maturity below 360 days. Previously, a 5.38 per cent tax rate applied only to debts with average tenors below 90 days. A week later, the minimum average tenor for IOF exemption was further increased to 720 days.[30]

Empirical evidence suggests that the IOF on external credit inflows was effective in lengthening the tenors of external credit for residents, therefore achieving its macro prudential goals (see Figure 7.8). Despite the increase in the IOF tax rate, the net inflow of external credit

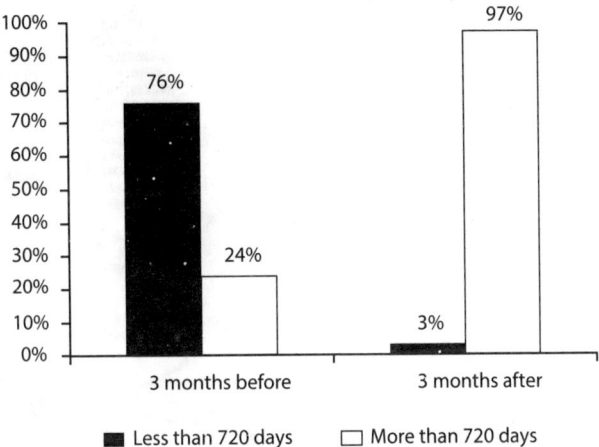

FIGURE 7.8   External Credit Profile 3 Months Before/After IOF
Source: BCB and authors' calculations.

---

[29]   Law 4,131/62 requires that the total amount borrowed abroad by a resident to be fully internalized in the country.

[30]   To provide more effectiveness to the measure, it was imposed on the performance of simultaneous foreign exchange operations for renewal, renegotiation, and assumption of obligation of external loan (including securities) under registration requirement with the central bank.

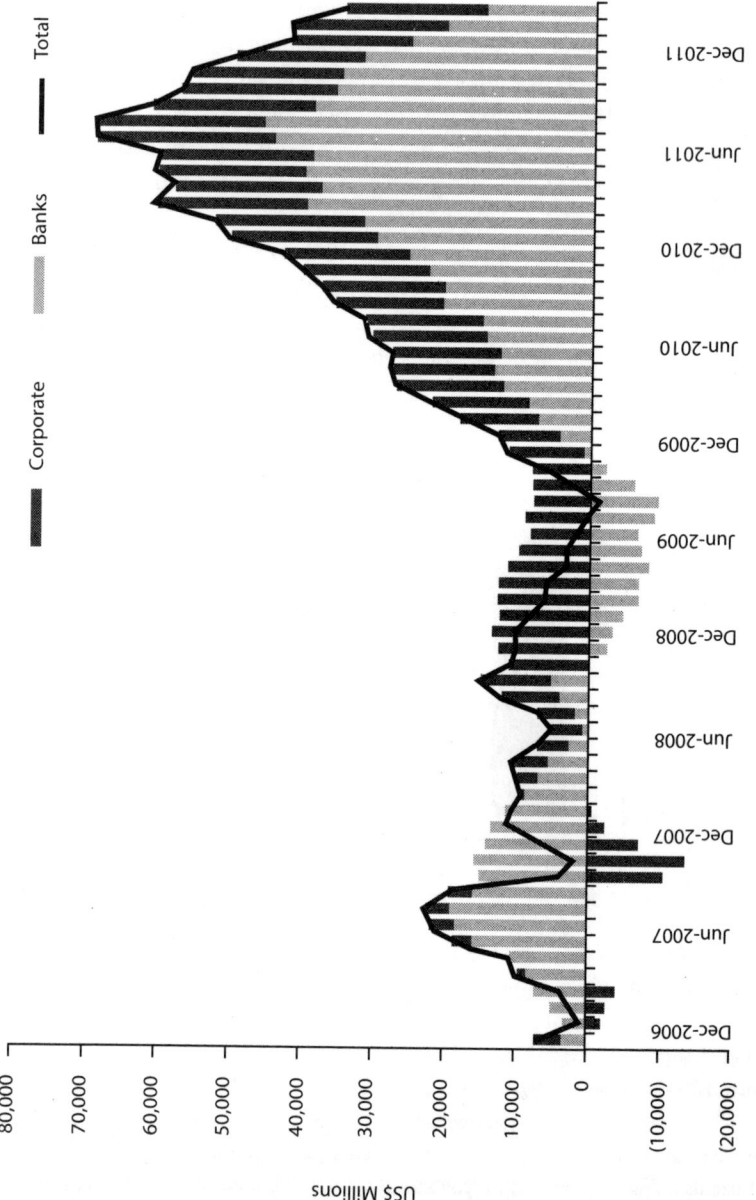

FIGURE 7.9 External Credit by Issuer, 2006–11
Source: BCB and authors' calculations.

amounted $49.6 billion in 2011[31], a 14.6 per cent increase compared with 2010, reflecting the global liquidity and strong foreign appetite for Brazilian assets (Figure 7.9).

The hike of the IOF tax rate on external credit also had a complementary function. As mentioned earlier, according to Brazilian foreign exchange regulations[32], when a bank borrows abroad through a direct loan or a securities issue, it actually opens a long foreign exchange position. Local banks used this channel as a way to circumvent the reserve requirement on short positions while keeping their arbitrage trades.

As shown in Figure 7.10, upon the adoption of the $3 billion limit on short positions in January 2011, the authorities allowed banks to comply with the new rule and recompose their positions until April 2011. As a consequence, from January to March 2011, banks raised $ 19.6 billion in

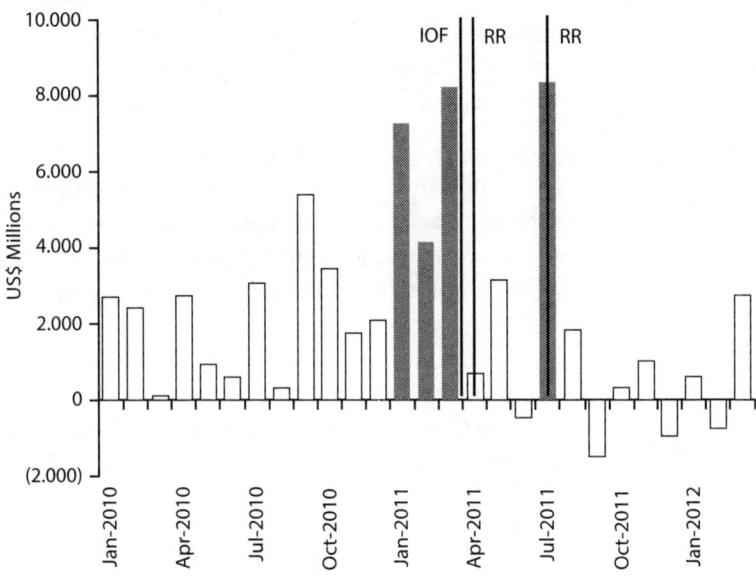

FIGURE 7.10 Net External Credit Inflows to Banks
Source: BCB and authors' calculations.

[31] The authorities further extended the taxable average tenor from 720 days to 1,080 days on 1 March 2012 and to 1,800 days in 9 March 2012. In 13 July 2012, it returned to 720 days and in 4 December 2012 it withdrew back to 360 days.

[32] External credit flow rules are established by Resolution 3,844/2010.

net external credit. In July, the limit was tightened to $1 billion, but this time banks were given only one week for compliance. Banks raised an additional $8.4 billion in external net borrowing in July.[33]

IOF Tax on FX Derivatives

In July 2011, the authorities announced two new prudential measures aimed to curb excessive and concentrated short positions that could cause detrimental effects to financial stability and speculative pressures on the exchange rate.

The first was a provisional measure dated 26 July 2011[34], which authorized the National Monetary Council (Conselho Monetário Nacional; CMN) to establish specific conditions for the negotiation of derivatives contracts, for monetary and exchange policy purposes, regardless of the nature of the investor, with powers to (a) determine deposits over the notional value of the derivatives contract; and (b) set forth limits, terms, and other conditions for the negotiation of such contracts.

The measure also amended the IOF legislation, to clarify that:

- In the case of securities transactions involving derivatives contracts, the maximum IOF rate would be 25 per cent. Up to this ceiling (25 per cent), the executive branch can change the applicable rate at any time, considering its monetary and exchange policy goals. However, the current applicable IOF rate for derivatives transactions is 1 per cent, as explained later; and
- The amount of the securities transaction, for IOF purposes, is the adjusted notional value of the derivatives contract. The adjusted notional value is the reference value of the contract (notional value) multiplied by the factor resulting from the derivative's price variation with respect to the underlying asset's price variation.

It also established that to be valid, all derivatives contracts must be registered with duly authorized entities, that is, clearing houses or data repositories that have been accredited by the central bank or by the

---

[33] Foreign exchange transactions related to direct investment in Brazilian companies remains subject to a rate of 0.38 per cent on the inflow.

[34] Provisional Measure 539/2011, later approved by the Brazilian Congress and converted in the Law 12,543 of 8 December 2011.

Brazilian Securities and Exchange Commission (Comissão de Valores Mobiliários; CVM) to operate with clearing, settlement, and registry.

The second measure was a decree[35], also dated July 26, 2011, which amends the IOF regulation approved by a 14 December 2007 decree.[36] The new decree repeats many of the terms defined in the 2011provisional measure described earlier, then states that the current applicable IOF rate to derivatives contracts is 1 per cent and it is due upon the purchase, sale, or maturity of financial derivatives contracts, whenever its settlement amount is affected by the exchange rate variation and results in an increase in the net short exposure in relation to the amount calculated at the end of the previous business day. It applies both to resident and nonresident positions.

The applicable rate is reduced to zero if the purchases, sales, or maturities of derivatives contracts, at the end of the day, result in net short exposure below $10 million. Above this figure, the 1 per cent rate will apply.

The decree created a level playing field between the underlying cash market and the derivative market for nonresidents' carry trades. As mentioned earlier, initially the authorities adopted a 1 per cent[37] tax rate that, although deemed insufficient to apply a burden equivalent to the 6 per cent tax on fixed income instruments, apparently was enough to discourage short positions, as shown in Figure 7.11.

The empirical basis for judging the effectiveness of restrictions on derivative positions is limited, given that their effects were mixed with the worsening of the global economic situation, since August 2011, and that they were imposed in conjunction with other measures. However, there is anecdotal evidence that the latitude given to the CMN to adopt further measures on derivatives market for monetary and exchange policy purposes, and also the establishment of the maximum IOF rate at 25 per cent, had an important psychological impact on investors' mindset that resulted on dismantling excessive positions in the derivatives market.

[35] Decree N° 7,536.
[36] Decree N° 6,306.
[37] The Law 12,543/2011 allows the IOF tax rate on derivatives up to 25 per cent.

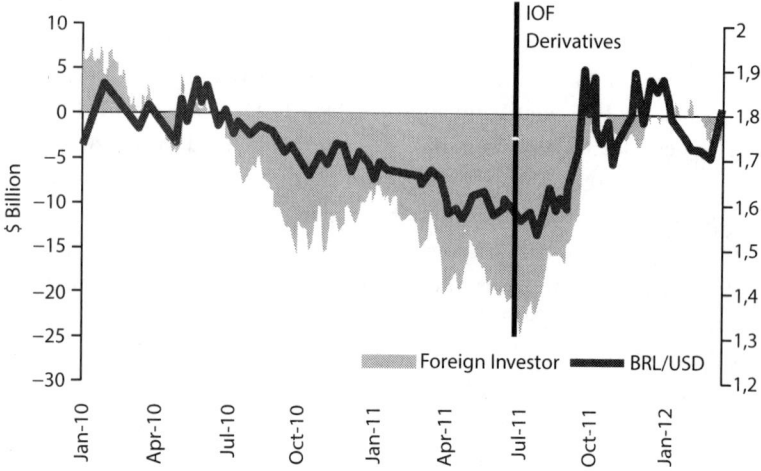

FIGURE 7.11   FX Derivatives Exposure and Exchange Rate
Source: BCB and authors' calculations.

All these measures were taken without losing sight of the fact that that there were important trade-offs in taxing foreign exchange markets. First, the cost of hedging might increase for the real economy.[38] Second, the development of domestic derivatives markets, which is often a difficult-to-achieve stage of financial deepening, could be impaired or even reversed by excessive imposition of market restrictions.

Advanced Receipts of Export Agreements

In March 2012, the Central Bank of Brazil amended the rules applicable to export financing transactions involving the advancement of payment to the Brazilian exporter, commonly known as 'advanced payment' (Pagamento Antecipado; PA).[39] This trade-financing modality is specifically designed to finance production by Brazilian exporters and for that

[38] On 15 March 2012, the government exempted certain exporters from the 1 per cent financial operations tax levied on FX derivatives as long as they can provide evidence that the volume of their FX derivatives trades are below 1.2 times the export contracts they had in the previous year.

[39] Central Bank of Brazil Circular 3,580.

reason it enjoys favorable tax treatment (0 per cent rates for IOF and for income tax on interest payments).

Pursuant to the new regulation, qualifying advanced payments can be carried out only by the importer (the foreign buyer of the Brazilian goods or services) for a limited period of 360 days[40]. Before this amendment, the advanced payment could be made by any legal entity, such as the importer or a foreign financial institution, and without any time limitation.

The amended central bank rules state that for values sent to Brazil as PA, one of the following situations shall occur within up to 360 days: (a) the shipment of goods or the provision of the service; (b) the conversion by the Brazilian exporter, with the prior written consent of the foreign payer, into direct investment (paying the corresponding 0.38 per cent IOF tax) or external credit[41] (paying 6 per cent IOF tax for operations with average maturity below 1,800 days); or (c) the return of the values sent to Brazil as PA, observing the tax regulations applicable to resources not destined to exports (paying 6 per cent IOF tax on external credit and 10–25 per cent income tax on interest payments).

This measure was prompted by concerns that the 'advanced payment' had been diverted from its main function. It also had a complementary scope to previous measures on foreign exchange inflows inasmuch as it prevented regulatory arbitrage and closed a loophole that could otherwise be used to circumvent the 6 per cent IOF tax on external credit operations. In fact, there was a strong growth of this kind of operation in January and February of 2012, when PA volume grew 46 per cent as compared with the same period in 2011, while exports did not advance at a comparable pace.

Figure 7.12 summarizes the main channels for foreign inflows to Brazil and government actions to curb its excesses and improve its composition.

---

[40] By means of Circular n° 3604, of 4 December 2012, this period was extended from 1 to 5 years.

[41] Registered with the Central Bank of Brazil pursuant to Law No. 4131, of 3 September 1962, as amended by Law No. 4390, of 29 August 1964, and relevant regulation.

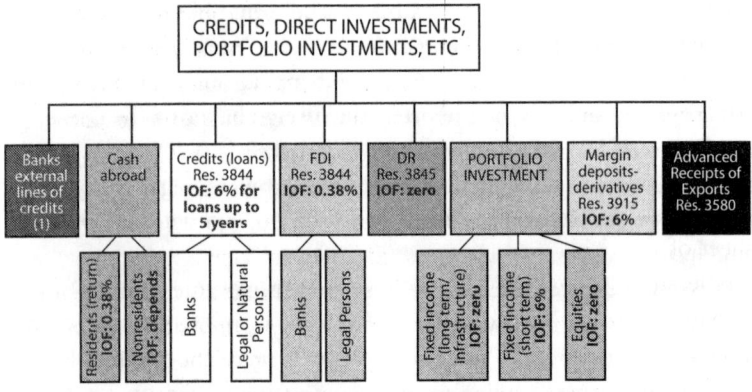

(1) There is no IOF, but short FX position reserves requirements may apply

FIGURE 7.12   Foreign Inflows' Channels and Main Government Measures
Source: Authors' calculations.

The Complex Conjuncture of the Second Half of 2011 and Early 2012

The results of the tightening cycle of 2010 and the first half of 2011 were positive. The policy settings were adjusted in a timely manner and were instrumental in cooling overheating pressures and gradually bringing inflation—after it reached a peak of 7.3 per cent YOY in September 2011—down toward the target midpoint. Brazil was then and remains well prepared to withstand changes in the global scenario in terms of robustness of its financial sector, available liquidity buffers in local and foreign currency, and space to conduct countercyclical demand-management policies in either direction.

Macroeconomic Policies with Global Volatility and Rapid Changes in Risk Perceptions

Policymakers in Brazil were justifiably cautious as they observed the developments in the global economy in the second quarter of 2011. The global mood was one of confidence that the recovery in advanced economies (the United States in particular) was taking hold, especially after the initial boost to market sentiment brought on by the new battery of unconventional monetary easing measures, which visibly permeated through stock markets. The S&P 500 jumped from 1,286 in January 2011 to 1,320 in June 2011 and activity was indeed rebounding in the United States. Nevertheless, in Brazil, local experience with debt crises suggested that the ensuing recoveries were taking longer than usual, and could be marked by volatility. Brazilian policymakers were concerned that many structural characteristics of advanced economies had not been fully appreciated: the new levels of debt on the balance sheet of the public sector, compounded by the fiscal cost of both the rescue and the slowdown in activity, could become a serious drag on growth prospects, especially in countries with significant built-in budgetary commitments to high levels of welfare spending.

That was the case in the Eurozone, aggravated by the lack of a federal fiscal framework (especially with the discredit of the Maastricht treaty targets), lack of policy coordination, and the particular fragility of the countries at the periphery of the monetary zone. Those weaknesses were seen as having the potential to undermine the recovery and subject markets to new waves of heightened risk aversion, if not outright panic. That overall assessment was one of the reasons behind the reduction in the pace of rate hikes toward the end of the tightening cycle of early 2011 (the three last moves of that cycle, in April, June, and July, were all hikes of 25 bps each).

Toward the end of July 2011, things deteriorated rapidly. A succession of idiosyncratic policy stalemates (notably, the debt ceiling in the United States) together with a worsening in market sentiment, triggered by the Greek situation but reaching more systemic economies of the Eurozone (Spain and Italy) as well, revealed that the prevailing combination of political economy factors in the United States and in the Eurozone was pushing the balance of risks to the downside. The data coming from US activity in July and August were also instrumental in affecting consumer sentiment, already negatively dented by stubborn levels of unemployment, the absence of a turnaround in the US housing market, still-high levels of household debt, high gas prices reflecting buoyant commodities markets, and the downgrade of US debt by one rating agency.

In that context of global deterioration, the Central Bank of Brazil was the first among its peers to reverse its stance. At the end of August 2011, it started to reduce the base policy rate. In the seven monetary policy committee meetings held since then, the SELIC (overnight) rate was cut by 400 bps (including two cuts of 75 bps each in March and April 2012). Monetary policy relaxation was accompanied by the tightening of fiscal policy in September (with the announcement of an increase of 0.1 per cent of GDP in the primary surplus target), as the worsening of the debt crisis in advanced European economies discouraged any form of fiscal complacency. Despite the accumulating evidence that global economic conditions were taking a serious turn for the worse, monetary relaxation was widely criticized by market analysts who were focused on the still- high inflation headline YOY in the last quarter of 2011, despite its declining trend initiated in September.

However, by the end of 2011, domestic economic activity in Brazil was showing signs of deceleration. Eventually, growth figures surprised analysts on the downside. Vindicating the chosen policy strategy, not only did activity slow as had been expected by policy makers, but the above mentioned worsening of global conditions affected business sentiment in Brazil by even more than anticipated, resulting in GDP growth of only 2.7 per cent in 2011. Besides the obvious dent to business confidence, domestic factors may also have contributed to making the slowdown more pronounced than originally expected, including the cyclical dynamics of certain segments of the credit market (itself compounded by confidence effects) and the detrimental impact of a stronger exchange rate on industrial production. In the first half of 2012, domestic activity indicators remained as if suspended at a protracted inflexion, with flat industrial production indicators, subdued investment and business confidence, and smaller volumes of trade, while consumption continued to expand on the back of still-robust overall credit growth, resilient consumer confidence, as well as buoyant labor-market conditions, including record-low unemployment rates and rising household incomes. Activity was expected to pick up with the economy regaining momentum during the second half of 2012, led by private domestic demand, as the transmission of the monetary easing and other stimulus measures gradually gathers strength—notwithstanding some delay in transmission as rising NPLs blunted the response of lending rates to monetary policy. After growing by 2.7 per cent in 2011, output did expand in the last quarter of 2012 at a faster pace but still below what was iniatially expected.

Inflation has been falling, but expectations—albeit decreasing marginally—remain that it will rise above the 4.5 per cent target for the end of 2012, and continue to rise in 2013. After its 7.3 per cent peak in September 2011, headline inflation fell to 4.99 per cent YOY in May 2012. This decline reflects the activity slowdown, transitory supply factors, the progressive removal of particularly adverse inflation readings from the one-year trailing window, and the effect of the regular periodic updating of the inflation index weights. The lagged impact of moderating growth and the negative output gap on more sticky components of the index—including services—has also exerted some downward pressure on inflation. Conversely, wholesale price inflation picked up in April, reflecting pass-through—albeit moderate—from the exchange-rate depreciation observed since March.

The year 2012 saw a volatile, risk-off, risk-on environment for policy makers. After the European Central Bank's (ECB's) inauguration of long term refinancing operations (LTROs) at the end of 2011, the new year began (as 2011 had) in a positive mood. But the implementation difficulties of the Greek program, the political economy debates about the pace of fiscal consolidation in many Eurozone countries and the missing of fiscal targets by Spain at the end of February 2012 threw markets in a downward spiral again. This negative external environment, notably the intensifying crisis in Europe, presents the most prominent downside risk in the near term. Important spillover channels include the potential for tighter external financing conditions and lower commodity prices should shockwaves from Europe lead to significantly lower global growth prospects.

Fine-Tuning Macro Prudential Instruments

With these negative macroeconomic developments, by the end of 2012, the credit market was growing at a more suitable rate and the average maturities for vehicle financing had declined. The average delinquency rate for vehicle financing in the first half of 2011 also declined to 27.6 per cent compared with the same period in 2010. In November 2011, the central bank decided to adjust the macro prudential measures adopted in 2010, not only to simplify the implementation and monitoring of the regulation but also to tailor it to the new economic outlook. It reduced from 150 per cent back to the earlier 75 per cent, the risk- weight factor (RWF) used for capital requirement calculation on all collateralized car loans with maturities below 60 months, regardless of loan-to-value

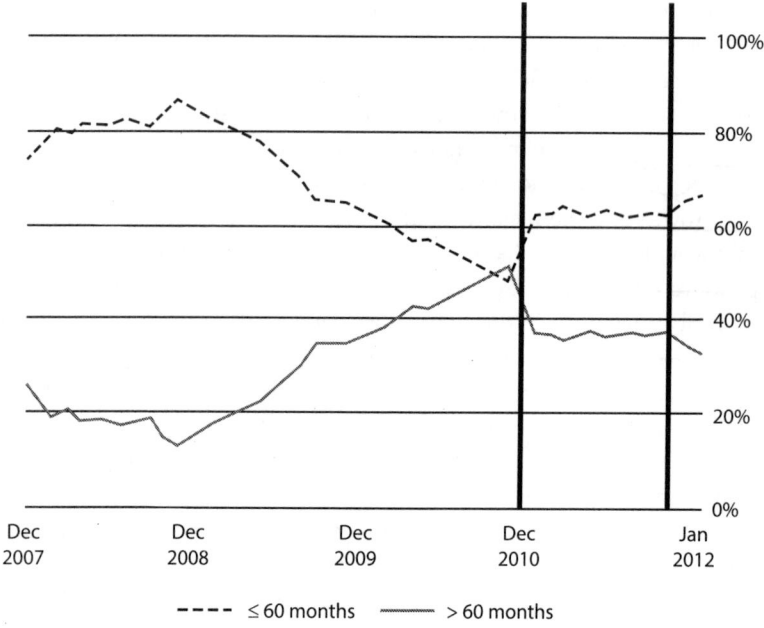

FIGURE 7.13   Percentage of New Vehicle Financing Loans, by Maturity Date
Source: BCB and authors' calculations.

ratios.[42] However, for car loans with maturities above 60 months, deemed to be riskiest, the RWF was kept at 150 per cent (Figure 7.13).

For the payroll-guaranteed consumer loans market, the diagnosis was that the measure implemented in December 2010 to increase to 150 per cent the RWF on loans above 36 months had only a modest temporary effect on the volumes of longer and riskier loans, falling well short of the desired impact. As shown in Figure 7.14, the share of longer-tenor loans in the payroll-guaranteed segment declined in the months immediately following the implementation of the measure, but even that was a weak and short-lived effect, as they soon resumed the upward trend.

As a consequence, the central bank decided to increase the RWF for payroll guaranteed loans above 60 months from 150 to 300 per cent,[43] and reduce it to 75 per cent for the other contracts. To avoid

[42] Circular 3,563/2011.

[43] On 4 March 2013, this RWF was reduced back to 150 per cent.

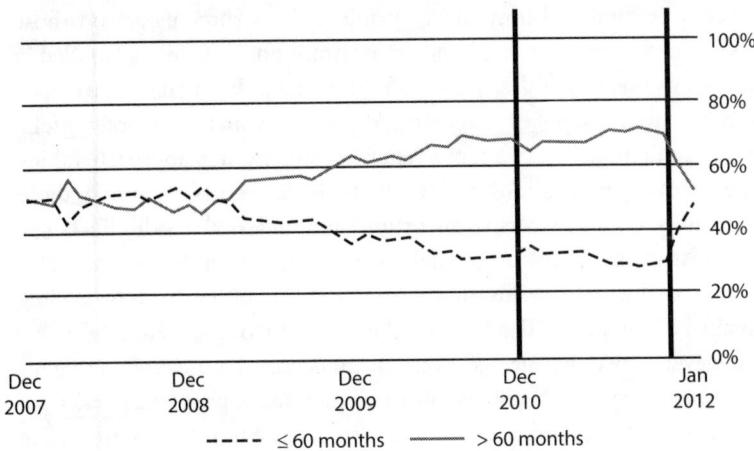

FIGURE 7.14 Percentage of New Payroll-Guaranteed Loans, by Maturity Date

Source: Central Bank of Brazil.

any regulatory arbitrage or distortion in the personal consumer credit market, it also increased to 300 per cent the RWF for loans above 60 months in other modalities of nonearmarked consumer credit.

In December 2011, along with other government measures to stimulate the domestic economy, the of the IOF legislation was amended[44] with respect to consumer credit transactions, reducing the rate to 0.0068 per cent[45] per day (previously 0.0082 per cent) for loans to individuals.

Policy Going Forward

Brazil will continue expanding its macro prudential toolbox on a precautionary basis, to increase its capacity to deal, whenever necessary, with exceptional foreign exchange volatility, destabilizing capital inflows, credit booms, and asset price bubbles. However, calibrating existing or new measures has proven to be difficult because of the economics profession's incomplete understanding of how risks to the financial

[44] Decree 7,632/2011.
[45] On 21 May 2012, Decree n° 7,726 further diminished it to 0.0041 per cent.

system develop and how macro prudential instruments act on those risks. Sometimes, as a result, decisions cannot be as firmly grounded in theory as one might desire; instead, Brazilian policy makers have been required to make policy judgments, drawing on analysis, market intelligence, and modeling to adopt a tentative, step-by-step approach, taking the necessary precautions, and weighing the trade-offs inherent to those measures to avoid excessive distortions and undesirable side effects.

Most of the macro prudential measures applied in Brazil since 2010 related to the time dimension of systemic risk, in other words to 'leaning against the wind' and dealing with the cyclicality of the financial system. However, experience gained from the 2008 crisis has illustrated that, as the financial system becomes more complex and sophisticated, risks can arise not only in a single sector but also as an interlinked, systemwide issue. In fact, the Brazilian financial system is characterized by a high degree of conglomeration and concentration. It is organized around a few financial conglomerates that control over 75 per cent of the system's assets. Therefore, another challenge is to develop effective indicators and to monitor cross-sectional risks related to the interconnectedness of the financial system and the real economy. The main tasks will be to assess network effects, enhance stress tests, expand the supervisory scope to include nonbank financial intermediaries, and to distill the findings from various analytical strands into a consistent macro prudential perspective on policy. Information on exposures between institutions and on exposures commonly held by institutions is crucial. Much of this information will need to be obtained not only from financial institutions, data repositories, and central depositories, but also from corporations. This aspect reinforces the understanding that the mandate that allows the Central Bank of Brazil[46] to access relevant information should be expanded to adequately fulfill its macro prudential supervisory role. Closer coordination and action between the various Brazilian supervisory agencies will, thus, be increasingly important.

In that spirit, Brazil is committed to the full and timely implementation of the Basel III framework and has reiterated its position in all G-20 fora (see Figure 7.15). Most Brazilian banks can raise sufficient capital

---

[46] The Central Bank of Brazil's mission is defined as 'to ensure the stability of the purchasing power of the currency and the soundness and efficiency of the financial system'.

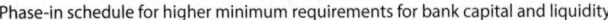

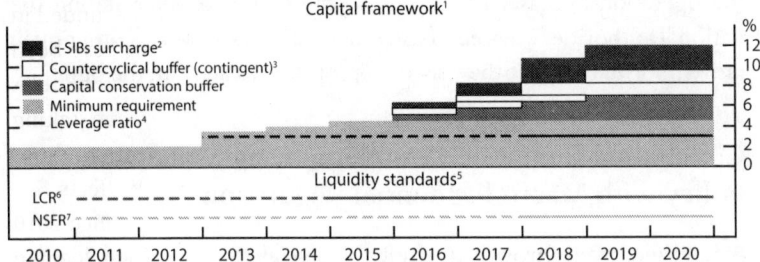

Phase-in schedule for higher minimum requirements for bank capital and liquidity

The dashed lines indicate observation periods and the solid lines indicate the maximum standard.

[1] Common equity capital requirement as a percentage of risk-weighted assets. [2] Maximum of the countercyclical buffers to be met with common equity or other fully loss-absorbing capital, implemented according to national circumstances. [3] Based on the results of the parallel run period, adjustments to be carried out in the first half of 2017 with a view to migrating to a Pillar 1 treatment on 1 January 2018 based on appropriate review and calibration. [4] Capital surcharge applicable to the top bucket of systemic importance. [5] Liquidity ratios to be monitored during the transition period. [6] Liquidity coverage ratio. [7] Net stable funding ratio.

FIGURE 7.15   Implementation of the Basel III Capital and Liquidity Rules

to meet Basel III requirements in the agreed timeframe mainly through retained earnings but, given new definitions and requirements, some adjustment of instruments to be eligible for Tier 1 capital will be needed. In Brazil, the traditional nonrisk-based measure of leverage, given by the ratio between total assets and equity, stands at low levels. The leverage ratios of Brazilian banks are particularly conservative considering the fact that our accounting rules are restrictive compared with international standards when it comes to netting of short and long positions. In addition, off-balance sheet exposures are not significant. Most banks should have no trouble meeting the new Basel III requirements on leverage; therefore no deleveraging process is expected in the near future.

Some refinements will need more work. On the countercyclical capital buffer requirements,[47] for example, further work may be required on its appropriate definition for a country undergoing structural changes and financial deepening because it normally relies on an automatic adjustment based on a 'credit gap' indicator.[48] In line with this, the

[47] The size of the countercyclical capital buffer varies over time and can amount from 0 to 2.5 per cent of the bank's risk-weighted assets.

[48] The countercyclical capital buffer relies on a formula that considers the relation between the total lending to the country's GDP and the size of its deviation from a long-term trend.

Basel Committee on Banking Supervision (BCBS) issued guidance on the operation of Basel III's countercyclical capital buffer stating that national authorities are free to use other variables as well as other qualitative information that they deem appropriate to activate the buffer.

Concluding Remarks: Complementing Monetary Policy with Macro Prudential Regulation

Brazil sailed well through the global financial storm. It used standard aggregate demand management instruments (combining tight fiscal and monetary policies) to deal with inflationary pressures arising from its V-shaped recovery in 2010. It maintained and reinforced its strong financial sector regulation and supervision, endorsed as a conclusion of the 2012 IMF mission conducting Brazil's Financial Sector Assessment Program (FSAP). In banking, the risk-based supervisory process is robust and with a high degree of compliance with the Basel core principles, together with insurance and capital markets supervision. Brazil also took measures to manage credit growth risks, appropriately introducing various macro prudential measures to contain financial risks in specific market segments. The Central Bank of Brazil has made clear that macro prudential measures are not a replacement for monetary policy action and are primarily geared at addressing financial stability risks.

Brazil's large macro financial linkages grew *pari passu* with improvements in the strength of the system. Brazil's FSAP stress tests show that the banking system can withstand severe shocks. After a public consultation process that ended in May 2012, the implementation of Basel III starting in 2013 will enhance the strength of the system. The interaction with the industry indicates that banks should be able to generate sufficient internal capital to manage this transition, including the replacement of deferred tax assets in their core capital base. Brazil's financial sector can also well manage shocks to liquidity and market conditions. Over 20 per cent of assets in required liquid reserves are held as buffers at the central bank, and liquidity and market stress tests run by the FSAP find the system is well positioned to manage strains, including those that could arise from tail risks such as in the Lehman Brothers episode or a new bout of severe stress in the Eurozone. It is true that credit has grown quickly in the last decade (Brazil's credit-to-GDP ratio rose from 26 per cent in 2004 to 49 per cent in 2011) and cross-country studies have associated expansions of this duration and magnitude with risks to stability. However, as noted by the FSAP, a significant portion of the credit increase in Brazil reflects financial deepening, helped by institutional and legal reforms that have substantially strengthened creditor rights. Finally, the overall level of financial development remains low by international standards, which is associated with lower stability risks. Brazil was also innovative during and after the peak of the global financial crisis in exploring the boundaries of Tinbergen's separation principle (see Table 7.7): on the one hand, we saw strong and established results that monetary policy is effective in addressing the transmission of excess demand into inflation; on the other hand, we knew that macro prudential instruments are effective in addressing the build-up of excessive financial risk. The less-explored areas were the effects of monetary policy (respectively, macro prudential policies) on financial risk (respectively, inflation and activity), and the interaction between these policies on both inflation control and financial stability. In the present stage of the global financial crisis, under the separation principle, Brazil employed two instruments (the central bank's base rate and a set of macro prudential tools) to address two objectives (the inflation target and a composite set of financial stability indicators). On the macro prudential side, a bias toward reducing excess credit growth and financial systemic risk requires a greater reliance on tighter regulation (around the Basel III framework) to reduce procyclicality.

TABLE 7.7 The 'New' Separation Framework

	Monetary Policy (MP) One Instrument: CB Base Rate	**Macro-Prudential (MaP)** Various Instruments: RR, LTVs, DTIs, K req (Basel rules), etc.
Price Stability (Inflation)	Effective on Activity/Inflation (e.g., Flex IT, divine coincidence, etc.)	Effects known but issues of anchoring expectations, timing and communication?
Financial Stability (Risk)	Old debate about Lean Against vs Clean After	Effective on Risk (credit and asset excess growth)

Source: BCB and authors' calculations.

Other related issues are under discussion. Financial stability remains in the mandate of many central banks but should it be conducted by a unified agency (the central bank itself) or by two separate agencies? Finally, communicating this new separation clearly to agents is important for an adequate anchoring of expectations.

Brazil had to address these issues with pragmatism, since it was painfully aware of the destabilizing effects of excessive levels of global liquidity, particularly when it transmits to domestic credit growth. Excessive capital inflows present several risks to recipient countries. They are potentially disruptive for emerging markets' price and financial stability. In the absence of any policy response, the economy may lose competitiveness and experience unsustainable trade account deficits. There is also a risk of financial instability. Banks tend to increase their foreign currency exposure and become more lenient in their credit standards when faced with higher foreign liquidity. Surges in capital inflows can lead to higher inflation and to credit and asset price bubbles. Beyond those points, the issue is whether monetary policy itself needs to be expressly concerned with financial stability objectives. And then, if the answer is affirmative, to what financial indicators monetary policy should respond? And what new set of instruments should be used as an additional component of the policy framework aimed at preventing financial crises? In short: To what extent should regulatory rules and monetary policy be combined to ensure both macroeconomic and financial stability?

That discussion is evolving alongside the emergence of analytical research, testing, and studying how these policies interact.[49] This analysis explores the roles of macro prudential regulation and monetary policy in mitigating procyclicality and promoting macroeconomic and financial stability. One avenue is to bring the qualitative insights into

---

[49] For a summary of the literature see Agénor and Pereira da Silva (2012a). For an analytical solution see Agénor et al. (2011, 2012). The stabilizing effect of a central bank reaction function with a credit rule is stronger than that of alternative rules following a classical Taylor-rule specification even when augmented by a set of macro prudential regulations. These results hold for an open economy with a flexible exchange rate, incorporating the interaction between capital inflows (sudden floods), credit creation, and the macroeconomy.

typical dynamic stochastic general equilibrium framework with explicitly modeled credit markets featuring some countercyclical (Basel-type) rules. There are some promising results suggesting that when both macroeconomic stability and financial stability are properly defined by quantitative benchmarks (for example, the volatility of stock or housing prices for the latter) monetary policy could go beyond its conventional mandate under inflation-targeting frameworks and address the time dimension of systemic risk—if only during a transitory period, while more is learned about the implementation and performance of the new macro prudential rules that are currently being discussed. Hence, there are promising arguments in favor of monetary policy reacting in a state-contingent manner to a credit growth gap measure, because of financial stability considerations. Nevertheless, monetary policy is not a replacement for macro prudential regulation because monetary policy cannot, in any event, address the cross-section dimension of systemic risk.

The broad direction of the new strand of literature that emerged after the crisis can be summarized in the following way: 'leaning against the financial cycle' (that is, stemming excessively rapid growth in credit) can be done through a combination of monetary and macro prudential policies to avoid financial fragility and some prevention is not only recommended but achievable in an effective way. A combination of policies is effective in involving monetary and macro prudential policies to act in a complementary fashion to ensure both macroeconomic and financial stability.

Brazil's recent experience with monetary and macro prudential policies to lean against the financial cycle and deal with systemic risks is an example of this new approach. We need more time to measure and assess properly whether this policy direction can be generalized and replicated with success. The present context of the global economy is challenging but it has also triggered new thinking among regulators and central bankers to be ahead of the curve for the ongoing and the next episodes of financial stress.

Epilogue: Exit from Unconventional Monetary Policies, currency dynamics and policy responses

Since the FED began communicating in May 2013 that it could start moderating its assets repurchase program (QE), global financial markets became more volatile and began a process of a re-pricing of risk sometimes leading a sell-off of emerging market assets. Since then, while Treasury yields began to increase, emerging market economies (EMEs) have generally seen depreciating exchange rates, increasing sovereign bond yields, and credit default swap spreads, and in many cases falling stock prices. In fact, market perceptions toward emerging economies seen to have shifted in a more dramatic way than fundamentals might suggest and the optimistic view of the post-crisis was replaced by a gloomy pessimism.

However, by September 2013, it appears that the difficulties of exiting from unconventional monetary policies (UMP) are still present and FED announced that the process of exiting would proceed more slowly than originally priced by markets. One particular concern was that if the long-term real interest rate rises too steeply, the US recovery could stumble, in which case the negative effects would be felt worldwide. On the other hand, prolonging QE would compound the risk of triggering asset bubbles, future inflation, and vulnerabilities in the financial sector.

Nevertheless, the exit from UMP, at an adequate timing, is overall, a welcome transition to more normal global monetary policy conditions. Since the exit would be a result of economic recovery in the world's largest economy, it shall be a net positive for emerging market economies, which will benefit including through global trade. Besides, EMEs are now in a much stronger position than in the past to withstand turbulence, given their improved fundamentals, more flexible exchange rates, and higher international reserve buffers.

In Brazil, in addition to our long experience with 'sudden stops' and much improved fundamentals, we prepared ourselves for this transition. First, our above-mentioned pragmatic policy response left us much better prepared for the eventual exit from UMP. We built strong policy buffers to protect financial stability and prepare for the exit, including international reserves up to about $380 billion, capable of absorbing shocks and provide for a predictable and smooth adjustment of asset prices, including the nominal exchange rate. Our international liabilities position is more robust, with more FDI and less portfolio investment, more equity and less debt. Foreign exchange exposure is limited. The financial system is strongly capitalized and provisioned and relies little on external sources of funding. Credit market expansion has moderated to sustainable levels. Second, we also took measures to strengthen financial system resilience and address fragilities revealed by the global financial crisis, over and above our existing, robust prudential–regulatory framework. We promoted significant improvements in credit and derivative reporting systems, enhancing our ability to monitor financial institutions operations in real time[50]. Even though derivatives in Brazil are mostly centrally cleared, we also enhanced reporting requirements for OTC derivatives. Finally, we have published—as alluded to earlier—the necessary regulations for the implementation of the Basel III framework in Brazil, in accordance with the internationally agreed-in phase-in schedule.

In Brazil's case, the sell-off has manifested itself mostly as a search for hedge and FX protection, not as actual outflows. In fact, portfolio debt flows in June and July have actually been positive at about $11.5 billion, while portfolio equity flows are negative at about $3.5 billion. In part, these numbers reflect a shift from equity to debt due to the removal of the capital inflow tax on portfolio debt instruments early in June. Most of the selling pressure has come from foreign real-money investors seeking to hedge their portfolios from currency devaluation, Brazilian companies hedging their foreign exchange liabilities, and foreign companies hedging their exposure to local assets. There is no foreign currency shortage in the domestic spot market, which the Central Bank monitors continually.

Therefore, our response has focused on removing risk from the economy during this transition period. We have policy buffers and an ample policy toolkit. Some of these tools were used successfully during the global financial crisis of 2008. The policy buffers we have in place give us ample room to steer the economy through this turbulent transition period. Finally, to deal specifically with excessive exchange rate volatility and to provide hedge and liquidity to the domestic foreign exchange market, the Central Bank of Brazil committed to a $60 billion (equivalent) program through the end of the year based on derivative instruments, in such way that safeguards our international

---

[50] The crisis also revealed vulnerabilities in the funding and business models of certain small and medium-sized banks. These banks comprised a small fraction of the small and medium-sized bank segment in Brazil. Even so, we took measures, including the resolution of a number of institutions, and the vulnerabilities have been eliminated.

reserves. The strategy is comprised of daily $500 million (equivalent) FX-Interest rate swap auctions, Monday through Thursday, as well as $1 billion in FX Repo auctions on Fridays. The program has proved successful in curbing volatility and could be extended beyond year end if necessary.

Brazil will continue to strengthen its macro-financial framework while implementing a wide range of reforms to enhance productivity and competitiveness in order to consolidate its economic growth model with social inclusion.

Annex 6A: Categorizing Brazil's Macro Prudential Instruments

Tools	Risk dimensions	
	Time dimension	Cross-sectoral dimension
Category 1. Instruments developed specifically to mitigate systemic risk		
	• Minimum capital ratio requirement above international standards (Circular 3360 - 12 Sep 2007)	• Higher capital charges for trades not cleared through CCPs (Circular 3360 - 12 Sept 2007)
	• Countercyclical change in risk weights for exposure to auto and payroll loans related to longer maturities and higher LTV ratios (Circular 3515 - 3 Dec 2010)	• Increase capital risk weights to exposures to mutual fund's quota (Circular 3563 - 11 Nov 2011)
	• Prohibit payroll loan's maturity above 60 months (Circular 3563 - 11 Nov 2011)	
	• Increase financial transaction tax on consumption credit operations for individuals (Decree 7456 - 6 Apr 2011)	
Category 2. Recalibrated instruments		
	• Loan loss provisioning incorporates expect losses but also incurred losses' data (Resolution 2682 - 21 Dec 1999)	• Financial transaction tax on derivatives' positions that increase fx short net exposure (Decree 7536 - 26 Jul 2011)

- Increase financial transaction tax on foreign inflows for fixed income investments (Decree 7330 - 18 Oct 2010)

- Increase reserve requirements on demand and time deposits and exempt "Letras Financeiras" (Circular 3513 and 3514 - 3 Dec 2010).

- Increase financial transaction tax on inflows related to foreign credit with maturities below 720 days (Decree 7457 - 6 Apr 2011)

- Unremunerated reserve requirement on currency short open positions above certain limits (Circular 3520 - 6 Jan 2011 and Circular 3,548 - 8 Jul 2011)

- Stressed VaR to build additional capital buffer against market risk during a boom for internal and standardized models (Circular 3478 - 24 Dec 2009 and Circular 3568 - 21 Dec 2011)

- Remunerated reserve requirements on time deposits conditioned upon acquisition of medium and small banks' credit portfolio (Circular 3569 - 22 Dec 2011)

Annex 6B: IOF Tax Measures on Foreign Exchange Transactions

IOF

TAX ON CREDIT AND EXCHANGE TRANSACTIONS, INSURANCE, AND SECURITIES

MAIN MEASURES INVOLVING NONRESIDENT OPERATIONS

FINANCIAL AND CAPITAL MARKETS	Dec. 6,306	Dec. 6,391	Dec. 6,613	Dec. 6,983	Dec. 7,011
	14.12.2007	17.03.2008	22.10.2008	19.10.2009	18.11.2009
Fixed income	zero	1.5%	zero	2%	–
Fixed income Law 12, 431 art. 1 and 3	–	–	–	–	–
Variable income (stocks)	zero	zero	zero	2%	–
IPO	zero	zero	zero	2%	–
Emerging companies Investment Funds (FIEE)	zero	1.5%	zero	2%	–
Private Equity Funds (FIP)	zero	1.5%	zero	2%	–
FDI to variable income / stocks (migration)	zero	zero	zero	zero	–
Margin deposits	zero	0.38%	0.38%	0.38%	–
Cancellation of DR into local shares	zero	zero	zero	zero	–
BDR / secondary market	–	–	–	–	–
Deliver of Brazilian shares to issue DR[1]	–	–	–	–	1.5%

1/ This is not IOF on foreign exchange operation, but IOF on securities

EXTERNAL LOANS	Dec. 6,306	Dec. 6,339	Dec. 7,456
	14.12.2007	03.01.2008	28.03.2011
Tax rate	5%	5.38%	6%
Taxable maturity	90 days	90 Days	360 days

CREDIT CARD	Dec. 7,412	Dec. 7,454
	30.12.2010	25.03.2011
Credit card company obligation for client's purchase abroad	2.38%	6.38%

Date format: dd.mm.yy

Dec. 7,323	Dec. 7,330	Dec. 7,412	Dec. 7,456	Dec. 7,632	Dec. 7,683	Dec. 8,023
04.10.2010	18.10.2010	30.12.2010	28.03.2011	01.12.2011	01.03.2012	04.06.2013
1%	6%	6%	6%	6%	–	zero
–	–	–	–	zero	–	–
2%	–	2%	2%	zero	–	–
2%	–	2%	2%	zero	–	–
4%	6%	2%	2%	zero	–	–
4%	6%	2%	2%	zero	–	–
zero	–	2%	2%	zero	–	–
0.38%	6%	6%	6%	6%	–	zero
zero	–	2%	2%	zero	–	–
–	–	–	–	6%	zero	–
–	–	–	–	–	–	–

Dec. 7,457	Dec. 7,683	Dec. 7,698	Dec. 7,751	Dec. 7,653
06.04.2011	01.03.2012	09.03.2012	13.06.2012	04.12.2012
6%	6%	6%	6%	6%
720 days	1,080 days	1,800 days	720 days	360 days

DERIVATIVE CONTRACTS[1]	Law 12,543[2]	Dec. 7,536	Dec. 7,563	Dec. 7,699	Dec. 8,027
	08.12.2011	26.07.2011	15.09.2011	15.03.2012	12.06.2013
Exposure: long exposure reductions/ short exposure increases	Max IOF 25%	1%[3]	1%*	1%[5]	zero

1/ This is not IOF on foreign exchange operation, but IOF on FX derivatives.

2/ Law converted from Provisional Measure 539, de 26.07.2011

3/ Tax applies on adjusted national value, which results from national value x price variation of derivatives with respective to the price variation of underlying assets. Applied to increases on short exposure.

4/ It details the calculation of the adjusted notional value and makes some additional adjustments to this value in order to disregard foreign exchange variation (which are not related with opening or liquidation of positions).

5/ Tax = 0 on positions that increase the net short exposures acquired by exporters for purpose of hedging, upon specific conditions established in the decree.

FOREIGN DIRECT INVESTMENT[1]	Dec. 6,306	Dec. 8,339	Dec. 7,412
	14.12.2007	03.01.2008	30.12.2010
FDI	zero	0.38%	0.38%

1/ General rule tax on foreign exchange operation is 0.38%, unless specified differently.

References

Agénor, Pierre-Richard, Koray Alper, and Luiz A. Pereira da Silva. 2009. 'Capital requirements and business cycles with credit market imperfections', *Policy Research Working Paper 5151*, World Bank, Washington, DC.

———. 2011. 'Capital regulation, monetary policy and financial stability', *Working Paper 154*, Centre for Growth and Business Cycles Research [place].

———. 2012. 'Sudden floods, macroprudential regulation and stability in an open economy', *Working Paper 267*, Central Bank of Brazil, Brasília.

Agénor, Pierre-Richard, and Luiz A. Pereira da Silva. 2010. 'Reforming international standards for bank capital requirements: A perspective from the developing world', in S. Kim and M.D. McKenzie (eds) *International Banking in the New Era: Post-Crisis Challenges and Opportunities*, IFR [spell], Vol. 11, Bingley: Emerald.

Agénor, Pierre-Richard, and Luiz A. Pereira da Silva. 2012a. 'Macroeconomic stability, financial stability, and monetary policy rules', forthcoming, *Journal of International Finance* 15(2): 205–24.

———. 2012b. 'Cyclical effects of bank capital requirements with imperfect credit markets', *Journal of Financial Stability* 8 (January): 43–56.

BCBS (Basel Committee on Banking Supervision). 2010. 'Group of governors and heads of supervision announces higher global minimum capital standards', 12 September. Available online at: http://www.bis.org/press/p100912.pdf. Accessed in 2014.

Bean, C. 2003. 'Asset prices, financial imbalances and monetary policy: Are inflation targets enough?' *Working Paper 140*, Bank for International Settlements, Basel, Switzerland.

Bernanke, Ben. 2002. 'Asset-price 'bubbles' and monetary policy', in *Proceedings of New York Chapter of the National Association for Business Economics*. Available online at: http://www.federalreserve.gov/boarddocs/speeches/2002/20021015/default.htm Accessed in 2014.

———. 2010. 'The effects of the Great Recession on central bank doctrine and practice', *Speech at 56th Economic Conference*, Federal Reserve Bank of Boston, 18 October, Boston, Massachusetts.

Bernanke, B., and M. Gertler. 1999. 'Monetary policy and asset volatility', *Federal Reserve Bank of Kansas City Economic Review* 84: 17–52.

———. 2001. 'Should central banks respond to movements in asset prices?' *American Economic Review* 91: 253–57.

BIS (Bank for International Settlements). 2009. 'Capital flows and emerging market economies', *Working Paper 33*, Committee on the Global Financial System, BIS, January.

———. 2010. 'Macroprudential instruments and frameworks: A stocktaking of issues and experiences', *Working Paper 38*, Committee on the Global Financial System, BIS, May.

Blanchard, O. 2000. 'What do we know about macroeconomics that Fisher and Wicksell did not?' *Working Paper Series 7550*, February, Cambridge, Massachusettes: National Bureau of Economic Research.

Blanchard, O., and J. Galí. 2005. 'Real wage rigidities and the new Keynesian model', *Working Paper 11806*, November, Cambridge, Massachusettes: National Bureau of Economic Research. Available online at: http://www.nber.org/papers/w11806. Accessed in 2014.

Blanchard, O., G. Dell'Ariccia, and P. Mauro. 2010. 'Rethinking macroeconomic policy', *Staff Position Note 10/03*, February, International Monetary Fund, Washington, DC.

Blanchard, O., D. Romer, M. Spence, and J. Stiglitz. 2012. *In the wake of the crisis*. Cambridge: Massachusetts Institute of Technology Press.

Blinder, Alan S. 1998. 'Central banking in theory and practice', Cambridge: Massachusetts Institute of Technology Press. [au is this a book? If not give type of publication]

———. 2010. 'How central should the central bank be?' *Journal of Economic Literature* March: 23–133.

Borio, C. 2011. 'Central banking post-crisis: What compass for uncharted waters?' *Working Paper 353*, September, Bank for International Settlements, Basel, Switzerland.

Borio, C., and P. Lowe. 2002. 'Asset prices, financial and monetary stability: Exploring the nexus', *Working Paper 114*, Basel, Switzerland: Bank for International Settlements. Available online at: http://www.bis.org/publ/work114.htm. Accessed in 2014.

———. 2002. 'Assessing the risk of banking crises', *BIS Quarterly Review*, December.[vol? pages?]

Borio, C., and P. Disyatat. 2011. 'Global imbalances and the financial crisis: Link or no link?' *Working Paper 346*, May, Basel, Switzerland: Bank for International Settlements.

Brunnermeier, Markus, Andrew Crocket, Charles Goodhart, Avinash D. Persaud, and Hyun Shin. 2009. 'The fundamental principles of financial regulation', International Center for Monetary and Banking Studies, *The Geneva Report on the World Economy 11*, 6 January. Available online at: http://www.princeton.edu/~markus/research/papers/Geneva11.pdf. Accessed in 2014.

Caballero, Ricardo, Emmanuel Farhi, and Pierre-Olivier Gourinchas. 2008. 'Financial crash, commodity prices and global imbalances', *Discussion Paper 7064*, Center for Economic Policy Research, London.

Canuto, Otaviano, and Swati Ghosh. 2013. 'Dealing with the Challenges of Macro Financial Linkages in Emerging Markets', *World Bank Study*.

Cecchetti, S., H. Genberg, J. Lipsky, and S. Wadhwani. 2000. 'Asset prices and central bank policy', *Report 2, Geneva Reports on the World Economy*, International Centre for Monetary and Banking Studies, Geneva, and Centre for Economic Policy Research, London.

Central Bank of Brazil. 2011a. 'Relatório de Estabilidade Financeira', April.

———. 2011b. 'Relatório de Inflação', June.

CIEPR (Committee on International Economic Policy and Reform). 2011. 'Rethinking central banking', September, The Brookings Institution. Available online at: http://www.brookings.edu/research/reports/2011/09/ciepr-central-banking. Accessed in 2014.

Cooper, Richard N. 2007. 'Living with global imbalances', *Brookings Papers on Economic Activity 2*, pp. 91–107.

Dooley, Michael P., David Folkerts-Landau, and Peter M. Garber. 2009. 'Bretton Woods II still defines the international monetary system', *Working Paper*

14731, February, National Bureau of Economic Research, Cambridge, Massachusettes.

Financial Services Authority. 2009. *The Turner Review: A Regulatory Response to the Global Banking Crisis*. London: Financial Services Authority.

Financial Stability Board. 2010. 'Overview of progress in the implementation of the G20 recommendations for strengthening financial stability: Report of the financial stability board to G20 leaders', Financial Stability Board, 18 June. Available online at: http://www.financialstabilityboard.org/publications/r_100627c.pdf. Accesssed in 2014.

Galati, G., and R. Moessner. 2011. 'Macroprudential policy—A literature review', *Working Paper 337*, February, Bank for International Settlements (BIS) Basel, Switzerland.

Goodhart, Charles A.E. 2000. *Which Lender of Last Resort for Europe?* London: Central Banking Publications.

Greenspan, A. 2002. 'Economic volatility', *Proceedings of Federal Reserve Bank of Kansas City Symposium*, Jackson Hole, 30 August. Available online at: http://www.federalreserve.gov/boarddocs/speeches/2002/20020830/default.htm. Accessed in 2014.

———. 1996. 'The challenge of central banking in a democratic society', Remarks by Alan Greenspan at the Annual Dinner and Francis Boyer Lecture of the American Enterprise Institute for Public Policy Research, 5 December. Available online at: http://www.federalreserve.gov/boarddocs/speeches/1996/19961205.htm. Accessed in 2014.

IMF (International Monetary Fund). 2011a. 'Recent experiences in managing capital inflows—Cross-cutting themes and possible policy framework', [type of publication?]14 February, Washington, DC: IMF.

———. 2011b. 'Macroprudential policy: An organizing framework', Working Paper, March, Monetary and Capital Markets Department, Washington, DC.: IMF.

———. 2011c. 'Toward operationalizing macroprudential policies: When to act?' in *Global Financial Stability Report*, Chapter 3, September, Washington, DC.: IMF.

Kohn, Donald. 2005. 'Financial markets, financial fragility, and central banking', remarks at a symposium sponsored by the Federal Reserve Bank of Kansas City, Jackson Hole, 27 August.

Lim, C., F. Columba, A. Costa, P. Kongsamut, A. Otani, M. Saiyid, T. Wezel, and X. Wu. 2011. 'Macroprudential policy: What instruments and how to use them? lessons from country experiences', *Working Paper 11/238*, October, Washington, DC.: International Monetary Fund. Available online at: http://www.imf.org/external/pubs/ft/wp/2011/wp11238.pdf. Accessed in 2014.

Mesquita, Mário, and M. Torós. 2010. 'Considerações sobre a Atuação do Banco Central na Crise de 2008', *Working Papers Series 202*, Central Bank of Brazil, March, Brasillia.

Mishkin, F. 2008. 'How should we respond to asset price bubbles?' Speech at the Wharton Financial Institutions Center and Oliver Wyman Institute's Annual Financial Risk Roundtable, Philadelphia, 15 May. Available online at: http://www.federalreserve.gov/newsevents/speech/mishkin20080515a. htm. Accesssed in 2014.

———. 2010. 'Monetary policy strategy: Lessons from the crisis', paper presented at the 6th European Central Bank Conference, 'Monetary Policy Revisited: Lessons from the Crisis', Frankfurt, 18–19 November. Available online at http://www.ecb.europa.eu/events/conferences/html/cbc6. en.html. Accessed in 2014.

Montoro, C., and R. Moreno. 2011. 'The use of reserve requirements as a policy instrument in Latin America', *BIS Quarterly Review* March: 53–65.

Moreno, R. 2011. 'Policymaking from a "macroprudential" perspective in emerging market economies', *Working Paper 336*, January, Bank for International Settlements, Basel, Switzerland.

Obstfeld, M., and K. Rogoff. 2009. 'Global imbalances and the financial crisis: Products of common causes', November, *Discussion Paper 7606*, Centre for Economic Policy Research London. Available online at: http://www.cepr. org/pubs/dps/DP7606.asp. Accessed in 2014.

Roubini, Nouriel, and Brad Setser. 2005. 'Will the Bretton Woods 2 regime unravel soon? The risk of a hard landing in 2005–2006', *RGE Monitor*, 1 February. Available online at: http://www.roubini.com/analysis/38641. php. Accessed in 2014.

Stark, Jürgen. 2010. 'In search of a robust monetary policy framework', speech at the 6th ECB Central Banking Conference [Is this the official name or should it be 'European Central Bank Conference' Same conference as in Mishkin 2010 above?]Frankfurt, Germany, 19 November.

Svensson, Lars E.O. 2010a. 'Inflation targeting', *NBER, Working Paper 16.654*.

———. 2011b. 'Inflation targeting and financial stability', Keynote lecture at the CEPR/ESI, [spell] 14th Annual Conference, hosted by the Central Bank of Turkey, October [days].

Terrier, G., et al. 2011. 'Policy instruments to lean against the wind in Latin America', *Working Paper 11/159*, July, Washington, DC.: International Monetary Fund.

Trichet, Jean-Claude. 2010. 'Reflections on the nature of monetary policy non-standard measures and finance theory', Speech at the 6th ECB Central Banking Conference, [Is this the official name or should it be 'European Central Bank Conference']Frankfurt, Germany, 19 November.

8

HARTADI A. SARWONO

Managing Capital Flows: Indonesia's Experience[1]

1. Introduction

Volatility in global capital flows has continued to corner the attention of policymakers in recent years. The onset of the Global Financial Crisis (GFC) in 2008 resulted in a sudden stop of capital flows to emerging economies. However, this trend reversed the very next year, resulting in a resurgence of capital inflows to emerging economies driven by attractiveness of investing rewards in these economies and loose monetary policy in advanced economies. The high volatility of capital flows have raised issues related to appropriate management of these flows. There exists enough empirical evidence to suggest that proper management of capital flows generates a number of benefits for an economy. However, the failure to manage these flows is likely to jeopardize both internal and external balance.

Indonesia as a small, open economy has also been exposed to the challenges related to managing of capital flows. The resurgence of capital inflows since 2009 resulted in a number of policy challenges as there was a considerable change both in the size and composition of

[1] Presented in RBI–ADB Conference on Managing Capital Flows, Mumbai, India, on 19 November 2012

capital flows. The overarching policy challenge has centered on how to maintain internal and external balances in a fast-growing economy amid the presence of the classic open economy policy trilemma.

The policy trilemma constitutes the need to balance three equally challenging tasks of managing the volatility of capital flows, responding to the ensuing exchange rate overshooting, and containing domestic liquidity expansion, wherein two of these are unavoidably conflicting. Accordingly, Bank Indonesia (BI) as the central bank and the Government should conduct policy to derive the maximum benefit from the surge of capital flows while managing the contemporaneous risks. As a result of remaining vigilant, thus far, the policies have managed the various risks associated with surges of capital flows, and contributed to the solid economic development.

This paper presents Indonesia's experience in dealing with capital flows, particularly since 2008. The reminder of this paper is organized as follows. The second section elaborates on the policy background in managing the capital flows while the third section describes the implementing strategy as well as various instruments used to manage capital flows. This is followed by the fourth section, which focuses on the various policy outcomes. Finally, the fifth section highlights the experience of capital flow management during the most recent period of capital reversals.

2. Policy Background

It is widely acknowledged that capital flows provide several benefits to the recipient countries. Kawai and Lamberte (2010) highlights the experience of several country experiences in Asia, which have benefited from greater volume of capital flows, prior to the GFC. Indonesia, as a small economy, also derived numerous benefits, both at the microeconomic and macroeconomic levels, from greater integration with global capital markets (Cadarajat 2009; Goeltom 2008). At the microeconomic level, capital inflows have contributed to enhance efficiency in resource allocation and the competitiveness of domestic financial sector. Capital inflows, particularly in the form of FDI, have also facilitated the transfer of technology and management practices. At the macroeconomic level, capital inflows have, in part, filled the saving-investment gap, smoothened consumption, diversified risks, and promoted economic development.

Notwithstanding their beneficial effects, the surge in capital flows has also posed several policy challenges. As discussed, large capital flows, if not managed properly, can exacerbate existing risks in recipient countries. Firstly, unbridled capital inflows may result in excessive credit expansion leading to an overheated economy and an overvalued real exchange rate, which, in turn, could trigger macroeconomic instability. Secondly, such inflows tend to create risks of balance of payments crisis and induce financial instability in a short span of time, especially in the event of reversal of these capital inflows. However, managing these risks is not an easy task.

Indonesia experienced a great deal of financial instability both during the Asian financial crises of 1997 as well as the more recent GFC in 2008. During the GFC, the extent of deleveraging and capital flight resulted in extensive pressure in the foreign exchange market as well as in the equity and government bond markets. Given the thin domestic financial market, capital reversal has triggered sharp exchange rate depreciation accompanied by increasing volatility of the currency. The Rupiah dropped by 21.7 per cent to around Rp 12,000 in November 2008 from around Rp 9,400 at the end of 2007 (Figure 8.1). At the same time, in November 2008 Jakarta stock exchange index plunged to its lowest level since 2006, and was more than 60 per cent lower than its peak level (Figure 8.2). Similarly, the yields on the benchmark government bond rose to around 20 per cent in October 2008 from 10 per cent in December 2007 (Figure 8.2).

Given the various benefits and risks associated with the foreign capital flows, the key policy challenge for BI as well as the government is to derive the maximum benefit of the capital flows while minimizing the costs. This is an onerous task given that there does not exist a single solution to the varied risks associated with capital flow surges. Thus, a multiple instrument approach needs to be adopted to counter these risks. The task becomes even more difficult for a small, open economy like Indonesia as these capital flows tend to be volatile and the quantum of flows large relative to domestic financial market. For instance, since 2009, the bulk of the foreign capital flowing into Indonesia has been in the form of portfolio investment flows which tend to be short-term in nature and prone to reversals. Accordingly, the key challenge facing the policymakers is to transform these short-term inflows into longer term flows and channel them to productive

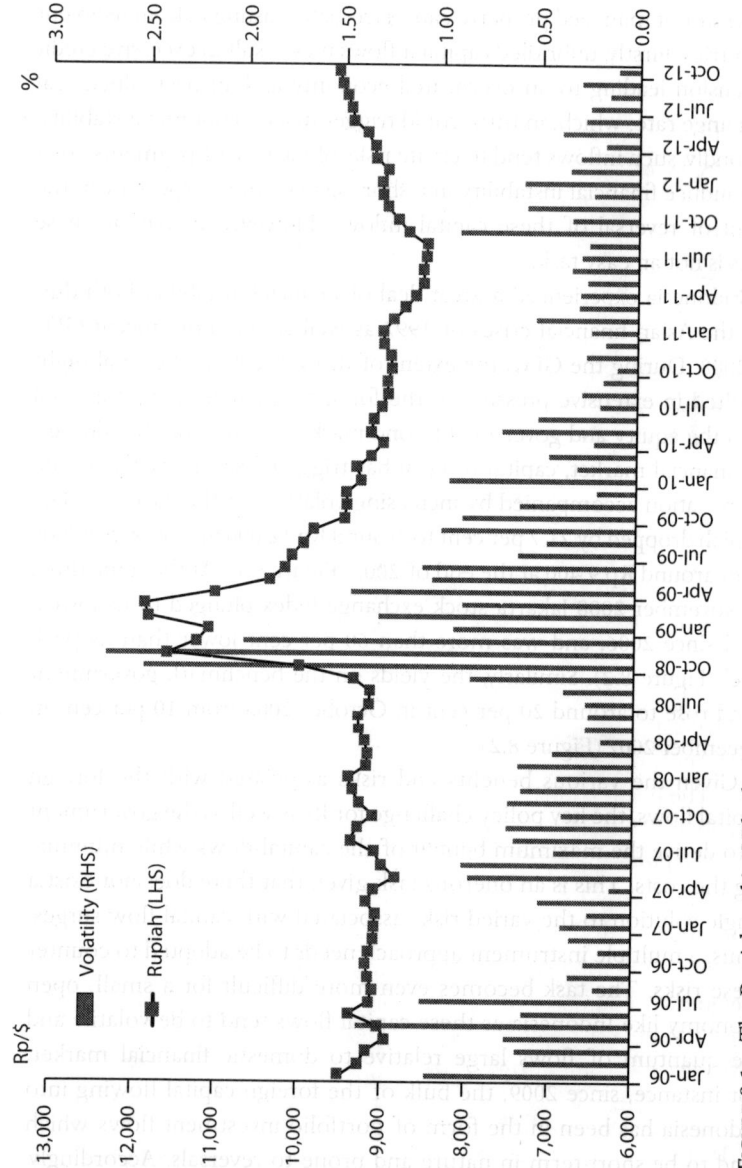

FIGURE 8.1   The Rupiah and its Volatility

Source: Bank Indonesia.

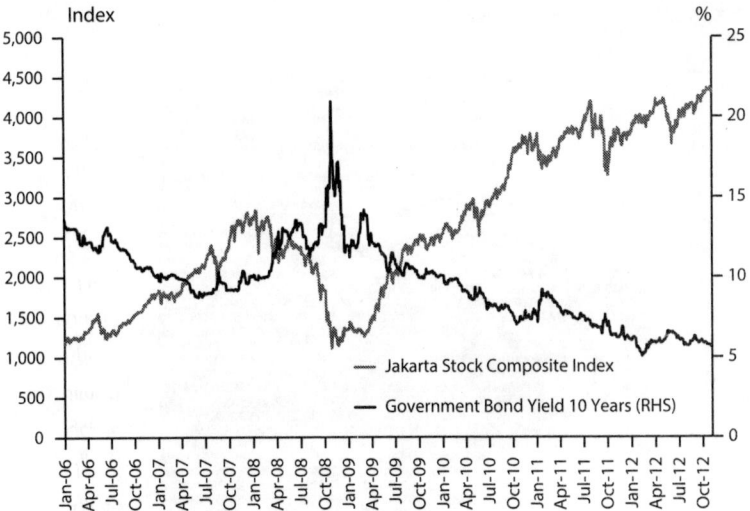

FIGURE 8.2   JSCI and Government Bond Yield
Source: Bank Indonesia.

sectors of the economy to support economic growth in a sustainable manner.

Trends in the capital and financial accounts under the balance of payments indicate that the net portfolio investment inflows in 2009 rose significantly to $10.3 billion in 2009, nearly double the inflows received in 2007. The portfolio investment inflows have been directed towards not only equities but also the public fixed income assets, namely government bonds (SUN) and central bank bills (SBI). Foreign investment in government bonds rose from $8.3 billion (16.6 per cent of total government bond issuance) at the end of 2007 to $21.6 billion (29.3 per cent of total government bond issuance) in December 2010 (Figure 8.3). Similarly, foreign ownership of central bank bills steadily increased from $2.9 billion (11.41 per cent of total central bank bills) at the end of 2007 to $6.1 billion (27.4 per cent of total central bank bills) in December 2010.

3. Policy Responses

Both the BI and the Government have implemented a series of policy measures to effectively manage the consequences of a resurgence of

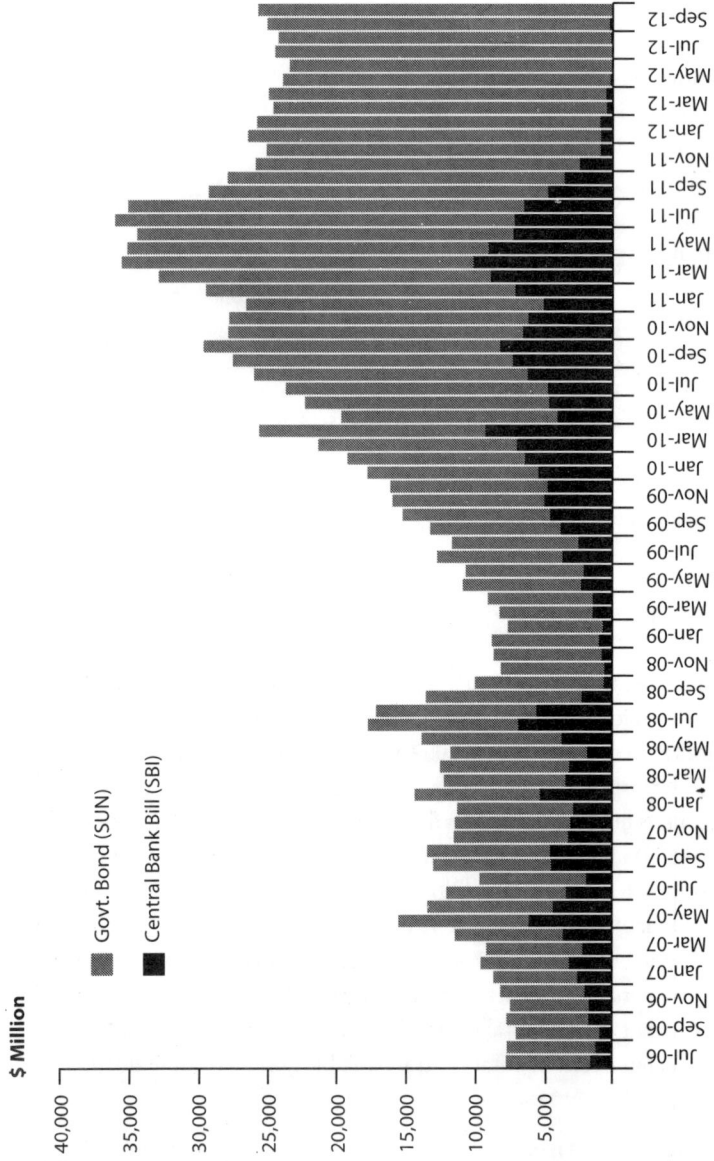

FIGURE 8.3   Foreign Investor in Government Bond and Central Bank Bills

Source: Bank Indonesia.

capital inflows since 2009. The authorities have ensured that sound and sustainable macroeconomic and financial policies are in place to create conducive environment for capital inflows. The BI has implemented prudent monetary policy that is consistent with its overall stance under Inflation Targeting Framework. Meanwhile, the government has succeeded in pursuing a sustainable fiscal policy by containing the budget deficit to less than 2 per cent of GDP, resulting in a declining trend in the government debt-to-GDP ratio (Figure 8.4).

The monetary policy stance is guided by the desire to strike an optimal balance between achieving targeted inflation and supporting economic growth, while at the same time also mitigating risks emanating from massive capital inflows. The BI rate is the policy rate reflecting the monetary policy stance adopted by Bank Indonesia. BI has gradually lowered the BI Rate from 9.5 per cent in November 2009 to 5.75 per cent in May 2013 due to lower inflation expectation as well as the desire to contain massive capital inflows. BI also adjusted the money market interest rate corridor to stimulate the interbank money market transaction in the midst of excess liquidity in banking sector. In June 2010, the corridor was widened from 100 basis points (bps) to 200 bps. In 2011, the corridor was further widened to 250 bps by lowering the bottom limit from BI Rate—100 bps to BI Rate—150 bps, while retaining the

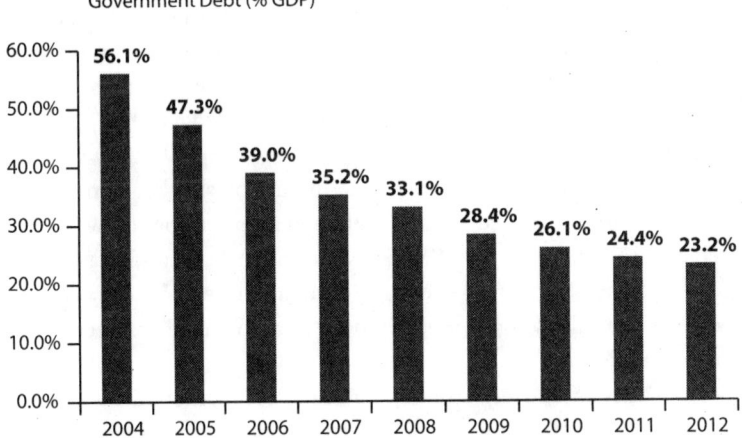

Government Debt (% GDP)

FIGURE 8.4   Government Debt to GDP Ratio (Percentage of GDP)
Source: Bank Indonesia.

upper limit at BI Rate + 100 bps. In August 2012, the bottom limit was slightly raised to BI Rate − 125 bps to respond to the uncertainty in the financial market that could have triggered capital outflows.

Nonetheless, the experience of Indonesia, as well as those of other EMEs, has clearly shown that while maintaining strong fundamental is a necessary condition to prudently cope with surges in capital flows, it is not a sufficient condition. Judicious management of capital flows requires several other prudential measures to be an integral part of the overall policy mix aimed at maintaining macro financial stability. These prudential measures are not aimed at controlling the volume or composition of capital flows, but are designed to reduce risks emanating from the volatility of these capital flows and sustain financial stability.

In this regard, the broad and comprehensive policy mix that the central bank has pursued mainly include: (a) maintaining flexible exchange rate with selective sterilized foreign exchange intervention, (b) enhancing monetary operation strategy, and (c) conducting capital flows management, introducing targeted macro-prudential measure. Each of these policies is briefly elaborated as follows.

Flexible Exchange Rate with Selective Sterilized Foreign Exchange Intervention

The role of exchange rate flexibility in managing capital flows in Indonesia's framework is extremely critical. A flexible exchange rate has the ability to serve as an important shock absorber that would eventually reduce the extent of overheating and dampen pressures on other asset prices. However, it has been acknowledged that excessive appreciation of rupiah during periods of rapid capital inflows would disrupt the economy and amplify the impact of shocks. Considering these risks, BI has also conducted sterilized intervention in the foreign exchange (FX) market. The FX intervention has been undertaken in a measured pace to contain excessive exchange rate volatility, while at the same time allowing the rupiah move in accordance with economic fundamentals.

The policy of actively intervening in the FX market during periods of excessive capital inflow has helped to enhance the stockpile of international reserves. As shown in Figure 8.5, this strategy has reserves increasing to an all the time high of $124.6 billion in August 2011, from

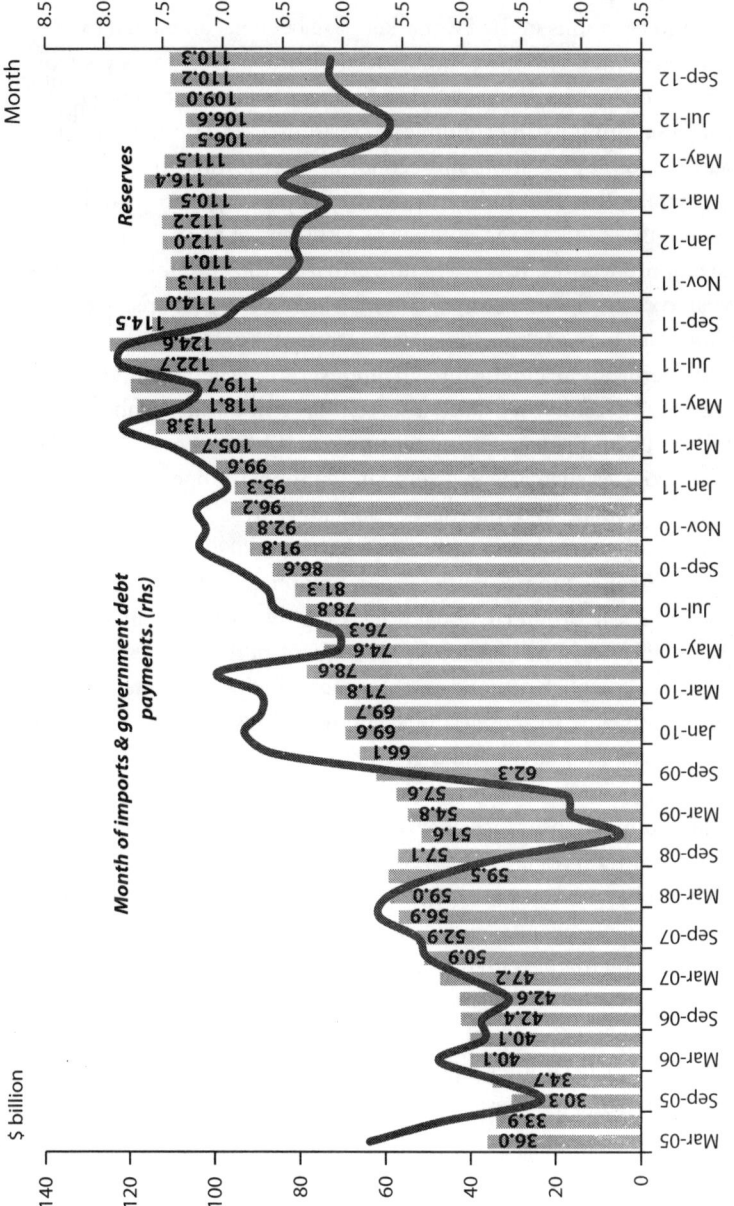

FIGURE 8.5 Indonesia's Foreign Exchange Reserves
Source: Bank Indonesia

around $50 billion in November 2008 in the aftermath of the collapse of Lehman Brothers.

The interventions in the FX market have been accompanied by sterilizing these interventions to mitigate their impact on money supply and inflation. Sterilized intervention has been widely used instrument in many emerging Asian economies to resist excessive nominal and real exchange rate appreciation and economic overheating in the face of large capital inflows. In Indonesia, as the supply of government bonds is limited, BI issued a large number of SBI, central bank securities, for sterilization purposes. It is well known that sterilized intervention has associated costs, the most important of which is the cost arising due to the difference between the domestic interest rates paid on SBI securities used for sterilization and the foreign interest rate earned on international reserves. Therefore, sterilized intervention is not a sustainable policy tool for large and persistent capital flows, and has to be accompanied by other policies such as enhancement of monetary operation, capital flows management, and macroprudential measures.

The rapid accumulation of reserves between 2009 and 2011 helped to create a self-insurance buffer from unintended shocks in the FX market. The role of international reserves as self-insurance instrument has been effectively recognized in subsequent periods of capital flow reversal. Amid higher demand and shortage of supply of international assets, BI was able to recycle the accumulated reserves to reduce the pressure in the FX market and thereby smooth exchange rate volatility. Consequently, international reserves carry numerous benefits. Apart from providing an insurance against sudden reversal of capital inflows, international reserves also allow countries to garner greater flexibility vis-à-vis monetary and exchange rate management while being integrated with global capital markets. Aizenman et al. (2012) show that Asian emerging markets used foreign exchange reserves to mitigate the binding constraints of the 'impossible trinity', that is, the difficulty of simultaneously attaining monetary independence, exchange rate stability, and full financial integration. They observe that Asian emerging markets, including Indonesia, achieved intermediate levels of monetary independence, exchange rate stability, and financial integration.

In addition, along with sterilized intervention in the FX market, the policy in 2011 involved intervention in the government bond market. During the capital flow reversal caused by heavy selling of government bonds by foreign holders, BI used some of the rupiah absorbed from the FX market to purchase government bonds in the secondary market. BI's intervention strategy in the government bond market prevented a significant drop in the bond prices, which could have undermined investors' confidence in the bond market and lead to systemic risks in the financial system including bank and nonbank financial institutions.

The strategy of intervening in both the FX and bond markets successfully stabilized both these markets and prevented further drop in the currency and government bond prices, compared to the experiences in 2008. These measures helped restore the yield of government bonds, as represented by 10-year bonds, to a reasonable rate of around 6.0 per cent after an increased to more than 7.5 per cent in September 2011, and at the same time helped reduce the volatility of the exchange rate (Figure 8.1 and Figure 8.2). Moreover, BI's strategy in the bond market could also buttress BI's policy to accumulate the stock of government bond to be used as a monetary instrument in the open-market operations accompanying SBI securities. Currently, BI has been quite active in utilizing those bonds as reverse repo instrument in day-to-day open market operations.

Monetary Operation Strategy

BI also strengthened its monetary operation strategy to sterilize the liquidity generated from FX intervention and to prevent the undue impact of short-term capital inflows. Apart from this, BI has also augmented monetary instruments in its monetary operation tools kit to better manage the liquidity in the in the economy.

In 2010, BI has lengthened the maturity of SBI up to nine months. This move also strengthened the effectiveness of the previous strategy to reduce the frequency of SBI auctions from weekly to monthly auction. In addition, BI also introduced nontraded monetary instruments to absorb excess liquidity using the Rupiah Term Deposits (Rupiah TD). This instrument is nontransferable, thereby reducing foreign investor intention to accumulate tradable monetary instrument such as SBI. However, banks could undertake early redemption if they required temporary liquidity, subject to certain conditions.

The strengthening of the monetary operation enhancement helped not only to improve the ability of the central bank to absorb excess liquidity, but also avoid capital flows being invested in the monetary instruments, as well as eliminate carry trade and arbitrage (Hendarsah 2010). Moreover, effective monetary operation has altered the composition of the liabilities from being predominantly consistent of SBI (tradable instruments) to one where Rupiah TD (nontradable instruments) made up a significant part of liabilities (Figure 8.6).

Capital Flow Management and Macroprudential Measures

In order to effectively manage the impact of heightened volatility in capital flows, macroeconomic policy measures and conventional open-market operations such as sterilized intervention need to be combined with capital flow management and macroprudential measures. However, capital flow management and macroprudential measures are basically reinforcements of previous policies and do not act as a substitute for the basic macro policies.

Capital Flow Management (CFM) and Macroprudential (MP) measures, though often perceived as being similar, their primary objectives do not necessarily overlap (IMF 2011). In Indonesia, CFM measures were administrative measures aimed to contain the scale or influence the composition of capital flows. In particular, these measures sought to limit short-term and volatile capital flows. In contrast, MP measures sought to limit the build-up of systemic financial risks, irrespective of whether the origin of the risk is domestic or cross-border.

As the part of CFM, BI issued the policy month holding period (MHP) up to six months recently. This was driven by the desire to prevent a sudden reversal of capital flows on a large scale, and to channel the capital inflows from SBI into more productive instruments such as government bonds, equities, and FDI. Under the MHP policy, a buyer of SBI is obliged to hold the instrument for a minimum period of 6 months. This is applicable for both primary and secondary market purchases of all tenors, and covers both residents and nonresidents. Thus, the regulation of the six-month holding period in SBIs locks in foreign investments in SBIs for at least six months. This measure incentivized foreign investors' to reduce their investment in SBI, which is primarily a monetary instrument and not an investment instrument, and channel their investments to bond and stock markets.

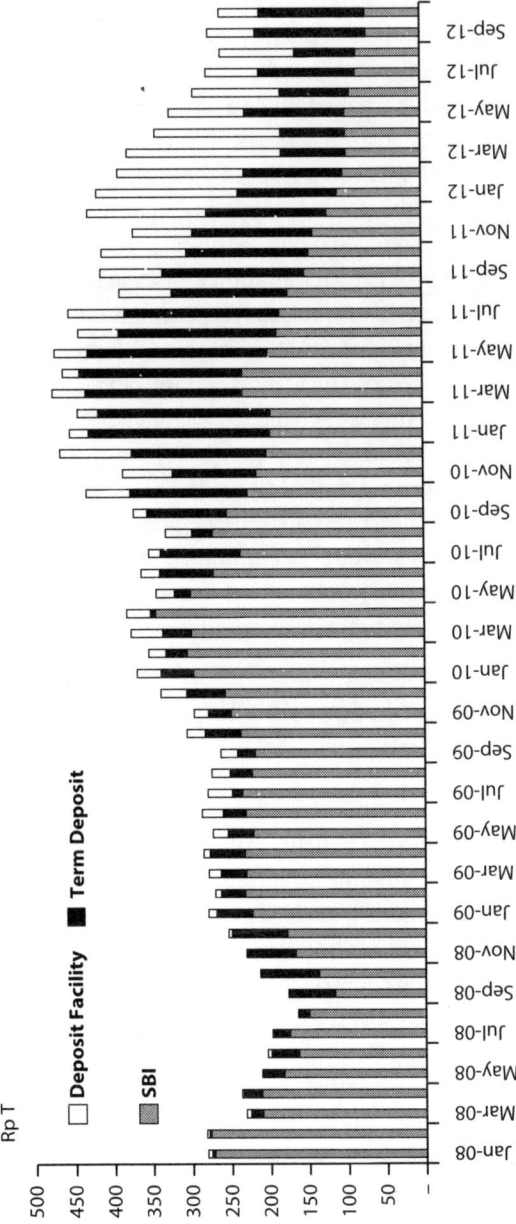

FIGURE 8.6 SBI, Term Deposit, and Deposit Facility
Source: Bank Indonesia.

Apart from introducing new policy measures, BI's existing policy on CFM also helped to control capital flows. A number of regulations were implemented in 2001 and subsequently strengthened in 2005 to curb the speculative transactions undertaken by foreign investors through rupiah and/or derivative transaction and also to facilitate noninternationalization of Rupiah.

In the context of MP measures, BI used the reserve requirement policy as an instrument to absorb undue liquidity stemming from substantial capital inflows and excess liquidity in banking system. In November 2010, BI raised the Rupiah Primary Statutory Reserve Requirement to 8 per cent from 5 per cent. BI also raised reserve requirement for foreign currency up to 8 per cent in June 2011. In addition, BI imposed statutory reserve requirement based on the loan to deposit ratio (LDR) in March 2011, which was aimed at helping banks to maintain their lending practices within prudential norms.

Recently, BI implemented other MP measures to manage excessive credit growth to certain sectors by strengthening the implementation of the loan-to-value (LTV) ratio to automotive and property sectors. The LTV policy is expected not only to shift the funds into more productive sectors but also strengthen the soundness of the banking sector.

4. Policy Outcome: Indonesia's Experience during Capital Inflows

As mentioned earlier, the policy mix introduced by the central bank was aimed at maximizing the benefits from integration with the global financial markets while minimizing the risks. Accordingly, the policies implemented have been quite beneficial in sustaining capital inflows and mitigating the inherent risks. The policies helped to maintain the trend of capital flowing into the country, shift the composition of investment in financial instruments, expand the stock of FDI, and eventually contain the exchange rate volatility.

The data supports the view that the policies introduced to maintain healthy volume of capital inflows were successful in achieving their objective. Capital inflows were on the rise since 2009 until mid-2012, before slightly weakening recently due to the prolonged uncertainty in the global financial market. The policies were also able to alter the composition of the portfolio investment in financial instruments towards a more productive portfolio. Among the financial instruments, the foreign ownership of SBIs dropped markedly from 39 per cent in May 2011 to only 1.2 per cent of total SBI's issuance in September 2012 (Figure 8.7). In contrast, foreign ownership of government bonds have remained strong around 30 per cent after reaching a peak level of around 34.5 per cent of the total issuance in July 2011. The policies also helped to attract FDI inflows, which became the dominant form of capital inflows in the Balance of Payments since 2010 (Figure 8.8).

The policies have also helped contain exchange rate volatility without deviating too far from the fundamental level. The Rupiah had recovered from the 2008 crisis by mid-2009. Since then, the Rupiah appreciated gradually by around 3–4 per cent per year, and was moving in line with the other regional currencies during the period of surge in capital inflows (Figure 8.1 and Figure 8.9).

The policy measures used to manage capital flows also contributed to buoy economic activity and maintain macroeconomic stability. Economic growth remained strong with inflation being contained within acceptable range. By end of 2011, economic growth remained

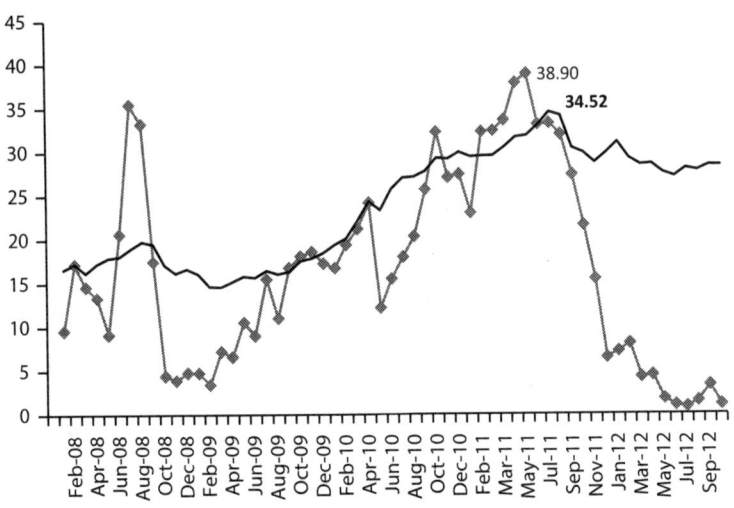

FIGURE 8.7   Foreign Ownership in SBI and Government Bond
Source: Bank Indonesia.

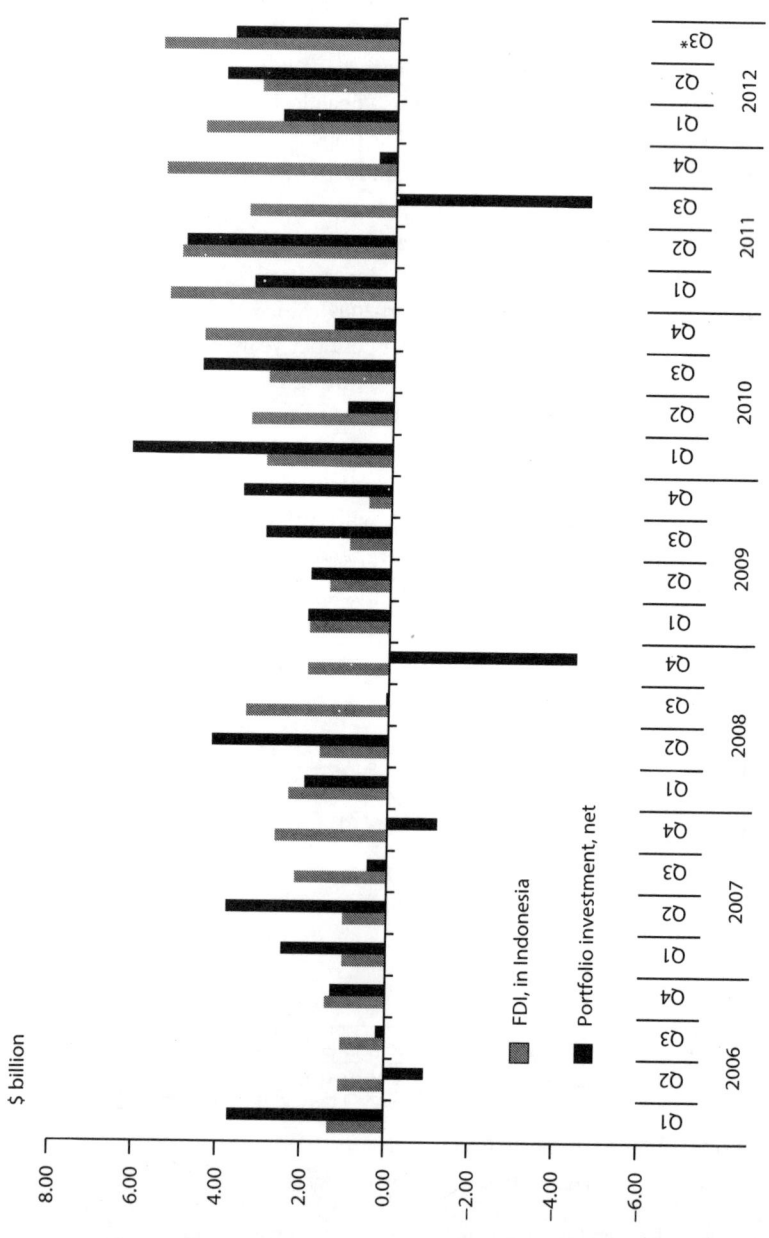

$ billion

FIGURE 8.8 Portfolio Investment and FDI
Source: Bank Indonesia.

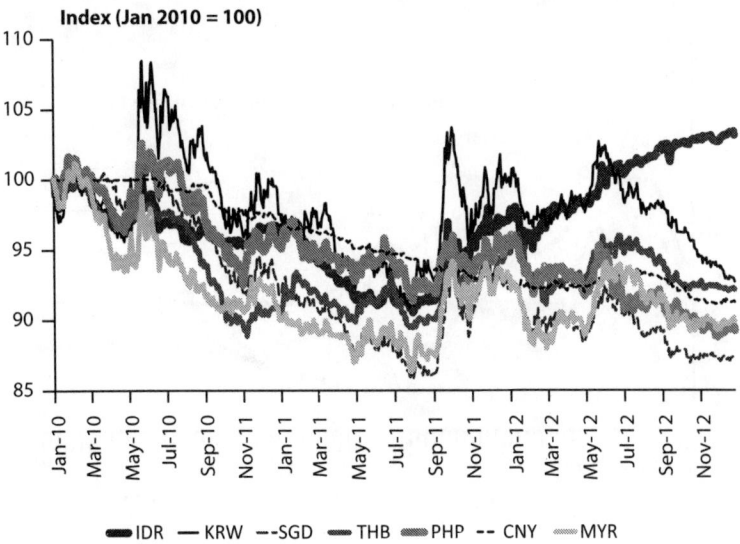

FIGURE 8.9   Index of Regional Currencies
Source: Bank Indonesia.

robust at 6.5 per cent, although it declined marginally to 6.2 per cent in 2012 due to weakening external demand. Meanwhile, the inflation was well positioned at the center of inflation target, and remained stable at around 4.3 per cent by the end of 2011 (Figure 8.10).

5. Policy Outcome: Recent Development in Indonesia's Financial Market

Starting from the second half of 2012, the Rupiah came under pressure, triggered by lingering global financial market uncertainty and the impact of a widening current account deficit arising from an expansion of imports due to the robust domestic demand coupled with slackening exports. Indonesia is currently confronted with managing two major shifts in the global environment. First, an economic slowdown in emerging markets such as PRC and India, and a pronounced fall in commodity prices adversely affected Indonesia's exports. Second, quite recently, signals of a gradual exit from the extraordinary accommodative monetary policy in the United States has prompted a marked shift

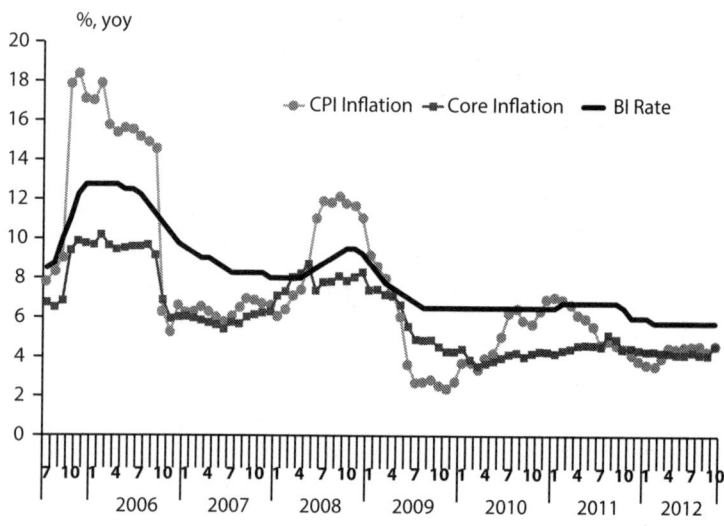

FIGURE 8.10   BI Policy Rate and Inflation
Source: Bank Indonesia

in financing conditions for emerging markets like Indonesia. After a prolonged period of strong portfolio inflows during 2009–11, Indonesia is currently facing risks from capital outflow due to a transition to more volatile external conditions and higher risk premiums.

Current conditions have put greater emphasis on how to recalibrate monetary and financial policies to a changing balance of payments situation. The current account balance has shifted into a deficit, the exposure to capital reversal has increased, the depreciation of exchange rate has accelerated, and foreign exchange reserve losses have mounted. These unfavorable conditions have put mounting pressures on the performance of Indonesian trade and financial market as well. Capital reversals combined with increasing risks in investment led to stock prices declining, bond yields rising, and the exchange rate weakening.

Pressures on Indonesia's balance of payments have continued to persist despite decelerating in intensity. The current account deficit in the second quarter of 2013 reached $ 9.9 billion or 4.4 per cent GDP, significantly different from a surplus of around $ 1.7 billion in 2011. The deficit was mainly driven by higher oil imports for domestic consumption. The capital and financial account witnessed a net surplus of

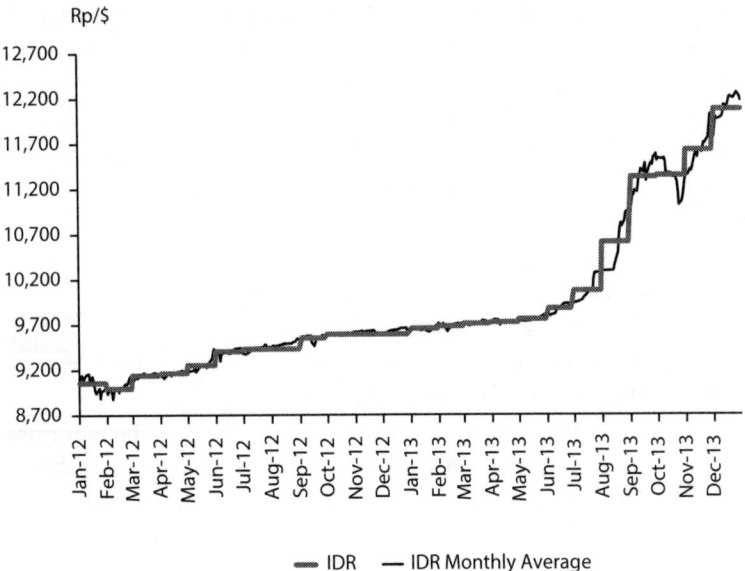

FIGURE 8.11   The Rupiah Depreciation Trend
Source: Bank Indonesia.

around $ 8.4 billion through capital inflows in the form of FDI and portfolio inflows, mainly in government securities while capital outflows emanated from the stock markets. Thus, overall there was a balance of payments deficit, which led to the exchange rate depreciating. By end of Q3 2013, Rupiah closed at Rp 11.580 per US dollar, having depreciated by 14.3 per cent from end of 2012.

Capital Flows Management during the Period of Capital Reversals

As discussed before, there is no single solution to solve the problems posed by volatile capital flows, and authorities need to utilize all available instruments. A mix of policy measures, covering monetary and exchange rate policy, sterilized intervention, and administrative capital flow management including macroprudential measures are needed to tackle the impact of these flows. The policies and measures to prudently manage capital flows have short, medium terms, and even longer term perspectives. Some of those measures may go beyond the central bank's purview but will have significant bearing on the impact on the composition of flows, stability, and the real sector of an economy.

The deepening of the financial markets is among the medium term priority agenda. In this regard, the different measures are to be designed to create a deep, sound and liquid financial market by introducing a greater variety of instruments. Measures such as the promotion of corporate bonds issuance will prove to be very crucial in taking advantage of the potential capital inflows and channeling them to productive sectors, especially the vital infrastructure sector. On the other hand, a deep financial market would also stimulate a more resilient economy against unanticipated shocks in the financial market.

Against this backdrop, BI decided to bolster its continuing monetary and financial policy mix to manage capital flows in the period of capital reversals. First, BI gradually raised the BI policy rate by 150 basis points since June 2013, which reached 7.25 per cent in October 2013. The rate hikes were aimed to further strengthen control over inflationary expectations and risk mitigation against the possibility of a depreciation–inflation spiral. This policy is also part of efforts to ease the current account deficit back to a sound and sustainable level.

Secondly, BI continued to allow exchange rates to remain flexible and respond to the changing fundamentals. However, there is a need to guard against the risks of disorderly adjustment through intervention to smooth excessive volatility. To ease the FX supply shortage, BI has selectively provided liquidity by recycling the accumulated reserves in the FX market and thereby reduced the volatility of rupiah. This policy response has inevitably led to a depletion of international reserve holdings from a peak of $120 billion in June 2011 to around $ 93 billion in August 2013, before it climbed back to $ 96 billion in October 2013.

BI also continued to provide 'Dual Intervention' through foreign exchange supply and tradable government securities purchases in the secondary market in a measurable manner. Exchange rate, along with bond yields, continued to be allowed to reprise to facilitate an orderly adjustment and absorb external shocks. Figure 8.13 shows the government bond yield curve gradually shifted up to provide incentive for the investors to place their funds in the medium to longer term instruments.

To promote financial deepening, BI has issued new instruments and introduced other measures. BI introduced 'Foreign Exchange Term

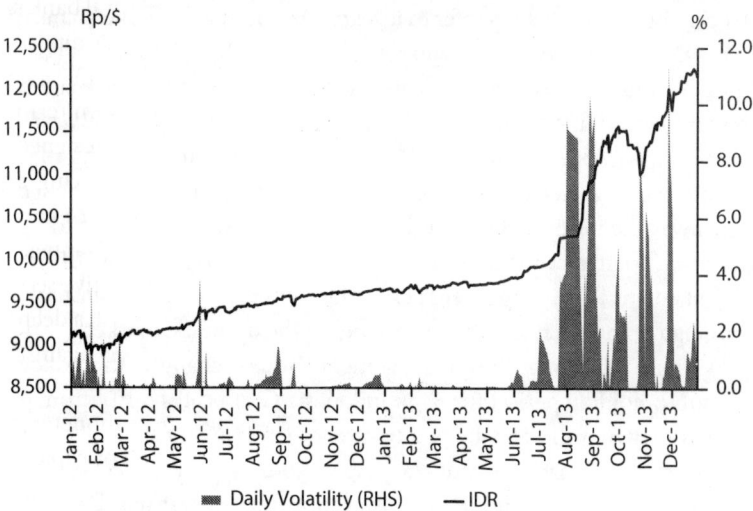

FIGURE 8.12 The Exchange Rate Volatility
Source: Bank Indonesia.

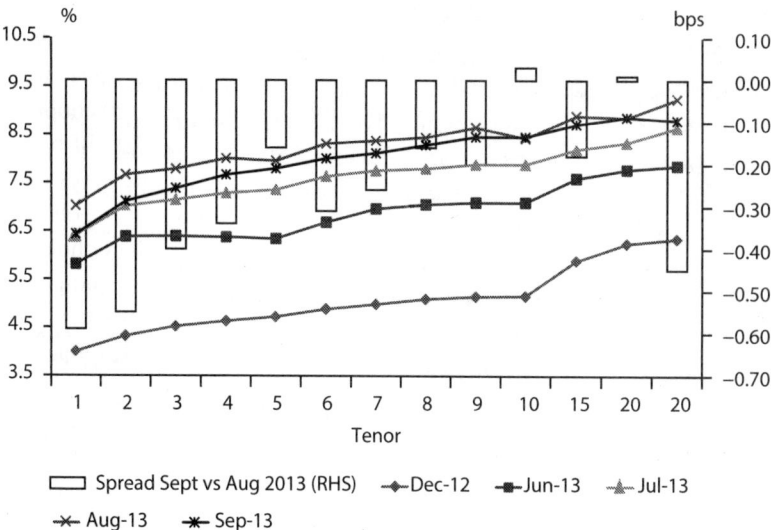

FIGURE 8.13 Government Bond Yield Curve
Source: Bank Indonesia.

Deposit' (TD Valas) which refer to foreign currency placement of banks' excess Dollar liquidity in the central bank. Under a tight FX market condition, BI will recycle the accumulated foreign currency to lessen market pressure. In addition, BI also relaxed the regulation on *nonresident's forward transaction's maturity* from a minimum of three months to a minimum of one week. This is expected to encourage investors to hedge their investment and subsequently could also deepen the FX market. Moreover, to attract repatriation of foreign exchange proceeds, BI has relaxed norms for buying foreign exchange by the exporters against sale of foreign exchange from export earnings in the domestic market.

As a part of capital flow management, BI also changed the policy of 'month-holding period for Bank Indonesia Certificates (SBI)' from 6 months to 1 month. This helped to strengthen liquidity management and boost the efficacy of monetary operations as well as deepen the financial markets. In addition, to bolster monetary operations, banking liquidity management, as well as follow-up measures for the financial market deepening, BI introduced 'Bank Indonesia Deposit Certificate (SDBI)' auction with 1-month and 3-months tenor. SDBI are monetary instruments issued by the central bank to absorb banks' excess liquidity that can be traded among the banks domestically.

Finally, BI also strengthened the macroprudential measures to contain rapid credit growth due to the excessive capital flows to both financial system and the economy. The LTV requirement on specific types of mortgage loans was introduced. The LTV/FTV ratio is the ratio between the value of loan that can be allocated and the corresponding value of collateral in the form of property. Property includes real property that includes houses, vertical housing (apartments, flats, condominiums, and penthouses), home offices, and home stores. The measure aims to improve financial system stability and bolster banking resilience by prioritizing prudential principles. This is achieved by, among others, slowing the concentration of credit risk in the real estate sector as well as promoting the application of prudential principles when disbursing credit.

6. Concluding Remarks

Rising volatility of capital flows has made appropriate management of capital flows a complex and challenging task. In particular, emerging economies like Indonesia have had to focus on maintaining an internal and external balance in a fast growing economy amid the presence of a policy trilemma. The policy trilemma constitutes the need to balance three equally challenging tasks of managing the volatility of capital flows, responding to the ensuing exchange rate overshooting and containing domestic liquidity expansion, wherein two of these are unavoidably conflicting. Large capital flows, if not managed properly, can exacerbate underlying risks in the recipient countries. It may generate macroeconomic risks through excessive credit expansion, overheating economy, and an overvalued real exchange rate, and eventually could trigger macroeconomic instability. Capital flows could also create risks of currency crisis and induce the financial instability risk within a short period, particularly in the events of sharp capital flows reversal.

This chapter argues that the central bank should consider sound and sustainable macroeconomic and financial policies as the first line of defense to create conducive environment for capital flows. Nonetheless, while maintaining strong fundamentals is necessary, it is not sufficient to cope with surges in capital flows. It requires a set of other measures as an integral part of the overall policy mix to maintain stability. These measures are prudential in nature and do not aim to control the volume of portfolio inflows. Rather, they are designed to reduce the risks associated with volatility of capital flows and sustain financial stability. In this regard, the broad and comprehensive policy mix that BI has pursued mainly include: (a) maintaining flexible exchange rate with selective sterilized foreign exchange intervention, (b) enhancing monetary operation strategy, and (c) conducting capital flows management, as well as imposing targeted macroprudential measures.

This paper shows that the implementation of BI policy mix has been quite beneficial in sustaining capital inflows and reducing the inherent risks. The policy mix helps to maintain robust capital inflow trends, shift the composition of investment in financial instruments, expand the extent of FDI, and eventually contain exchange rate volatility.

BI believes that the policy mix could be advantageous during the episode of capital reversals. Recently, the Rupiah has come under pressure, triggered by lingering global financial market uncertainty and the impact of widening of the current account deficit. After a prolonged period of strong portfolio inflows during 2009–11, Indonesia is currently facing capital outflows due to a transition to more volatile external conditions and higher risk premiums.

Responding to the downside risks, BI expanded the policy mix to ensure an orderly adjustment in the external balance so that these adjustments would not pose uncontrollable risks to the overall macroeconomic stability. In this regard, BI has continued to let the exchange rate move in an orderly manner, and intervened in the foreign exchange market if necessary to smooth out the volatility. BI also introduced measures under capital flow management to strengthen liquidity management, boost the efficacy of monetary operations, as well as deepen the financial markets. In addition, BI also pursued targeted macroprudential measures to contain rapid credit growth due to the excessive capital flows to both financial system and the economy.

References

Aizenman, J., M.D. Chinn, and H. Ito. 2012. 'The Financial Crisis, Rethinking of the Global Financial Architecture and the Trilemma', in Masahiro Kawai, Peter J. Morgan, and Shinji Takagi (eds) *Monetary and Currency Policy Management in Asia*, p. 143. ADB Institute and Edward Elgar Publishing, Cheltenham Glos GL50 2JA UK.

Bank Indonesia. 2008. *Economic Report on Indonesia*.

———. 2009. *Economic Report on Indonesia*.

———. 2010. *Economic Report on Indonesia*.

———. 2011. *Economic Report on Indonesia*.

Cadarajat, Yayat. 2009. 'Capital Flows and Their Implications for Central Bank Policies in Indonesia', in Min B. Shrestha and Choon-Sen Lim (eds) *Capital Flows and their Implications for Central Bank Policies in the SEACEN Countries*, The SEACEN Centre.

Goeltom, Miranda. 2008. 'Managing Capital Flows in Rapid Changing Environment', *Indonesia's country paper at the BIS Deputy Governor Annual Meeting*, Basel, January.

Hendarsah, Nanang. 2010. *Challenges and Policy Options in Managing Portfolio Investment Flows: Bank Indonesia's Recent Experiences*, Bank Indonesia, Mimeo.

IMF. 2011. *Recent Experiences in Managing Capital Inflows-Cross Cutting Themes and Possible Guidelines*, February.

Kawai, Masahiro and Mario B. Lamberte. 2010. *Managing Capital Flows: The Search for a Framework*. UK: ADBI and Edward Elgar Publishing.

Index

Editors and Contributors

Editors

Bruno Carrasco is currently the Director of South Asia Public Management, Financial Sector and Trade Division (SAPF) of the Asian Development Bank (ADB). He first joined ADB in 1993 as a Young Professional and in 2003 he served as Principal Financial Economist in South Asia Department. He became Director, Country Coordination and Regional Cooperation in 2008. Two years later, he was appointed Director of SAPF. Prior to rejoining ADB, he worked as Senior Economist at the European Central Bank from 2000 to 2003. Carrasco has a PhD in Economics from the University of Essex, UK, and Masters in Economics from the University of British Columbia, Canada.

Subir Gokarn is currently Senior Fellow and Director of Research, Brookings India. His research interests lie broadly in the areas of macroeconomics and development. Prior to this, he was Deputy Governor of the Reserve Bank of India (2009–12). Earlier, he was Chief Economist of Standard & Poor's Asia-Pacific (2007–09), Executive Director and Chief Economist of CRISIL (2002–07), Chief Economist at the National Council of Applied Economic Research (NCAER), New Delhi (2000–02), and Associate Professor at the Indira Gandhi Institute of Development Research (IGIDR), Mumbai (1991–2000). He contributes a fortnightly column on current economic issues to the *Business Standard*, a leading financial daily of India. He is currently serving a two-year term as member of the National Security Advisory Board.

Hiranya Mukhopadhyay is currently working as a Senior Public Management Economist at the Asian Development Bank (ADB). Prior to joining ADB in 2001, he worked at the National Institute of Public Finance and Policy, New Delhi. Mukhopadhyay holds a PhD degree in economics from Jawaharlal Nehru University, New Delhi. He has also visited Boston University and the University of Oxford as a Post-Doctoral Fellow and completed research projects. Mukhopadhyay's areas of specialization are open economy macroeconomics and public finance (with special emphasis on subnational finances). He has published several articles in Indian and international journals. He has co-edited *Dimensions of Economic Theory and Policy* published by the Oxford University Press.

Contributors

Kristin J. Forbes is the Jerome and Dorothy Lemelson Professor of Management and Global Economics at MIT's Sloan School of Management. She regularly rotates between academia and economic policy positions. From 2003 to 2005, Forbes served as a Member of the White House's Council of Economic Advisers and she is currently a Member of the Governor's Council of Economic Advisers for the State of Massachusetts. From 2001 to 2002, she worked in the US Treasury Department. Her academic research addresses policy-related questions in international macroeconomics. Forbes was named a 'Young Global Leader' as part of the World Economic Forum at Davos. She is a research associate at the NBER and a member of the Bellagio Group, Trilateral Commission, and Council on Foreign Relations. She is on the Panel of Economic Advisers for the Congressional Budget Office and the Academic Advisory Board for the Peterson Institute for International Economics and the Center for Global Development.

Joseph E. Gagnon, senior fellow at the Peterson Institute for International Economics since September 2009, was visiting associate director, Division of Monetary Affairs (2008–09) at the US Federal Reserve Board. Previously he served at the US Federal Reserve Board as Associate Director, Division of International Finance (1999–2008), and senior economist (1987–90 and 1991–97). He has also served at the US Treasury Department (1994–95 and 1997–99) and has taught at the Haas School of Business, University of California, Berkeley (1990–91). He is the author of *Flexible Exchange Rates for a Stable World Economy* (2011) and

The Global Outlook for Government Debt over the Next 25 years: Implications for the Economy and Public Policy (2011). He has published numerous articles in economics journals, including the *Journal of International Economics*, the *Journal of Monetary Economics*, the *Review of International Economics*, and the *Journal of International Money and Finance*, and has contributed to several edited volumes. He received a BA from Harvard University in 1981 and a PhD in Economics from Stanford University in 1987.

Ricardo Eyer Harris is currently an adviser at the Prudential and Foreign Exchange Regulation Department at the Banco Central do Brasil. Previously, he was head of division at the securities and settlement systems oversight and bank rediscount divisions at the Department of Banking Operations and Payments System. In the private sector, Harris worked in several mergers and acquisitions and project finance operations. He holds a degree in Accounting from the State University of Rio de Janeiro and post graduated in Business Strategy from Fundação Getúlio Vargas. In 2004, he was certified as a Chartered Financial Analyst by the CFA Institute.

Michael W. Klein is the William L. Clayton Professor of International Economics Affairs at the Fletcher School, Tufts University. He is also a Research Associate of the National Bureau of Economic Research and a Nonresident Senior Fellow of the Brookings Institution. He served as Chief Economist in the Office of International Affairs at the United States Treasury from June 2010 to December 2011. His research interests include international macroeconomic policy, international capital markets, the effects of international factors on United States labour markets, exchange rate policy, and foreign direct investment. He has published extensively in scholarly journals, and is the co-author of two economics scholarly books, *Job Creation, Job Destruction and International Competition* (2003) and *Exchange Rate Regimes in the Modern Era* (2010). He holds a BA from Brandeis University and a PhD in Economics from Columbia University.

Jonathan D. Ostry is Deputy Director of the Research Department at the IMF. His current responsibilities include leading staff teams on: IMF-FSB Early Warning Exercises; multilateral exchange rate surveillance; capital account management; fiscal sustainability; and inequality. Past positions include leading the division that produces the *World Economic Outlook*, and leading country teams on several Asian countries, including Japan. Ostry is the author/editor of a number of books on international macro issues, and numerous articles in scholarly journals. Ostry earned his BA (with distinction) from Queen's University (Canada) at the age of 18. He then went up to the University of Oxford (Balliol College) where he earned a BA in Philosophy, Politics and Economics. His MSc is from the London School of Economics and his PhD from the University of Chicago.

Hartadi A. Sarwono currently serves as a President Director & CEO of The Indonesian Banking Development Institute. He was formerly Deputy Governor of Bank Indonesia and appointed for the first five years' period of 2003–08, and reappointed for the second period of 2008–13. During his career, he dealt mostly in macroeconomics, monetary policy formulation, and international affairs. Sarwono received his Industrial Engineering degree from Bandung Institute of Technology (ITB 1979). Later, he earned an MA degree in Macroeconomics (1985) and a PhD in Monetary Theory and Policy (1989) from the University of Oregon, Eugene-Oregon, USA.

Abhijit Sen Gupta is currently an Economist with the Indian Resident Mission of the Asian Development Bank. Prior to this he has worked with Jawaharlal Nehru University (Associate Professor), World Bank (Consultant), and International Monetary Fund (Intern). He obtained his PhD in International Economics from the University of California, Santa Cruz, and has published more than a dozen academic articles in both refereed international journals and conference volumes, together with a host of op-ed articles for the general public

Rajeswari Sengupta is a Visiting Fellow at the Indira Gandhi Institute of Development Research (IGIDR) in Mumbai, India. Her research focuses on International Finance and Open Economy Macroeconomics. She has held research positions at the Institute for Financial Management and Research (IFMR), Reserve Bank of India, the World Bank in Washington, D.C. and the International Monetary Fund (IMF). She has published in reputed international journals such as *Journal of International Money and Finance, the World Economy, Emerging Markets Review* among others.

Sengupta completed her MA and PhD in Economics from the University of California, Santa Cruz (UCSC).

Luiz Awazu Pereira da Silva is currently Deputy-Governor at the Central Bank of Brazil, in charge of International Affairs, Corporate Risk and of Financial Regulation. Before that, in Brazil, he was Deputy-Finance Minister, in charge of International Affairs at the Ministry of Finance and Chief Economist of the Ministry of Budget and Planning. He was also Regional Country Director and Advisor to the Chief Economist at the World Bank and, in Japan, worked at the Institute of Fiscal and Monetary Policy of the Ministry of Finance and as Country Risk Director at the Japan Bank for International Cooperation. He has worked and published on development economics, macro-modeling, financial regulation, and monetary policy.

Bhupal Singh is Director in the Department of Economic and Policy Research of the Reserve Bank of India at Mumbai, India. He holds an MPhil degree in Economics from Jawaharlal Nehru University, New Delhi and is currently pursuing PhD from University of Mumbai, Mumbai, India. His research interests include policy oriented research in international economics, monetary economics, financial markets, and asset prices.